Dream Zones

Anthropology, Culture and Society

Series Editors:
Professor Vered Amit, Concordia University
and
Professor Christina Garsten, Stockholm University

Recent titles:

Claiming Individuality:
The Cultural Politics of
Distinction
EDITED BY VERED AMIT
AND NOEL DYCK

Community, Cosmopolitanism
and the Problem of Human
Commonality
VERED AMIT AND
NIGEL RAPPORT

Home Spaces, Street Styles:
Contesting Power and Identity
in a South African City
LESLIE J. BANK

In Foreign Fields:
The Politics and Experiences of
Transnational Sport Migration
THOMAS F. CARTER

A World of Insecurity:
Anthropological Perspectives
on Human Security
EDITED BY THOMAS ERIKSEN,
ELLEN BAL AND
OSCAR SALEMINK

A History of Anthropology
Second Edition
THOMAS HYLLAND ERIKSEN
AND FINN SIVERT NIELSEN

Ethnicity and Nationalism:
Anthropological Perspectives
Third Edition
THOMAS HYLLAND ERIKSEN

Small Places, Large Issues:
An Introduction to Social and
Cultural Anthropology
Third Edition
THOMAS HYLLAND ERIKSEN

What Is Anthropology?
THOMAS HYLLAND ERIKSEN
Discordant Development:
Global Capitalism and the
Struggle for Connection in
Bangladesh
KATY GARDNER

Organisational Anthropology:
Doing Ethnography in and
Among Complex Organisations
EDITED BY CHRISTINA GARSTEN
AND ANETTE NYQVIST

Border Watch:
Cultures of Immigration,
Detention and Control
ALEXANDRA HALL

Corruption:
Anthropological Perspectives
EDITED BY DIETER HALLER
AND CRIS SHORE

Anthropology's World:
Life in a Twenty-First
Century Discipline
ULF HANNERZ

Humans and Other Animals
Cross-cultural Perspectives on
Human–Animal Interactions
SAMANTHA HURN

Cultures of Fear:
A Critical Reader
EDITED BY ULI LINKE AND
DANIELLE TAANA SMITH

The Will of the Many:
How the Alterglobalisation
Movement is Changing the
Face of Democracy
MARIANNE MAECKELBERGH

Cultivating Development:
An Ethnography of Aid Policy
and Practice
DAVID MOSSE

The Gloss of Harmony:
The Politics of Policy Making
in Multilateral Organisations
EDITED BY BIRGIT MÜLLER

Contesting Publics
Feminism, Activism,
Ethnography
LYNNE PHILLIPS
AND SALLY COLE

Food For Change
The Politics and Values
of Social Movements
JEFF PRATT AND
PETER LUETCHFORD

Race and Ethnicity
in Latin America
Second Edition
PETER WADE

Race and Sex
in Latin America
PETER WADE

The Capability of Places:
Methods for Modelling
Community Response to
Intrusion and Change
SANDRA WALLMAN

Anthropology at the Dawn
of the Cold War:
The Influence of Foundations,
McCarthyism and the CIA
EDITED BY DUSTIN M. WAX

Dream Zones

Anticipating Capitalism and
Development in India

Jamie Cross

First published 2014 by Pluto Press
345 Archway Road, London N6 5AA

www.plutobooks.com

British Library Cataloguing in Publication Data
A catalogue record for this book is available from the British Library

ISBN   978 0 7453 3373 1   Hardback
ISBN   978 0 7453 3372 4   Paperback
ISBN   978 1 7837 1038 6   PDF eBook
ISBN   978 1 7837 1040 9   Kindle eBook
ISBN   978 1 7837 1039 3   EPUB eBook

Library of Congress Cataloging in Publication Data applied for

10   9   8   7   6   5   4   3   2   1

Typeset from disk by Stanford DTP Services, Northampton, England
Text design by Melanie Patrick

Contents

Maps and Figures

Series Preface

Anthropology is a discipline based upon in-depth ethnographic works that deal with wider theoretical issues in the context of particular, local conditions – to paraphrase an important volume from the series: large issues explored in small places. This series has a particular mission: to publish work that moves away from an old-style descriptive ethnography that is strongly area-studies oriented, and offers genuine theoretical arguments that are of interest to a much wider readership, but which are nevertheless located and grounded in solid ethnographic research. If anthropology is to argue itself a place in the contemporary intellectual world, then it must surely be through such research.

We start from the question: 'What can this ethnographic material tell us about the bigger theoretical issues that concern the social sciences?' rather than 'What can these theoretical ideas tell us about the ethnographic context?' Put this way round, such work becomes about large issues, set in a (relatively) small place, rather than detailed description of a small place for its own sake. As Clifford Geertz once said, 'Anthropologists don't study villages; they study in villages.'

By place, we mean not only geographical locale, but also other types of 'place' – within political, economic, religious or other social systems. We therefore publish work based on ethnography within political and religious movements, occupational or class groups, among youth, development agencies, and nationalist movements; but also work that is more thematically based – on kinship, landscape, the state, violence, corruption, the self. The series publishes four kinds of volume: ethnographic monographs; comparative texts; edited collections; and shorter, polemical essays.

We publish work from all traditions of anthropology, and all parts of the world, which combines theoretical debate with empirical evidence to demonstrate anthropology's unique position in contemporary scholarship and the contemporary world.

Professor Vered Amit
Professor Christina Garsten

Acknowledgements

This book has been driven by a commitment to what I understand as public anthropology, a commitment fostered by a number of people and institutions but anchored in my experience as a postgraduate student at the University of Sussex. In finishing this book I feel a considerable debt of gratitude to those who once taught me and have supported me since, in particular to James Fairhead, Jon Mitchell, Geert de Neve, Filippo Osella, Jeffrey Pratt and Jock Stirrat.

Of course the material in this book carries the legacy of conversations with many people, including those who have read and commented on the material here in its various early forms. I would particularly like to thank Jonathan Parry, whose methodological commitment to empirical research, to questions of work, labour and industry in India, and to ethnographic writing as a genre has been particularly influential. In addition I would like to thank Sharad Chari, Laura Bear, Mukalika Banerjee, Akhil Gupta, Asseem Srivastava, Amita Bhaviskar, A.R. Vasavi, Alpa Shah, M. Vijayabaskar, S. Seethalakshmi, Madhumita Dutta, Patrick Osscarson, Michael Levien, Anant Maringanti, M. Vijayabaskar, Rebecca Prentice and Dinah Rajak, Lotte Hoek, Ward Berenschot and Malini Sur.

This book would not have been possible without the long-term support of many people in Visakhapatnam. I would like to thank, in particular, G. Jai Kisan, K.E. Raj Pramukh and P.D.S. Pal Kumar in the Department of Anthropology, and M. Nalini and Meena Rao in the Department of Politics and Public Administration, Andhra University. My very special thanks to Indira Gummiluri, my guide to Telugu language and literature, and Ram Babu for their hospitality over several years. Thanks to Suneetha and Mani – my long lost comrades – and to Chakri for his research assistance. Thanks also to J.V. Ratnam, E.A.S. Sharma, V.S. Krishna and Radha Krishna, whose activism animates the city in diverse ways.

Most of all I would like to thank those people who I first met on the floor of the Worldwide Diamonds factory in 2005 and whose various commitments to the future shaped the perspective from which this book is written. The book is dedicated to you: Chandrakala (Chinni), Geetha, Rama Lakhsmi, Lakshmi, Prakash, Patnaik, Laxman Rao, Kondal Rao, Appala Raju, Suresh, Srinivas, Bhaskar Rao and Nageswar Rao. I would also like to thank those civil servants and government officials whose support facilitated my research in north coastal Andhra Pradesh but who have chosen to remain anonymous.

In writing this book I have had the good fortune to be hosted at several institutions. At the National Institute of Advanced Studies in Bangalore I would like to thank Carol Upadhya; at the University of Amsterdam I would like to thank Mario Rutten and Jan Breman; at the National University of Ireland, Jamie Saris, Chandana Mathur, Steve Coleman and Thomas Strong; at the Australian National University, Alan Rumsey and Francesca Merlan, Philip Taylor, Assa Doron and Nicholas Peterson. At the School of International Labor Relations, Cornell University, special thanks to Sarosh Kuruvilla, Rebbeca Given and George Boyer.

At Pluto Press my thanks to David Castle for his enthusiasm for my project and his considerable patience, to Jonathan Maunder, and Sophie Richmond for her copy-editing. Thanks also to Ciaran Cross whose reading primed the final text.

The research on which this book is based has been financially supported by doctoral and postdoctoral fellowships from the UK's Economic and Social Research Council (2003–7 and 2009–10) and a Leach Postdoctoral Fellowship from the UK's Royal Anthropological Institute (2008–9). It has also been wittingly or unwittingly subsidized at various moments by Paul and Jo Cross, Ismene Stalpers and Oliver Maxwell.

Finally, I thank my fellow traveller Alice Street, without whom there would be no book and no point, and Robinson, from whom these acknowledgements are keeping me.

Glossary and Abbreviations

ADB	Asia Development Bank
aakshalu	aspirations
Andhra Jyoti	*Shining Andhra*, Telugu newspaper
ayupettu	strengths
benami	third party or false name in transactions
bhavodvegaalu	passions and sentiments
CPI	Congress Party of India
CPI (M)	Communist Party of India (Marxist)
D. Form *patta*	title document for land redistributed to the poor
Dasara	annual harvest festival
dastaks	Mughal-era duty-free pass
dharnas	relay-hunger strikes,
Eenadu	*Today*, Telugu newspaper
firmans	Mughal-era imperial decree
gram panchayats	village-level governing body
grama sabhas	village-level assembly
GTZ	German Development Agency
hawa	air, wind
kalalu	dreams
karikalu	aspirations
katnam	groom price
Mandal	village-level administrative area
Nagula Chauvithi	South Indian festival associated with the worship of snake goddesses
NAPM	National Alliance of People's Movements
nirgiva prantham	dead zones
Nirvaasitulu Shanksema Sangham	Welfare Association for the Displaced
patta	private land title
puroni	advance payment agreement
pulli	tiger
putu	a unit of measurement

saravedi chetlu	silver trees
SEZ	special economic zone
Tahsildars	village secretaries
tapana	colloquial Telugu expression of obligation in exchange relations
taragarilu	brokers
TDP	Telugu Dessam Party
tikaadu	middlemen
uppu	air
valmeekam	snake pits
varnas	Hinduism's four-fold division of society
Zamindars	hereditary landlords

Note on Language

Throughout this text I follow the Rice Transliteration Standard in dispensing with the use of diacritics and representing modern Telugu using the Roman alphabet.

Map 1 The seven economic zones created by the government of India between 1965 and 1991; with the state of Andhra Pradesh highlighted

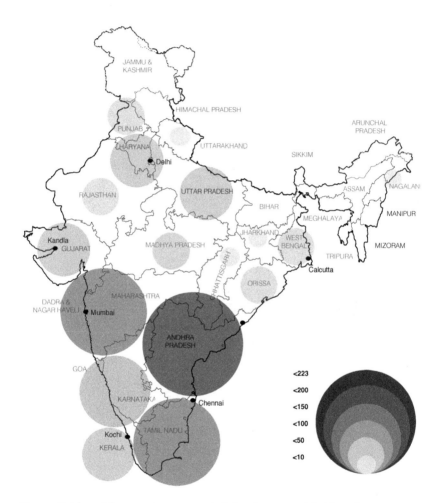

Map 2   Total special economic zones granted planning approval (mid 2013)

1

The Economy of Anticipation

Special Economic Zones are dream projects ... launched by the
Government of India with great fanfare as a growth catalyst ... in the
fond hope that they would help India replicate the Chinese success
story of rapid industrialisation ... But the reception amongst various
Indian stakeholders has not been on the expected lines.

Government of India Parliamentary Standing Committee,
Report on the Functioning of Special Economic Zones, August 2007

In the hours before daybreak on the morning of 14 March 2007, somewhere
between 10,000 and 20,000 people gathered on the southern banks of the
Haldi River, opposite the port city of Haldia, in Nandigram, West Bengal,
India. Men, women and children massed together on the edge of a canal
in a place called Sonachura. Facing them on the opposite bank stood
hundreds of armed police.

Less than twelve months earlier the Left Front government of West
Bengal, led by the Communist Party of India (Marxist), had earmarked
some 10,000 acres of agricultural land in Nandigram for a massive
programme of industrialisation driven by foreign investment.[1] The
government's plans for the region's growth and development saw the area
around Haldia transformed into a hub for the global petrochemical and
pharmaceutical industries. The engines of this transformation were to be
two special economic zones (SEZs), purpose-built enclaves that offered
preferential tax regimes and flexible labour policies to investors. These
zones were to be constructed by the state government under a public–
private partnership agreement with a number of transnational real estate
developers, led by the Salim Group of Indonesia.

For some 95,000 residents of Nandigram – the majority of them
low-caste Hindus and Muslims – the promises of jobs and development
attached to these zones came with few guarantees and little clarity. For
those directly affected by the proposals, including the residents of 27 *gram
panchayats* or villages who would be displaced by the zones, there was

confusion about how people would be compensated for the loss of their land and homes and about where they would be expected to go. There was also ambiguity and uncertainty over the kinds of employment the zones would create. Who would be employed in the zone, people asked visiting journalists? What kind of work would they have to do and what kind of skills would such work require? (See for example Dhara 2008.)

The scepticism and antipathy voiced by the residents of Nandigram also referenced past hopes and failures of industrialisation. The SEZs were not the first large-scale industrial infrastructure projects to promise mass employment and development to people living on the banks of the Haldi River. In 1977 – the same year that a Left Front government led by the Communist Party of India was first voted into power in West Bengal – the Kolkata Port Trust and a state-run engineering company acquired 400 acres of land from 142 families at a place called Jellingham for what promised to be a massive industrial venture. Plans for the complex here including a shipbuilding facility and an oil rig construction unit. Within months, however, the business venture had proved commercially unviable. By 1981 the site had been closed down, its buildings and equipment abandoned along with the promises of employment made to families from whom land for the project had been acquired. Twenty years later claims for compensation were still being pursued through the courts. Visitors to the site encountered an industrial graveyard: ramshackle buildings with broken windows and walls reduced to rubble; decaying cranes and bulldozers; heavy equipment and iron beams coated in rust and overgrown by vegetation.[2]

Such landscapes of ruination inscribe the unmet promises of past industrial development projects in the present.[3] As they documented rising opposition to the SEZs planned for Nandigram journalists and researchers recorded a sense of 'déjà vu' among Nandigram's residents, for many of whom the Jellingham port project had taken place in living memory.[4] West Bengal's main opposition parties lent their support to residents who opposed the project and helped establish a new organisation – the Committee against Land Evictions (*Bhumi Uchhed Pratirodh Committee*) – that set out to coordinate opposition to the zone in Nandigram and protect the right of farmers to their land and agricultural livelihoods.[5]

In late 2006 the Haldia Development Authority announced the beginning of a land acquisition process for the SEZs. Amid escalating confrontations between residents and the police the Committee against Land Evictions began to barricade the area. They dug up roads and culverts, damaged roads and bridges, and built ditches or bunds to prevent government officials from accessing the area or beginning the land acquisition process. In early 2007 they claimed to have sealed the area off and declared that Nandigram was now a *muktanchal*, a liberated zone free from government rule.

At public hearings held across India social activists urged the government not to acquire land from peasants without their consent. The Chief Minister of West Bengal, Buddhadeb Bhattacharjee, promised to proceed with caution but insisted that 'Haldia is our future' and that the zone would be built. The state's industry minister reiterated the position, telling journalists that the project was needed 'to remove the economic backwardness' of the population in the area and prevent it from remaining 'steeped in poverty'. This vision of West Bengal's social and economic future carried more than rhetorical force. At the beginning of March the state government transported over 3000 police into Nandigram and closed access roads into the area, preventing journalists and human rights activists from entering.

On the morning of 14 March the Committee Against Land Evictions mobilised their supporters at two major access points to Nandigram, following information about impending police action. The committee planned to prevent the police from entering by presenting the demonstration as a peaceful, non-violent and pious protest. Eyewitness reports describe how women and children were amassed at the front of the gathering, how Muslim men performed *namaz*, kneeling down in prayer to recite verses from the Koran, and how Hindus carried temple idols aloft and performed *pujas*.

Their efforts proved futile. As dawn broke over 800 police accompanied by some 500 political activists belonging to the ruling Communist Party, some of them dressed in police uniform, attempted to cross the Bhangabera Bridge near Sonachura in a coordinated attempt to take control of Nandigram and impose order. The police announced through loudspeakers that the assembly was illegal and proceeded to break it up. They fired tear gas and charged demonstrators with *lathis* (batons) and iron rods, before firing live rounds on the fleeing crowds. The day of violence that followed left 14 people dead, one person missing, at least 17 people hospitalised with bullet wounds, hundreds of men, women and children injured after being caught in stampedes or being beaten by the police, and accusations of rape and serious sexual abuse by police and

Communist Party activists against women and young girls (Dhara 2008; Sivaraman et al. 2007).

In November 2007 the Calcutta High Court declared that the decision of the police to open fire on the public was 'wholly unconstitutional' and declared that 'it could not be justified under any provision of the law'. The state was ordered to pay 500,000 rupees to relatives of the deceased, 200,000 rupees to victims of rape, and 100,000 rupees to the injured. Meanwhile, the Communist Party led government abandoned their plans for Nandigram and announced its intention to build the proposed chemical plant 30 km away, on a sparsely populated island in the middle of the Haldi River. In May 2008, however, state assembly elections in West Bengal saw the Left Front government collapse and the Communist Party of India (Marxist) voted out of office after 34 years.

*   *   *

SEZs assume an iconic significance in narratives of India's recent social and economic change (e.g. Corbridge et al. 2012), emerging as uniquely charged objects of conviction and anxiety about the capitalist future. Between the 1960s and the early 1990s the government of India built seven economic zones across the country. By the end of the 2000s there were over 500 zones in various stages of planning, construction and operation, financed under public–private partnership agreements or by real estate developers and corporations. While regional governments, politicians and industrialists have championed zone projects as engines of growth they have been met by public challenges over the terms on which land is being acquired for industrialisation and over the conditions of employment they create.

For many critical commentators India's SEZs have come to materialise the nightmares of capitalism, as market futures are imposed upon people and places through state-sanctioned acts of violence and coercion (Ray 2008). The events at Nandigram have come to mark out the contours of this analysis and cast a long shadow over its re-telling. In India, Nandigram has come to symbolise both the force with which market-oriented development policies are enacted and the potential for popular resistance to them. In the wake of Nandigram a new slogan could be heard on solidarity protests and demonstrations held across India's cities, echoing those once used during the Vietnam War: *Amar Naam, Tomar Naam,*

Shobaar Naam, Nandigram, Nandigram. My Name, Your Name, Everyone's Name is Nandigram, Nandigram (Maringanti 2008).

For activists, journalists and scholars who situate themselves within a tradition of Marxist political economy the appropriate critical response to India's SEZs has been to locate them in a logic of empire and capital. Invoking South Asian histories of imperialism, some present SEZs as neocolonial spatial formulations imposed on independent India by a complex of Bretton Woods institutions, transnational corporations, development donors and management consultancy firms. Others approach these projects as the coherent outcomes of a systematic historical process geared towards the single goal of territorial enclosure, unregulated markets, and capitalist accumulation.[6] India's SEZs, they argue, demand to be understood as part of a global land grab that finds state institutions forcibly securing the assets of the poor for the rich. In Marxist terms this is a process of primitive accumulation or 'accumulation by dispossession' (Harvey 2005) that has its precedents in the eviction of peasants from farmland and the enclosure of the commons in early modern England.[7] As sites of work SEZs also appear as analogues of the prison or the labour camp, creating spaces of incarceration and industrial work in which new populations can be abandoned to the market, stripped of their rights and entitlements, and reduced to a condition of bare life (Ong 2006; Roy 2009).

In this book I situate a critical engagement with large-scale industrial infrastructure projects within an ethnographic tradition that seeks to open up the social and material politics of capitalism. Rather than presume to know in advance that India's SEZs are coherent political or economic projects I explore how economic zones are made into particular places for capital by planners and politicians, corporate managers and executives, farmers, workers and activists as they pursue different futures.[8] In doing so I do not set out to reproduce triumphalist narratives that celebrate India's recent economic rise and new status as a global superpower (e.g. Balch 2012; Deb 2012). But neither do I aim to reproduce oppositional accounts that celebrate the struggles and protests against land acquisition or labour regimes as unequivocal evidence of subaltern resistance to the power of state and capital (e.g. Shrivastava and Kothari 2012). Instead this book reflects on the limits to a purely ideological refutation of market-oriented industrial development projects and challenges readers to engage with the divergent ways of knowing about, imagining and living towards the future that play out in these sites, restructuring relations of power in familiar and ambiguous ways.

The book is written, in part, for readers who are interested in how anthropology might conceptualise, engage with and apprehend the temporal politics of capitalism. For these readers it shows how large-scale industrial infrastructure projects like those in contemporary India are built on an economy of anticipation. At the same time it is written for those who want to put their shoulder to the wheel and challenge the terms and conditions under which projects of industrial development take place. For these readers, I set out to make the case for anthropology as a mode of engagement that can help focus the challenge ahead by rethinking the locations of power, agency and practice in capitalist economies.

The Futures of Capitalism

Contemporary capitalism is built upon dreams as well as nightmares.[9] These are the quintessentially modern dreams of economic and social re-ordering. They are the dreams of industrial modernity, of mass employment leading to prosperity and progress, and mass production eliminating scarcity. They are neoliberal dreams of market freedom, of private enterprise liberated from the constraints of government, politics and culture. They are corporate dreams of profit without responsibility and control without resistance. They are modest dreams of the good life, of everyday hopes and aspirations for improvements in ways of living, of upward movement through hierarchies of wealth and status, of social mobility and material wellbeing, of economic security and betterment. And they are oppositional dreams, of popular mobilisations against state and capital, of radical breaks with the present and of other possible worlds than this.

These dreamed-of futures have lives of their own and material effects upon which our current global moment depends.[10] In this book I explore how they converge with particular intensity upon large-scale industrial infrastructure projects, like the economic zones that have been planned and built across India today.

Much social theory has been written against the impulse to attribute a single logic, rationality or coherence to capitalism. In the words of sociologist Bruno Latour (1993) our critical narratives of political and economic rule create 'sleek' or 'filled-in surfaces' that cast states and markets as complete entities or invest them with an 'abstract but totalising power'. As Latour wrote:

> Take some small business owner hesitatingly going after a few market shares, some conqueror trembling with fever, some poor scientist tinkering in his lab, a lowly engineer piecing together a few more or less favourable relationships of force, some stuttering and fearful politician, turn the critics loose on them, and what do you get? Capitalism, imperialism, science, technology, domination – all equally absolute, systematic, totalitarian. (1993: 125–6)[11]

If the present day can no longer be modern in a utopian sense, he went on to argue, it can still be 'modern at least for the worst'.

Therein, of course, lie both the discursive power and limitations of dystopian accounts of industrialisation and development in the global South. The reduction of projects and policies to a totalising logic may focus the challenge ahead but they remain an 'ethnographically thin' kind of political praxis that impoverishes our understanding of power, culture and agency (Ortner 1995). Just as anthropologogists have challenged the optimistic teleologies of modernity, with their assumptions that social and economic transformations follow a linear trajectory into a future that is better than the past, so too they have challenged the counter-narratives that represent capitalist modernity as an inexorable process of ever increasing alienation or disenchantment (see Rofel 2007; Tsing 2005; Yanagisako 2002).

Current anthropology is driven by an 'aesthetic of emergence' (Miyazaki 2006: 139) that treats global economic processes as provisional, indeterminate and contingent. This is an anthropology of capitalism that re-conceptualises forces that were classically treated as distinct and opposing as reciprocally interactive and mutually constituting, in ways intended to destabilise monolithic portraits of power, domination and resistance (e.g. Tsing 2000b). It is an anthropology that apprehends capitalism as immanent in human action rather than as a system with 'a priori coherence' (Rofel 2007: 25). It is an anthropology that sees how projects of accumulation are constituted, redirected, diverted and undermined by elements that sometimes appear external to them (Mitchell 2002); an anthropology that is concerned with the ways that economic ideologies, rationalities and technologies are always local even as they travel globally (Ong and Collier 2005); and an anthropology that is focused on the encounters and engagements, connections and frictions between places and people, ways of knowing and ways of being (Tsing 2005). Writing in this vein about contemporary Indian economy and society, anthropologists have challenged us to consider the elements of collaboration, compromise and contingency, ambivalence and ambiguity in the relationships between the rural poor and the state, or between industrial workers and the corporation, rather than to assume 'the blunt imposition of political rule' or subaltern false consciousness (Mosse 2005: 6–7).

This book draws energy from these currents in anthropology and builds upon them by putting dreamed-of futures back into our analyses (cf. Appadurai 2008: 32). Just as the time of the present is constantly remade to accommodate the re-invented past (Hobsbawm and Ranger 1983) so too the present is remade around diverse and changing futures. Our global economy is underpinned by an 'abundance of futures' (Rosenberg and Harding 2005) that lie in our big narratives and our small acts: 'in every place where hopes and doubts are mobilised' (2005: 9).

The dreamed-of or anticipated future has been central to anthropology's engagements with the spaces and discourses of capitalist modernity.[12] The dream that industrial modernity can bring about an end of scarcity, an abundance of goods, permanent employment, prosperity and the fulfilment of personal happiness has played a vital role in political scripts and languages, underpinning twentieth-century blueprints for living the good life. In India, for example, historic projects of upward social mobility through hierarchies of caste and class have seen individuals and communities embrace a modernist orientation towards the future, and set out to realise goals of progress and development through the reform of cultural practices and the erasure of associations with degraded manual occupations, as well as through the accumulation of capital (Osella and Osella 2000b: 48). Just as these commitments to the idea of a different and better future have been inflected by globally circulating 'scripts' of social and economic development (Appadurai 1996: 63), and the linear concepts and forward-moving teleologies of modernity, so too have they been inflected with other deep-rooted and long-standing ideas about improvement, civility and virtue that are tied to agricultural history and organised religion (Pandian 2009: 6) as well as the valorisation of hard work, labour and toil (Chari 2004).

Anthropology also reminds us that dreamed-of and anticipated futures are what engender or renew commitments to capitalist political economy.

As recent studies of global financial markets show, judgements about the future that appear to be based upon the careful calculation of risk or complex statistical modelling can be inseparable from the whims and sentiments of individuals (e.g. Zaloom 2007). In Hirokazu Miyazaki's (2006) ethnography of Japanese derivatives traders, for example, dreams (*yuma*) of spectacular financial success that would allow people to escape a life of work are also dreams that commit people to remain at work in the present. As Miyazaki reminds us, it is the speculative exuberance of investors, the fantasy of endless expansion and boundless future growth, as much as their reasoned decision making that drives financial flows, 'taking capitalism in new directions and into new spaces' (Harvey 2000: 254–5 quoted in Miyazaki 2006: 163). David Graeber (2011) puts it even more forcefully in his history of debt. Faith in the eternal future of capitalism is what creates the capitalist economy's speculative bubbles, he writes, because under such conditions there is never any reason not to lend or give credit (2011: 381).[13]

This book shows how capitalism is made, sustained and disrupted in this economy of anticipation. Diverse ways of 'knowing about', imagining and 'living towards' the future (Adams et al. 2009) underpin contemporary political economy, shaping relationships of power and consent. Large-scale infrastructure projects like India's SEZs are 'exemplary sites of anticipatory practice' (Adams et al. 2009: 250). They are arenas in which people attempt to know and master the unknowable future with modes of planning, calculation and prediction; borrowing against the expectation of future profits or returns, mapping development visions, modelling growth trajectories or bracketing potential risks.[14] They are also arenas of imagination, hope, aspiration and desire in which people construct and assemble possible future worlds for themselves and others from existing ideas and images.[15] Finally, they are deeply affective spaces in which the future is felt, encountered and inhabited; in which the lived sensation of future prospects can seize bodies, persons and selves, gripping them with hope and desire, anxiety and fear.[16]

As I detail in the chapters that follow, it is the interplay between these ways of knowing about, imagining and living towards the future that makes India's SEZs into places of contemporary capitalism.[17] Attempts to realise diverse futures are what make enclave spaces into material and symbolic places, producing India's economic zones as a promissory infrastructure for capital and shaping political struggles over land and labour. At times apparently divergent dreams for the future are allied together in ways that make flows of capital more powerful and effective, shaping a politics of control, consent and acquiescence. At other times, the collision of different futures produces conflict and contestation. This economy of anticipation is what Anna Tsing (2005) has called the 'sticky grip' or friction in which all movements of capital are caught, and in which places like Nandigram become entangled.

Of course, the dreams and failures of capitalist modernity are tightly interwoven. Spaces of industrial decline and disinvestment, and experiences of abjection and abandonment, exclusion or disconnection do not lie outside of capitalist economies but are as much a part of them as booming zones of enterprise and prosperity.[18] In the twentieth century utopian dreams of future social and economic order had immense ideological and material power, driving projects of industrial modernisation in North America and Europe, as well as in the postcolonial world (Buck-Morss 2002; Ferguson 1999). Even when these promises and dreams lose their credibility they continue to have an enduring role and significance (Ferguson 2006; Sidaway 2007). This uneven geography of promise and loss is clearly visible across contemporary India. Structural adjustment policies and public sector restructuring has seen the de-industrialisation of India's old industrial heartlands and the incorporation into the global economy of centres of decentralised and informal manufacturing.[19]

Just as crisis is the ground on which capitalism regenerates itself, so too unrealised futures are the fertile grounds from which new hopes, dreams and desires arise. Crises of over-accumulation create the conditions for speculative investments in urban spaces or infrastructure development projects. Crises of security legitimate new forms of state surveillance, policing and violence. Crises of growth and debt are used to justify economic policies. Meanwhile, as Lauren Berlant (2011: 10) has argued, personal crises – whether of displacement or unemployment – become the stories with which individuals reflect upon the ways that they navigate through and adjust to change.

The futures invested in India's present-day infrastructure development projects are mediated by the dreams of futures past. In Nandigram – like other places across India – the unmet or unrealised promise of development is the ground in which politicians and planners plant new dreams of investment, industrialisation and employment. The lived experience of abandonment is the soil in which opposition parties and social movement activists plant the prospect of political change. Commitments to land and livelihoods among people threatened with eviction by infrastructure development projects are always more than ancestral or primordial attachments. They are active investments and commitments to other kinds of futures, built on the debris of the past, and shaped by personal histories of migration, labour and occupancy. Landscapes and dwellings are always inscribed with ideas and norms about how future generations should live as much as they are with memory (Carsten and Hugh-Jones 1995). Opposition to SEZ projects finds people struggling to hold on to ideas about how life should be lived, pursuing hopes and aspirations for a better life while confronting nightmare future scenarios that index fears of loss and dispossession, impoverishment and precariousness.[20] Against this backdrop some people come to see their futures firmly bound to plans for rapid industrialisation while others see their futures lying in struggles to oppose it.

Problem Spaces

The history of capitalism is sometimes told as the history of human interventions aimed at removing frictions to the mobility of capital. Perhaps more than any other twentieth-century spatial form, the economic zone – or what the *Financial Times* calls the 'capitalist enclave' – has held out the promise of realising this dream.[21] In the second half of the twentieth century, export-oriented manufacturing became central to visions of progress across the global South, promising growth without volatility, growth without limits and growth without end. Across South and South East Asia, Latin America and the Caribbean economic zones or enclaves became a key component of an emerging economic orthodoxy and were incorporated into diverse national programmes for social and economic development.

Economic zones are geographically defined territories within the nation-state that establish differential forms of governance and regulation to investors. Since the 1960s a patchwork of such enclave spaces has emerged across the global economy, from 'export processing zones' and 'free trade zones' to 'special economic zones'. In 1998 the UN's International Labour Organization counted 850 zones worldwide; by 2006 this figure had risen to over 3500 and by 2008 they were estimated to account for more than US$200 billion in exports and to directly employ over 40 million people.[22] These zones vary tremendously in terms of their size, organisation and success, ranging from the walled or ring-fenced *maquiladoras* dotted along the US–Mexico border to economic regions or city states like Shenzhen in China. As they have become hubs of manufacturing, assembly and data processing they have also incorporated new groups of men and women into the global labour force, and are frequently pinpointed as sites of flagrant abuse and repression by international trade unions and labour rights activists.[23]

As economic zones emerged as important sites of investment and production, they also emerged as unique 'problem spaces' (Collier and Ong 2005) from which to theorise contemporary capitalism. For many social theorists the zone has become symptomatic of powerful transformations in the organisation of time and space associated with both postmodernity and neoliberalism (see Jameson 2005; Giddens 1991; Harvey 1990b; Palan 2003). If the English factory once materialised the spatial and temporal utopias of eighteenth- and nineteenth-century industrial capitalism (Hetherington 1997) the economic zones and enclaves built across the global South have come to materialise the 'utopics' of late twentieth-century capitalism.

In David Harvey's (1990b) classic work, *The Condition of Postmodernity*, for example, free trade zones captured a speeding up of the global economy: an acceleration in the experience of time. For Harvey, zones were built for speed. By reducing red tape and increasing the connectivity of global locations, zones met the demands of capitalists for temporal efficiency. Moreover, by creating sites of experimentation and innovation in industrial organisation, zones enabled transnational corporations to re-order working space and time in ways that generate profits more efficiently.[24] These characteristics, coupled with the ease of capital mobility into, out of and between these zones, and the absence of state restraints on the organisation of labour, came to exemplify what Harvey called flexible accumulation (Harvey 1990a, 1990b, 2001).

These temporal qualities have been crucial to the ways that zones have been planned and marketed, with associations between pace and place constantly managed and re-affirmed by planners, politicians and administrators. Advertisements, brochures and websites designed to market economic zones to investors emphasise their 'fast-track customs clearance procedures' or the 'high-speed data connection links' presenting the zone as a space of action and immediacy, uniquely equipped for the demands of global business. The political and economic rational for economic zones has – everywhere – hinged on this contrast between the temporality of the market and the temporality of government. Just as capitalist zones or enclaves are sold, marketed and packaged as fast spaces of rapid and accelerated growth they make the state appear as a brake on the economy, and enact government as slow.

Across diverse works of geography, political science and anthropology economic zones have come to exemplify this neoliberal partitioning and re-inscription of space, and have become key sites for examining attendant transformations in sovereignty, governance and citizenship (see Ong 2006; Peck and Theodore 2012). The proliferation of enclave spaces has seen the selective application or uneven spread of market-oriented governance regimes, exercised by a wide swathe of non-state institutions – including transnational corporations, banks, regulatory authorities and international development agencies, as targeted populations come to be administered, managed and governed in relation to their potential for growth and productivity (Elyachar 2005; Ferguson 2006). In Aihwa Ong's (2006) book *Neoliberalism as Exception*, for example, economic zones are spaces that are carved out and 'encoded' for economic freedom and entrepreneurial activity.[25]

Today's economic zones and enclaves continue to be important locations from which to engage contemporary capitalism because they re-focus our attention on the economies of anticipation. Like other kinds of large-scale infrastructure projects – airports (Chalfin 2008) and roads (Masquelier 2002), new cities (James Holston 1989) and gated communities (Low 2001; Falzon 2004), dams, factories or hospitals (Street 2012) – economic zones face forwards, into the near and distant future, to promise a break or rupture with the present. Like roads or runways, zones are spaces of connection and futurity that make new connections between different places and different times. Like these other projects, their success and failure turn on the cultivation of futures of growth, profit and improvement, as well as the positioning of these projects as 'vehicles' for bringing these futures about (Ghertner 2010).

Like these other kinds of large-scale infrastructure projects economic zones mediate experiences of social and economic change and become sites of contradictory and overlapping discourses, narratives and realities. The possibility that zones might create exceptional conditions is precisely what makes them such politically charged spaces of anticipation for diverse communities of politicians and planners, corporate managers and executives, farmers, industrial labourers, and left activists. Yet, as I emphasise in this book, actually existing zones frequently fail to realise the futures invested in them.

India's Dream Zones

In the decades following its independence from Britain in 1947 India's political economy came to be defined by models of state-directed development and extensive state regulation and planning. Between the early 1960s and the early 1990s the government of India built seven 'export processing zones' in some of the country's largest cities and ports (see chapter 2). These early zones were spaces of cautious experimentation with liberalised trade regimes and business freedoms. Unlike those built at the same time elsewhere in South Asia – in Bangladesh (Kabeer 2000) and Sri Lanka (Hewamanne 2008; Lynch 2007), for example – India's zones remained subject to considerable government controls and did not prove particularly attractive to investors.

At the cusp of the 1990s, however, India's economic and political landscape began to be transformed. In 1991 the government of India responded to a balance of payments crisis by accepting the terms of a loan from the International Monetary Fund and introducing an accelerated programme of liberalising economic reforms.[26] New industrial, trade and investment policies increased India's openness to flows of investment; quotas and tariffs on imports were removed in ways intended to encourage foreign direct investment and to open up to private investment sectors of the economy formerly reserved for the public sector.[27] Over the next two decades, the priorities for public expenditure became re-focused on the creation of an enabling environment for business and the state's relationship to capital was re-worked in ways that favoured financial, business and agricultural elites (see Corbridge and Harriss 2000; Menon and Nigam 2007).

The post-liberalisation era in India saw shifts in the temporal language of Indian politics, with 'ultimate origins' and 'distant horizons' (Guyer 2007) coming to have a heightened importance in political discourse and public culture.[28] On the one hand a saffron wave of Hindu nationalism invoked ancient history and laid claim to the idea of a sovereign, disciplined national culture that was rooted in a superior, archaic Hindu past (Hansen 1999). At the same time India's economic reformers invoked vistas of the far-off future. Long-term visions of social and economic development became a vital part of politics and statecraft, and the rhetoric accompanying liberalisation was marked by 20-year or 40-year visions of growth, employment creation, poverty reduction and development

(Guyer 2007). The country's economic zones emerged as infrastructures of change capable of transporting places and people into the future and bringing the future into the present.

At the end of the twentieth century, China's booming economy made Indian politicians, planners and policy makers look east. In February 2000, the government of India Minister for Commerce and Industries, Murasoli Maran, led a delegation of policy makers to Beijing to promote India–China trade relations and to foster increased technical and scientific cooperation between the two countries. The trip included a visit to the Shenzen special economic zone and, on his return, he actively lobbied the government to include SEZs in its strategy for export-led economic growth. 'After studying the success of these special economic zones in China, I have decided to have similar SEZs in our country,' he told journalists (see Maran 2000).

In Maran's vision this new generation of economic zones would reaffirm India's position in the global economy, advertising the role of the Indian state as a facilitator or mediator for capital to an audience of international investors, and carrying the nation into the twenty-first century. 'SEZs', he said, 'are our best dream-projects.' They 'will act as magnet and glue', attracting foreign direct investment and binding different groups of people and organisations together 'creating a bright future for India' (see Maran 2002).

In 2000 a national coalition government (the National Democratic Alliance) led by the right-wing Bharatya Janata Party (BJP) propelled this vision into policy. New legislation paved the way for the creation of 'special economic zones' based explicitly on the Chinese exemplar, and by 2005 a further twelve zones were established across the country under public–private partnership agreements. These new zones were also expected to deepen a process of economic reform by acting as a vanguard of nationwide liberalisation. As former Prime Minister Atel Bihari Vajpayee explained, 'we see the SEZ not only as stimulating greater investment inflows but also as policy laboratories'.

For impatient reformists, however, the creation of economic zones was a temporary solution and they argued that these experiments be rapidly scaled up. Members of India's financial and business community complained that economic liberalisation had not yet gone far enough and they lobbied for a freeing of market forces, for the abolition of state subsidies, the private financing of infrastructure, the lifting of barriers on capital flight and disinvestment, and the removal of labour laws that protected workers. Yet as the social costs of liberalisation were subjected to increased public scrutiny such measures remained publicly divisive. India's economic liberalisation has been – like China's – 'halting, partially planned and ad hoc' (Rofel 2007: 23), driven by political expediency and regional politics as much as a single unified ideology. Here, as elsewhere, the economic zone emerged as a pragmatic planning technology that allowed state governments to support unfettered capitalism while at the same time denouncing it to their electorates (Palan 2003: 190).

In 2004 India's national elections saw the Indian Congress Party return to power at the head of a new coalition government (the United Progressive Alliance) promising neoliberalism with a human face. One of the new government's first major pieces of legislation was a new SEZ policy (the 2005 SEZ Act) again inspired by what the Minister of Commerce Kamal Nath called in its introduction, 'the Chinese model'. The new policy paved the way for a third generation of zones by offering investors the freedom from government controls and labour laws that neoliberal economists and business lobbyists considered the final structural impediments to growth. The new act dramatically amended the governance structure of these spaces, reducing the role of public finances in their development, increasing the scope for public–private partnerships and expanding the range of permissible business opportunities inside them to include a range of residential, commercial and banking activities.

In the mid 2000s there was an explosion of SEZ projects across India. Between 2005 and 2008 the government granted formal approval to 462 new zones (Aggarwal 2012) and by mid 2013 there was a total of 577 projects across India. Where India's first economic zones had been strategically located to speed up major ports and cities by creating new links to global markets, the SEZ Act invited investors to gravitate towards locations where they anticipated the fastest and highest return on their capital. While China's zones remained state spaces, with the central government deciding where zones should be built, India's zones were to be determined by the market, with private real estate developers and corporations able to propose new zones and to establish their locations, size and nature.

The rapid proliferation of SEZs reveals the uneven ways in which India's regions and communities have been made to accommodate market futures, offering a window onto the spatial and temporal politics of liberalisation. SEZs have not been rolled out across the country in a uniform manner. India is composed of 28 states, founded on the basis of language and self-determination, and across the country economic zones have distinct genealogies, shaped by regional geographies, histories and political economies. Parties from the right and left of the political spectrum – from the Hindu nationalist BJP in the state of Gujarat to the Left Front Communist government in the state of West Bengal – have both adapted and harnessed India's SEZ policy to agendas for development and change. In the post-liberalisation era these state governments have come to enjoy increased autonomy in terms of economic strategy and have become much more active in facilitating inflows of investment. As stronger states used the SEZ policy to offer potential investors a special package of subsidised land, tax breaks and incentives, weaker states, in the face of extraordinary competition for inflows of capital, have been compelled to do so too (Corbridge et al. 2012: 133; Gupta and Sivaramakrishnan 2011: 7).

As a model for industrialisation and growth SEZs have been widely challenged in India. Claims that economic zones catalyse social and economic development by increasing employment, exports and foreign exchange, while transferring skills and technology into the domestic economy, have been subjected to scrutiny and criticism. Meanwhile questions over the terms on which land is acquired for SEZs and the conditions of labour inside them have brought this vehicle of liberalisation into the arena of mass politics (Corbridge et al. 2012: 137; Jenkins 2011: 64). In the second half of the 2000s the rapid proliferation of SEZs saw them emerge as spaces of contestation, marking a frontline in struggles between workers, farmers, activists, businesspeople, investors and state governments over the meanings, beneficiaries and direction of 'development'. Like any large-scale infrastructure development project in India these projects have hinged on the state's power to acquire land for 'public purposes' and the deployment of this power in the name of 'the greater common good' has frequently concealed commitments to very specific interest groups that stood to benefit at the expense of the majority (Corbridge and Hariss 2000; Corbridge et al. 2012).

Nowhere has the contingency of these processes been more pronounced than in the South Indian state of Andhra Pradesh which, by 2013, had seen the approval, planning or construction of more economic zones that any other state.

Andhra Pradesh

Andhra Pradesh entered the international imagination at the end of the 1990s as a poster child for the promises and failures of liberalisation in India. The state had come to circulate both as a shining exemplar of what World Bank structural adjustment loans and the accompanying policies of deregulation, fiscal obedience and market-oriented development programmes hoped to achieve and, simultaneously, as another illustration of the violence, inequalities and new concentrations of power that have accompanied such attempts to re-order economy and society. As India's states competed against each other to encourage inflows of capital, Andhra Pradesh's Telugu nationalists had proved themselves to be among the 'most aggressive and sophisticated political players in the game of globalisation' (Rajan 2006), capturing a major percentage of all foreign direct investment in India. Here the changing relationship between the state and the market in India was manifested in state development policies that were 'equal parts management discourse and advertising spectacle' (Mazzeralla 2010), and the close ties of kinship and caste between a nexus of politicians, industrial capitalists and the agrarian nouveau riche. Just as Andhra Pradesh became synonymous with India's software industry and with innovations in e-governance information technology, so too it became renowned for rampant political corruption, indebtedness of the poor and farmer suicides.

For many social and political activists in India, Andhra Pradesh in the late 1990s was a cauldron of opposition to liberalisation. I first travelled to the state in 2002 as a participant in the Asian Social Forum, a regional offshoot of the World Social Forum (Baviskar 2008; Mertes 2002). This eclectic gathering brought together social and political activists from grassroots campaign groups, trade unions and non-governmental organisations (NGOs) under the banner of an emergent global justice movement with the slogan 'Another world is possible'. For three days, the Nizam College grounds in central Hyderabad were host to seminars, workshops and lectures on the social and economic impact of structural adjustment policies, lending conditionalities, privatisation and industrial development projects, biotechnology, as well the fall-out of communal violence that had rocked the state of Gujarat and strategies of resistance against George W. Bush's War on Terror.

For the forum organisers Andhra Pradesh had been a symbolic choice of venue. A few months before the Social Forum, an outlawed Maoist paramilitary organisation, the People's War Group, had attempted to assassinate the state's Chief Minister, Chandrababu Naidu. For some participants these recent events lent the Social Forum an air of considerable urgency and anticipation, with many social and political activists rejuvenated by the possibilities for progressive struggle that the bleak future seemed to portend.

It was at the Social Forum that I first learnt about the economic zones in the coastal plains of north coastal Andhra Pradesh, outside the state's second largest city Visakhapatnam. Earlier that year a global subcontracting company operating out of the Visakhapatnam SEZ was the subject of a test case submitted to the International Labour Organization alleging the violation of rights to the freedom of association and collective bargaining. In the corner of two giant tents and in hot lecture theatres, the forum's participants shared stories of oppressive working conditions, trade union repression, capitalist work discipline and worker insecurity across Asia's new economic zones, with activists from the Philippines, Malaysia, Sri Lanka and Bangladesh imagining the scope for new forms of regional collective action.

Over the following decade Andhra Pradesh became one of the most enthusiastic proponents of economic zones in India. The state government's investment arm, the Andhra Pradesh Industrial Infrastructure Corporation (APIIC), developed over 20 projects, providing financial support or entering into public–private partnership projects with an array of transnational property developers and industrial houses. By 2013 Andhra Pradesh was home to 20 per cent of all the zones built in India, with zones housing companies in biotechnology, pharmaceuticals, textiles and apparel, gems and jewellery, microelectronics, food, power, metal processing as well as the information technology sector. Official figures showed that close to 140 square km of land across the state had been acquired for the purposes of SEZs, while unofficial figures accounting for land held under different kinds of tenancy agreements, including land that had been granted to the poor, suggested that this figure was closer to 300 square km.

This massive expansion of enclave spaces in Andhra Pradesh has been particularly evident around the city of Visakhapatnam in north coastal Andhra Pradesh. One of India's first economic zones was built here in the early 1990s, one of the largest zones in India was built here a decade later and, by the end of the 2000s, there were another six. Between 2004 and 2012 I carried out some 26 months of ethnographic fieldwork here, working in Telugu and English. My fieldwork included brief visits in 2003, 18 months between 2004 and 2005, a month in 2007, 5 months in 2009 and another month in 2012. The fieldwork has been situated in particular places: in caste-segregated rural villages and small market towns at the frontiers of rural industrialisation; in resettlement colonies and townships populated by people displaced by or working in zones; in the offices of government administrators, trade unions and NGOs; and on the factory floor of a European-owned subcontracting unit for the global diamond industry where – in the spirit of industrial ethnography – I spent twelve months learning to cut and polish rough stones as an unpaid apprentice.

By focusing on this corner of India, this book sets out to reveal the context-specific ways in which attempts to know about, imagine and live towards the future congeal and collide. How is the future summoned and mobilised? How are some futures made to accommodate or constrain others? How do these spaces come to evoke new dreams and incite new desires? How do particular kinds of projects come to materialise collective and individual hopes for power, profit and progress? How do some dreams of profit and progress, social mobility and material success become possible? And what is the status of these economies of anticipation in the making of spaces of capital?

In 2005 a gigantic billboard was erected on the outskirts of Visakhapatnam, advertising the city's first SEZ with a promise to make 'ambitions … aspirations and dreams come true'. The slogan was illustrated with an image of a gleaming airliner taking off from the highway and soaring into the sky. Designed and painted by a Telugu advertising agency, the billboard perfectly captured the economy of anticipation upon which India's flagship industrial infrastructure projects are built. Large-scale industrial infrastructure projects like these are, as Frederick Errington and Deborah Gewertz (2004) once wrote, 'social facts'. Just as they physically dominate and organise the landscape so they shape and are shaped by the dreams and desires of people they attract and employ (2004: 1).

Structure of the Book

Each of this book's five substantive chapters focuses on a different mode of anticipation and follows a different constituency of human actors to explore the hopes, desires, dreams and aspirations that make India's SEZs.

In chapter 2 I follow the politicians and planners who have championed zones as friction-free environments for global capital. This chapter focuses on the political and ideological visions of the free market that are projected onto the economic zone as a space for global capital. In India neoliberal zones and enclaves are often seen through the prism of colonialism, and interpreted as reviving or reproducing colonial-era spatial forms. But modern spatial practices are always more than a reprise or re-establishment of imperial formations and this chapter argues that zones demand to be framed by regional histories and postcolonial genealogies of planned development and modernisation. Tracking the effects of a World Bank structural adjustment loan to Andhra Pradesh during the 1990s, the chapter shows how the state's new zones were part of an 'economy of appearances' (Tsing 2000a) designed to signal its commitment to business and investment. Yet structural adjustment policies overlapped with a resurgent Telugu nationalism and new SEZs were also monuments to a movement for regional autonomy. Struggles for statehood continue to transform India's political geography, with movements of capital and people in post-liberalisation India creating new resources and offering new impetus to regional struggles for statehood (Maringanti 2010). Economic zones, this chapter argues, have become contemporary India's political dream worlds: spaces in which regional politicians have sought to re-imagine, re-make and re-order their states.

Chapter 3 follows the rural communities who challenge or agree to the expropriation of their land as they contest or pursue visions of social and economic development. In India the compulsory acquisition of agricultural land by state governments for the construction of economic zones has repeatedly been met with conflict and violence as farmers and cultivators oppose the terms and conditions of 'industrial development'. Yet the politics of resistance to these zones is shaped less by some coherent or united opposition to 'development' per se than by opposing visions of what development might be. The chapter follows the acquisition of land for what was once touted as the largest economic zone in Asia across the predominantly rural district of Atchutapuram in north coastal Andhra Pradesh. While those government bureaucrats tasked with overseeing the acquisition of land cultivated promises of development and employment, those who stood to lose their land mobilised, leveraged and appropriated these promises to different ends. Moving between rural villages and a new SEZ resettlement colony, the chapter follows the negotiation of compensation payments and resettlement packages to show how different visions of development were invested in the zone. Against a backdrop of historic caste-based inequality in access to agricultural land, Dalit communities and landless cultivators imagined the zone as a harbinger of social mobility and empowerment. Meanwhile it was landowners and rural elites who mobilised opposition to the zone in ways that delayed its construction and allowed them to make new fortunes through speculative investments in real estate.

Chapter 4 focuses on the dreams of profit without responsibility and control without resistance that the managers of global subcontracting firms pursue inside the economic zone. The chapter follows the managers of a subcontracting unit inside the Visakhapatnam SEZ in coastal Andhra Pradesh as they set out to transform this into a globally competitive, world-class manufacturing facility. Tracing the everyday work of management across the shop floor, the chapter shows how attempts to realise corporate fantasies of control over space and people shaped systems of surveillance and supervision, and industrial relations. Here attempts to realise capitalist futures were underpinned by fears and anxieties at the fragility of the future, and managerial nightmares of resistance and the loss of control.

Chapter 5 focuses on the hopes and dreams that are forged in spaces of global manufacturing, and argues that factory labour here demands to be understood as both instrumental and aspirational. The chapter follows a diverse group of young Telugu men from villages and highway townships across coastal Andhra Pradesh as they enter the global workforce inside one of India's oldest SEZs. Through stories and narratives of work inside the region's SEZ factories, the chapter explores how these young people carry aspirations for full employment, personal development and gain onto the factory floor. It shows how family histories of migration and education, as well as filial ties of love and respect constitute a structural context within which these people make sense of low-waged, hyper-intensive manufacturing processes. As the chapter demonstrates, in this corner of provincial South India ideas about the dividends of hard work and toil that have shaped the agrarian economy are carried into the global factory, where they overlap with modern managerial discourses of 'entrepreneurship' and 'self-improvement'. Drawing on my first-hand experience as a machinist on the floor of the Worldwide Diamonds factory, this chapter engages with an established tradition of industrial ethnography, showing how low-waged labour processes here demand to be understood as consensual rather than simply coercive.

Chapter 6 follows the activists who produce India's SEZs as dystopian spaces of capitalism. This chapter shows how representations of the economic zone have come to play a pivotal role in mobilising opposition to neoliberal globalisation and development. As social and political activists work towards more just and democratic futures, they mobilise portraits of exploitation and dispossession that homogenise contradictory experiences and sanitise the politics of resistance. Following trade union rallies and a pan-Indian anti-SEZ campaign, this chapter examines the fields of protest around these spaces. Exploring how opposition to displacement and exploitation has created new alliances between farmers, industrial workers and an educated middle class, it also shows how these political movements reveal underlying tensions and frictions between rural landlords and tenant farmers, young men and women employed as factory workers, and the middle-class social activists campaigning on their behalf. Contrary to the frequent depiction of radical or progressive politics in and around India's SEZs, this book shows how struggles over land and labour transform the political terrain on which these zones exist without necessarily opposing them.

In the concluding chapter I return to the book's opening questions. What kind of effects do the diverse dreams of growth and freedom, profit and control, development and self-improvement that are invested in India's economic zones and enclaves have? In answer, I argue that it is in the pursuit of conflicting and contradictory dreams that people produce the relationships and meanings that make these spaces of global capital. The failure of India's economic zones to realise the hopes and dreams invested in them has not simply produced disenchantment and discontent. Rather it has also given rise to new hopes for the future and makes these zones spaces of continued experimentation and contestation. In India, like elsewhere, market-oriented development policies and projects have come to hinge on the deferred realisation of dreams for development. Indeed, as this book concludes, in much of the global South it is both the anticipation and perpetual postponement of hopes, dreams and expectations for development that has come to define experiences and understandings of capitalism. Here we see that failure is to modernity what crisis is to capitalism: the force through which dreams and desires for the future are renewed.

2

The Vision of Growth

To travel by state bus from the port city of Visakhapatnam into the peri-urban hinterland of north coastal Andhra Pradesh is to take a journey through India's colonial and postcolonial industrial history. The landscape is littered with monuments to successive eras of nationalist modernisation and liberalisation. The roads are heavy with tankers and trucks. The roadside is coated in thick layers of mineral dust and oil.

The journey begins in the city centre, where the statues of nationalist heroes and Telugu poets fight for space amid the micro-electronic bazaars, silk malls and jewellery emporia, before skirting the cranes and container terminals at the edge of the city's port.[1] First opened by Britain's Viceroy and Governor-General of India in 1933 the port drove the city's early growth, transforming what had been a regional outpost of British colonial government into a centre of nationalist industry. Or, as one local history book puts it, transforming a 'sleepy rural idyll' into a 'dirty industrial hub'. India's oldest modern shipbuilding yard was established here in 1941 by the Indian industrialist Walchand Hirachand Doshi and independent India's first steamship, an 8000-ton vessel called the *Jal Usha* or Water Dawn, was built and launched here in 1948 by the country's new prime minister Jawaharlal Nehru. The shipyard was nationalised in the 1960s and for the next 20 years a succession of massive public investments in shipping, maritime and heavy industry made Visakhapatnam one of the fastest growing urban centres in India (Amis and Kumar 2000).

As the bus journey continues you follow an elevated conveyor belt that carries iron ore pellets for 5 km above the city from a vast iron ore handling complex to the port. The bus passes the Hindustan Petroleum Corporation's refinery, epicentre of the city's worst industrial disaster. In September 1996 a vapour cloud of leaking liquid petroleum gas from the refinery exploded, killing 60 people. The bus winds past the city's biggest polluters, privately owned factories making plastics and polymers, nitrogen phosphorus and fertiliser, from which fluoride and nitrates leach into the groundwater supply and sulphur trioxide leaks into the air.

Figure 1   Industrial Visakhapatnam, with the city's steel plant on the horizon

Eventually the bus joins National Highway Number Five, one of India's major transportation routes that connects the east-coast mega-cities of Chennai and Calcutta. On the highway the bus speeds past the heavy metal units making zinc and heavy metal plates, past the industrial estates built in the 1970s to encourage small-scale private entrepreneurship, and through the settlements and townships with names like Auto Nagar and Zinc Colony that were built to house labour migrants and industrial workers. In 1961 Visakhapatnam had a population of just 211,000. Over the following 30 years the city's population grew at a rate of 7 per cent a year and its municipal boundaries were repeatedly extended inland to incorporate the urban townships emerging on its periphery. By the millennium the population of Visakhapatnam city and its peri-urban hinterland had swelled to some 2.6 million people, sandwiched between Benares and Bhopal in the list of India's major urban centres or 'second-tier cities'. The population of this entire municipal region is expected to surpass 3.5 million people by 2021.[2]

The most important local monuments to India's industrial history and its planned future lie just over an hour from the city's centre, 35 km inland, where Highway Number Five steamrolls through the small township of Kurumanapalem. The roadside is lined with licensed bars, cigarette stands, tea stalls, and tiffin stalls selling deep fried chillies, *dosas* (pancakes made

Figure 2   Gateway to the Visakha steel plant

from rice batter and black lentils) and *idlis* (steamed cakes made from rice and black lentil). The city's most prominent sites of industry, investment and work are signposted here. On one side of the road lies a grand archway emblazoned with the words 'Welcome to the City of Steel' that marks the entrance to the Visakha steel plant. This plant commemorates an era of postcolonial nationalism and a vision of industrial modernisation rooted in central planning and import substitution.

On the opposite side of the highway a road leads to one of India's oldest economic zones, a monument to ideologies of market-oriented development. For years the road to the zone was poorly signposted. But by the end of the 2000s the increased political significance of economic zones as drivers of Andhra Pradesh's regional development and industrialisation had been signalled by the construction of a gigantic red and black gateway that straddled the road. Today a gigantic banner hangs in the centre of this gateway with a larger-than-life portrait of Andhra Pradesh's late Congress Party Chief Minister Y.S. Rajshekhara Reddy striding forwards, welcoming investors to the Visakhapatnam Special Economic Zone.

The twin gateways that tower over National Highway Number Five on the outskirts of Visakhapatnam stand testament to the importance of large-scale industrial infrastructure projects in the landscape of provincial

Figure 3   Gateway to the Visakhapatnam special economic zone

India. Like India's steel plants the country's economic zones have become important reference points in narratives of social and economic transformation, and the hopes and expectations attached to them reflect local histories of industrialisation as well as past promises of growth and development. In an interview with me, a deputy officer in the Andhra Pradesh Industrial Infrastructure Corporation (APIIC) once summed up the enthusiasm for economic zones among the city's planners and public servants. As his comments made clear, the weight of expectation attached to these projects was oriented backwards in time to local social histories of development, and past promises projected onto ports, shipyards and steel plants, as much as it was oriented forwards into the future.

This city, Visakhapatnam, has always been talked of in big words. It's always been described as a city with potential. It's been called the City of Destiny, the City of Beauty, the City of Delight, the City of This and the City of That. But it never grew as much as it should have. Well now its time has come! Now it will start growing! With these new zones the government has committed itself to the promotion of the city. You watch! Within ten years this entire city will be changed beyond recognition. You won't be able to recognise it any more. That's the kind of potential it has now. In a decade this city will make its mark. These new projects are going to put this city on the international map!

*   *   *

In this chapter I explore the economic zone as a planned space and planning as a particular mode of anticipation through which states and governments articulate dreams for the future. In doing so I provide a background to this book by showing how India's SEZs are embedded in regional histories of industrialisation and liberalisation.

To their critics India's economic zones are frequently said to revive colonial-era spatial forms (Sidaway 2003, 2007). To be sure, the preferential conditions and tax exemptions that are offered to investors in India's SEZs, for example, might be said to have their antecedents in the *dastaks* (duty-free passes) and *firmans* (imperial decrees) wrung from India's eighteenth-century rulers by the British East India Company (Robins 2006). As the rulers of India's Mughal-era princely states sought to guarantee their continued international trade and political survival in the face of Britain's military-backed commercial expansion they frequently had little choice but to grant concessions and preferential trading conditions. Today, as India's state governments compete against each other for inflows of foreign direct investment, the special package of land, public subsidies and tax exemptions that comprise the SEZ frequently appear to reproduce these exchanges, as 'geo-bribes' or deal-making gifts aimed at satiating the demands of corporate investors (Roy 2009: 79).

Spaces of capitalism, however, are always more than a reprise of imperial forms or patterns and, as I explore in this chapter, India's SEZs are also rooted in 'regional modernities' (Sivaramakrishnan and Agrawal 2003) and a genealogy of spatial forms that tie them to postcolonial projects of industrial modernisation. Like other large-scale social and economic infrastructure projects – from factories to dams, cities built to a grid plan and centralised communication networks – India's SEZs represent the legacy of a 'modernist moment' in planning. The history of economic zones, as planned or state spaces, is anchored in political projects to imagine or re-imagine the nation. Indeed, as I explore, India's free trade zones are to liberalising India what steel plants and townships were to the postcolonial Nehruvian state.

Yet just as zones are always spaces of history they are also always spaces of novelty and innovation that give shape and form to particular visions of the future. In the ordering of space and people, the design of their built environments and the organisation of work both steel plants and zones anticipate and attempt to bring about particular kinds of future, new kinds of territory and new political subjectivities. Like the industrial infrastructure projects undertaken during a period of postcolonial nation-building, India's first zones were also projects of social engineering, intended to create new economic spaces and working subjects as much as to generate jobs, exports or foreign exchange. But while the grand designs inscribed in India's new towns, cities and industries during the 1950s and 1960s were oriented inwards, towards the nation and its citizens, those inscribed in its economic zones were oriented outwards, towards the global market and its investors.

As spaces of experimentation with social, political and economic organisation India's economic zones manifest ideas about planning and administration, science and technology that have defined India's experience of modernity and its mythologies of state building.[3] They have also brought these ideas into relationship with other globally circulating forms of knowledge and technical expertise, templates and models, around which states and populations have been reformatted in relation to the global market. As I show in this chapter, India's economic zones also demand to be understood in relation to the development imaginaries and political economies of regional political entities within the nation-state. Just as liberalising economic policies have been adapted, interpreted and negotiated by regional political actors so too India's SEZ policies have been harnessed to the ambitions and development imaginaries of its regional state governments.

As anthropologists remind us, the promises of modern planning are part of what produces place (Abram and Weskalnys 2011, 2013), and this chapter explores how economic zones are shaped by visions for social and economic development. In post-liberalisation India, as the barriers on capital flows began to be removed and state governments competed against each other to attract inflows of foreign direct investment, SEZs emerged as spaces onto which the spectacular potential of states for potential investors could be projected. As differences between state-level infrastructures and political environments have become important for investors, the qualities of time and space have become especially marked. For state governments to attract inflows of capital they have had to inspire investors, inducing their confidence and optimism by projecting spectacular possibilities for growth and profit making onto territory under their administration. Across South India large-scale infrastructure projects are also political performances that dramatise the potential of states as good places to do business. With economic zones state governments have been able to fashion places of as yet unrealised possibility, conjuring up the possibility of growth, profit and economic performance for audiences of potential investors in what Anna Tsing (2000a) has called the 'economy of appearances'.

After Steel

When Visakhapatnam's steel plant opened in 1984 it quickly became a defining feature, welded onto the identity of Andhra's second largest city. The distinctive profile of the plant's coke ovens and blast furnaces came to dominate the city's southern skyline, just as the wages and benefits enjoyed by the plant's 20,000 public sector workers came to dominate ideas of secure, stable employment in a local imagination.

The families of over 4000 steel plant workers live beside the plant in a purpose-built township, Ukkunagaram. This town, whose name literally means Steel-Town in Telugu, was one of the last steel townships to be built by India's central government after independence.[4] With its expansive tarmac streets, built in a large circular layout, its underground sewerage, storm water drains and underground power cabling, it resembles the suburbs of an indistinct North American town more than the unplanned highway townships. Each residential area is carefully linked to market places, parks, a theatre, leisure centre, marriage hall and welfare centres. There are three large Hindu temples, a Catholic and a Baptist church, and a mosque, which residents point to as evidence of the township's ecumenical spirit. Residents have established cultural associations and social clubs. The town is governed by an independent administration and is supplied with water from its own reservoir.

The steel plants and townships built by the Indian state between the 1950s and 1970s have an important place in India's postcolonial history. In their struggle for independence from Britain during the 1930s and 1940s India's nationalist politicians saw the state as a vehicle for re-imagining, re-engineering and materialising a postcolonial Indian nation. As they envisaged it, an independent Indian nation-state would not simply replicate or imitate. Instead, through its organisation, administration and organs of governance the independent Indian state would establish a modernity that differed from that of the West in ways that expressed India's coming into being and imagined a new national community. The postcolonial future was one in which technical expertise and development planning would accomplish for India what it had never been able to achieve for the colonial state, when this apparatus was tied to the commercial interests of Great Britain. As Gyan Prakash (1999) has written, forms of technical expertise and scientific knowledge were crucial to India's constitution and the Nehruvian state made a foundational commitment to development through planning, as a 'utopian practice that would make India a modern nation'.

In this spirit steel plants and townships were quintessentially modernist spaces that embraced the technical, scientific rationality of urban planning, architecture and design as a means with which to shed old social, cultural and conceptual ties and to build future-oriented forms of collective identity and association. The impetus for building steel towns and townships went far beyond the economic imperative for steel or a practical need to provide housing for a new public sector work force. Steel plants were, as anthropologist Jonathan Parry (1999a: 133) put it, 'crucibles of Nehruvian modernity' that would forge not just steel but new kinds of society. These industrial workplaces were to be symbols of the nation's integration, in which workers from different parts of the country would transcend their pre-modern or 'primordial' loyalties of caste, region and religion for new collective and patriotic identities. The townships built alongside them were, in historian Sirupa Roy's (2007: 134) phrase, 'dreamworlds': spaces that called forth the future of national time, re-worked the nationalist gaze and produced new kinds of citizen-subjects. Townships were imagined as self-sufficient enclaves, politically and economically autonomous in relation to their surroundings. For their planners and politicians they were 'new kinds of places inhabited by new kinds of people who would directly participate in the grand project of building the nation' (2007: 138). Townships were spaces in which the transition from dependent colonial economy to sovereign and planned national economy could take place and the transformation of the unfree subject to the productive citizen could be enacted.

What steel plants and townships were to India's Nehruvian state the free trade zone was to become to the post-Nehruvian (Menon and Nigam 2007) or liberalising state. In these planned capitalist enclaves a dramatic and substantial re-working took place of nationalist priorities and once-established ideas about territory and citizenship. Between the mid 1960s and the mid 1990s India's central government sanctioned a small number of what it then called 'export processing zones' that would offer foreign investors purpose-built factory units, office and administration facilities, upgraded transportation links, subsidised electricity, water and tele-communications, as well as long-term exemptions on import duties and export profits. The first of these was opened in 1965 by Prime Minister Lal Bahadur Shastri in the port of Kandla, Gujarat, and India claims it as the first special economic zone in Asia. In 1974 a second zone was built in Mumbai and during the 1980s four more zones were established, in Delhi, Chennai, Calcutta and Cochin, in Kerala, all of them strategically located close to major cities, seaports and airports. A final zone was built outside Visakhapatnam. A proposal to locate a free trade zone here was first raised by the government of Andhra Pradesh in the late 1980s as the then Congress government sought to rein in public spending and attract foreign investors. Planning permission was eventually granted at the very cusp of the 1990s and construction work began in 1991, the year in which a foreign exchange crisis, a loan from the International Monetary Fund and the announcement of a new programme of economic reform by Finance Minister Manmohan Singh marked a tipping point in India's liberalisation.

These first-generation economic zones were centrally planned public undertakings, overseen and administered by the Ministry of Commerce in Delhi. State governments could propose sites for a zone and had to provide land and meet the costs of construction, while the central government committed to administering and governing them. By contrast with the grand nation-building designs being inscribed in India's steel plants and steel townships, these new enclaves were relatively modest undertakings. The zones were all relatively small in size, somewhere between 0.5 km and 3 km square, the costs of building them were far less than that of a steel plant or township and their immediate impact on the surrounding landscape was far less spectacular. But these zones shared with other kinds of Nehruvian-era infrastructure projects a basic premise of modernist planning: that the organisation and form of the built environment was a means for re-ordering economy and society towards the future. Like steel plants and townships these early zones were projects of social engineering – generative infrastructure projects that were intended to create new economic spaces and working subjects as much as they were intended to generate jobs and foreign exchange, promote exports and accelerate industrialisation.

Where the planned industrial worlds of Nehruvian modernity had been tied to the imagination of the nation, of national space and nationalist working subjects, the planned capitalist enclaves that the Indian state began to build during the 1970s and 1980s were spaces in which the nation's territory and its working subjects were being re-imagined in relationship to the global economy. While India's investments in steel had been inward looking investments in the nation, the construction of its new export processing zones were oriented outwards, into the world. They were to be globally networked spaces that would materialise transnational flows of finance, commodities, information and people. For years the road to the Visakhapatnam zone was signposted with a billboard that captured the way it was being imagined as a transnational space with horizons and connections beyond South Asia: 'Vizag Special Economic Zone is VSEZ: Four Letters. Five continents!'

In the unadorned simplicity of their design and layout, these first zones encapsulated ideas of rationalised efficiency. Each zone was to be marked with a boundary wall which both demarcated the area for tax and customs purposes as lying outside the domestic tariff but also regulated the zone's built environment. Internally the zone was carefully organised and subjected to strong visual controls. Specific areas were demarcated for administration blocks or security compounds and kept separate from areas identified for designated industries, like garments or microelectronics. Trees, plantations and flower-beds created barriers between different internal zones, maintaining a careful segregation of different spaces and functions.

The zone at Visakhapatnam, for example, covers 365 acres and is surrounded by an 8 foot perimeter wall topped with broken glass. Inside the zone green belts of eucalyptus, bamboo, teak and neem trees are planted around purpose-built factory units. In maps and models of the zone everything beyond the perimeter wall is left blank. This image – of the zone as an isolated territory, lifted out of its surroundings, unmoored and cast adrift from the larger regulatory environment – was precisely how it had been conceived in legal terms and exactly how it appeared to local urban planners. 'It's like an island', some of them told me, 'cut off from the mainland'.

These first zones were also modelled on India's industrial estates (cf. Levien 2013). During the 1950s the Indian government acquired land on the edge of towns and cities to create estates for private industry and offered subsidies and low-rent manufacturing sheds as means of stimulating enterprise in particular locations. By 1961 there were 120 industrial estates across India where people manufactured basic consumer goods for domestic markets – things like safety razor blades, barbed wire, hair combs, dyes, paper bags and umbrella ribs – as well as components and parts for larger industries, things like switch boards and cinema equipment. Government administrators saw these industrial estates as 'excellent opportunities for controlled observation and experiments with private enterprise' that protected state-owned industries from the market (Alexander 1963: 49). By contrast, its new free trade zones were designed to insulate capitalists from the state. Rather than protecting the nation from the market, these zones were built to insulate India's nascent export economy from what were deemed uncompetitive rules and regulations.

The centrepiece of each zone was the 'standard design factory', an identikit building connected to power, water, telephone and waste disposal networks, which was designed so investors could move straight in and begin operations. Like the factory units built in India's industrial estates the 'standard design factory' was rooted in a functionalist architectural tradition. A high-ranking civil servant once described the aesthetic:

> An industrial estate should essentially have the features of a 'utility' building project. It is quite unnecessary to make them show pieces of architectural beauty or specimens of perfection in constructional style. This does not mean construction should be crude. Nor is cheapness a virtue to be achieved at all cost. What is required is simplicity in style. (Alexander 1963: 58)

Space inside these units was held on a renewable lease and investors were free to build cabins, add partition walls and install machinery according to their needs.

Just as these zones were imagined as transnational spaces through which the nation could be integrated into the global economy, they were also to be spaces in which Indian subjects could be re-moulded around the needs and demands of the global economy. In the Visakhapatnam SEZ a framed message hanging behind the desk of the zone's development commissioner encapsulated the kinds of personal conduct and values enshrined in the space: it read, 'God made man to work, Work is man's best duty'. Such proclamations of hard work as a 'moral, personal and social good' (Rose 1999: 103) have been central to the social organisation of these zones and to the labour regimes that they have fostered. In public sector industries like Visakhapatnam's steel plant the terms and conditions of work were the outcome of collective bargaining agreements between trade unions and managers. But inside the economic zone employers were exempted from complying with national labour policies. Until the mid 2000s employers in Visakhapatnam's economic zone, for example, did not need to keep a register of their employees or fix daily working hours; they were also not compelled to record or publish working hours,[5] wage rates,[6] employee tasks or shift details.[7]

For some commentators the social and economic impact of these early zones was unspectacular (e.g. Aggarwal 2012). Far from creating islands of freedom from the state and flexibility within a centrally planned economy these early zones remained tightly controlled by the Indian government. Zone authorities had few executive powers to approve new investors. New businesses were subject to tight checks and had to obtain licences and permissions from several different state and central government departments. Customs procedures were not streamlined, exports were often subject to long delays and there was little scope for private investment in the physical infrastructure of the zones themselves. Unlike the zones that were built at the same time in South East Asia (Malaysia, Indonesia, the Philippines) as well as those in neighbouring Bangladesh and Sri Lanka, India's zones remained relatively unexciting for investors. To the chagrin of India's business elites these zones remained far from the vision of a smooth, efficient market utopia. By the mid 1990s they remained at the bottom of international league tables that ranked zones in terms of the environment they offered to global business (Aggarwal 2012).

By the mid 1990s, however, the Indian state no longer held a monopoly over development planning. Processes of decentralisation had seen increased responsibility devolved to sub-national or state governments. At the same time an array of non-state agencies, including international development organisations and management consultancies, with claims to authority, knowledge and technical expertise in the design and implementation of economic reforms had become more closely involved in development planning. At the end of the 1990s economic zones re-emerged as symbols of the country's commitment to liberalisation and as engines that could drive spectacular rates of future growth.

Globally Mobile Zones

Just as India's economic zones have a distinct postcolonial genealogy so too have they been shaped by particular forms of knowledge and technical expertise associated with an era of economic reform. In the wake of India's economic liberalisation, international financial institutions like the World Bank and the Asian Development Bank (ADB), international donors like the UK's Department for International Development (DFID) and international management consultancy firms like Price Waterhouse Coopers and McKinsey emerged as sources of technical expertise on development planning and economic policy. These organisations have been vital conduits for the movement of knowledge and technical expertise associated with liberalisation across political, geographic and cultural borders. During the 1990s they played an important role in the global circulation of models for economic zones, not just encouraging governments to build zones but also giving expertise, advice and support aimed at showing how zones should be built.

The World Bank, for example, explicitly argued that economic zones in countries like India should be evaluated purely in terms of their contribution to a continuing project of economic liberalisation. The World Bank's commercial lending arm, the International Finance Corporation (IFC) was particularly instrumental in the transfer of knowledge about economic zones between policy makers across countries in South Asia, publishing a detailed practitioners guide for policy makers that offers guidance for creating what it called 'commercially viable economic zones'. Through capacity building projects and consultations the IFC worked to encourage 'market-oriented' rather than 'politically motivated decisions' and offered guidance on the design of a regulatory framework for such zones.

Meanwhile the ADB carefully monitored policy developments on economic zones in China and South East Asia by funding in-country research studies. Through their annual publication, *Asian Development Outlook* and regional 'technical cooperation' meetings, the ADB spread what they called 'good practices', encouraging the use of economic zones as a planning technology that could encourage foreign direct investment, promote exports and drive industrialisation. As international management consultancy firms and technical cooperation organisations set up new offices in Delhi, they offered advice to India's Planning Commission and regional state governments on economic restructuring. In 1994 the

Ford Foundation, for example, funded a fact-finding mission by a team of Indian researchers and policy makers to China.[8] The published findings of their visit (Gupta 1996) describe how the research team saw China's zones as a 'laboratory of experiment for the smooth transition of the Chinese economy' and how they set out to identify 'useful features of Chinese zones that could be adapted to Indian conditions'.

The normative prescriptions for success and failure that circulated through these organisations are eminently mobile. The organisation or structure of zones in different countries, as documented by international organisations, created a decontextualised technology of planning, a 'freestanding entity' or 'free floating' blueprint (Mitchell 2002: 231). The particular characteristics and qualities of zones like those in South Korea, Malaysia and the Philippines, for example, were lifted out of their regional contexts and political economies, standardised and codified, so that their features or qualities appeared to be neatly transferable to other states. In this way the economic zone became entirely disconnected from local political or historical contexts in ways that allowed policy makers to imagine that the zones could be easily replicated from country to country.

Life-cycle models of the economic zone designed by business scholars for policy makers to predict and plan a zone's growth over time have proved particularly popular in India. These models plot stages in a zone's development onto moments of regulation or inflows of investment, technology or human capital.[9] In one model (Srivastava and Rai 2007) the life of a zone is broken into four stages, a Launching Phase, a Ramp-up Phase, a Payback Phase and an Annuity Phase; each phase is superimposed onto a 'break-even' chart that shows two lines of costs and revenues. By lifting zones out of all local and historical time, and emptying them of geo-political context, such models lend themselves particularly well to standardisation and to universal applicability.

In India these life-cycle models have been particularly influential, regularly presented at business conferences on economic zones and frequently referred to by civil servants. Yet if such technologies purport to make the economic future of the zone knowable, exact and legitimate, they also invoke an indeterminate and unspecified future in ways that allow planners to hedge their bets. As the civil servant responsible for one massive multi-product zone in India put it to me:

> You will start with slow growth as people come to scout it out and then we will attract some anchor industries. Then growth will be gradual

following a normal curve, then peaking, then reaching saturation. But we can't say yet whether the life cycle for the zones will be eight years, or ten, or 15 or 20 years. All the zone projects are still new or are consolidating. It's too early to say.

Of course, development agencies and management consultancies in India are alert to accusations that their models or practices are simply 'imported' and they frequently emphasise the ways in which their work is adapted to 'local circumstance'. Like the global advertising agencies that adapt brand-name consumer goods to place for their corporate clients (e.g. Mazzarella 2003), the added value claimed by global consultancy firms in India is their ability to adapt globally circulating ideas, paradigms and concepts to the particularities of place. The regional director of a global management consultancy told me in Hyderabad:

Consultancy firms like ours do not simply import blueprints, we reshape the blueprints to fit the particularities of India's states. We don't just bring in concepts because they worked somewhere else. We look at similar situations elsewhere and we say, 'in this place, this has worked,' then we take that knowledge and we modulate it to a local environment and local requirements.

This adaptation of policies and programmes for liberalisation to place has been strikingly apparent in Andhra Pradesh. Here the 'rule of experts' (Mitchell 2002) was enlisted in struggles for regional autonomy, self-determination and a Telugu nation, or *Telugu-dessam*.

The Telugu Nation

In 1952 a 50-year-old Ghandhian activist, Potti Sreeramulu, began a fast-unto-death in an attempt to force the newly independent Indian government to integrate all Telugu-speaking people within a single administrative area. His suicide in the name of the mother tongue marked the modern rise of the Telugu language as the foundation of collective cultural and political identities (Mitchell 2009) and was followed by a popular agitation. In its wake Jawaharlal Nehru's government carved out a new linguistic state, named Andhra State, from two Telugu-speaking regions along India's east coast, previously part of Madras. Five years later, in 1957 the dissolution of one of India's last remaining princely states, Hyderabad, saw the addition of its Telugu-speaking districts merged into the new state, now renamed Andhra Pradesh.

At India's independence, economic and political power in the north coastal region of Andhra Pradesh was concentrated among strata of former peasant castes – Reddys, Kammas and Vysas – who controlled irrigated lands in the delta of the Krishna-Godavari river. In the post-independence period land reforms and increases in agricultural productivity enabled them to gain control of fertile land and irrigation facilities across the state, and invest their agricultural surplus in industry and politics (Srinivasulu 2002). During the 1970s and 1980s Kamma families began to diversify out of agriculture and began to re-invest their agricultural surpluses in urban centres and a range of urban businesses across the state, including transportation, real estate, education, the print media, the Telugu film industry, manufacturing and politics. The translation of Kamma capital into political power culminated with the entry of cinema star and matinee idol, N.T. Rama Rao (popularly known as NTR), onto the political stage. Rama Rao came to fame playing heroes and villains in big-screen versions of mythological Hindu epics, gaining particular acclaim for his roles as Rama and Krishna in the Ramayana and the Mahabaratha. In 1982, aged 59, NTR ended his cinematic career and formed a new party, the Telugu Dessam Party (TDP).

Since its formation as a separate state Andhra Pradesh had been ruled by the Indian Congress Party, a coalition of Brahmins and Reddys. But in 1983 the newly formed TDP swept the state's assembly elections and N.T. Rama Rao became its first Kamma Chief Minister. A year later, in India's 1984 national elections, the TDP became the second largest party in the Indian parliament, the *Lok Sabha*.

The rise to power of this intermediate caste, vernacular and agrarian elite in Andhra Pradesh was paralleled across India. During the 1980s a new wave of political movements gained control of regional state assemblies, fracturing the dominance of the Congress Party that had ruled India since independence. These movements were avowedly anti-Congress and appropriated the rhetoric of postcolonial Indian nationalism to assert their autonomy from central government. The emergence of these parties signalled the rise of caste communities who occupied an intermediate position in a Hindu ritual hierarchy but who were often the dominant social group in their area. Kammas were well-organised, landowning communities who had benefited from post-independence land reforms and green revolution agriculture. As they sought to translate these benefits into political power they celebrated their rustic and unsophisticated credentials and championed a new populism.

On the campaign trail in 1983 Rama Rao stoked popular resentment at the power of the Congress Party, telling voters that the 'great state of Andhra Pradesh would no longer be treated as a branch office of the Congress Party' and that 'Andhra's pride need not be pledged to Delhi but could be upheld in Hyderabad' (Guha 2007: 553). Meanwhile he played up his on-screen mythological persona, touring the state in a Chevrolet van modified to resemble a chariot, or *chaitanya ratham*, and appearing at political rallies dressed as Lord Rama. In doing so he echoed the opposition of other vernacular leaders to the upper-caste, secular-nationalist modernist discourse of the Congress Party and their erasure of caste and religious identities from the political field. Yet the Congress Party's 'modern universalist language' remained an important part of public politics and NTR worked to recruit educated professionals – including doctors, teachers and lawyers – to his campaign, as well as those caste communities that had been historically under-represented by political parties.

The rise to power of the Kamma-led TDP was accompanied by new assertions of Andhra Pradesh's territorial, cultural and economic unity. This was most evident in the party's campaign slogan '*aarukotla andhrula aatma garuvamu*' or 'self-pride for the 60 million people of Andhra', in which a demand for regional respect and dignity also reasserted the linguistic, demographic and geographical boundaries of the state. In Hyderabad new inflows of capital and people from the coastal districts of Andhra Pradesh saw the imposition of a more parochial 'Telugu' culture on the city. Housing colonies, places and institutions were renamed, statues and sculptures of Telugu heroes, poets and scribes were installed across the city, and the growing Telugu movie industry re-worked representations of a shared Telugu identity based primarily around a common language (Srinivas 2008, 2009).

In the mid 1990s increased frustration at the lack of opportunities for business led Kamma industrialists to lobby for significant changes in government policy. Andhra Pradesh's largest Telugu newspaper, *Eenadu* or *Today* – owned and run by Kamma entrepreneur Cherukuri Ramoji Rao, a former hotelier whose Ramoji Group was the state's largest Kamma-owned corporation – led demands for change. The paper appealed for a new vision in government, a no-nonsense administrative efficiency and purposeful decision making that would appeal to local, national and multinational capital (Damodaran 2008). In 1995 the influence and support of this Kamma pro-business lobby saw N.T. Rama Rao overthrown as leader of the TDP by his son in law, Chandrababu Naidu.

Under Chandrababu Naidu's leadership the TDP set out to redefine the interests of Andhra Pradesh. This was done not just by emphasising its territorial integrity and the idea of a unified Telugu community with a common heritage and shared linguistic identity but also by calling upon the language of planning and administration, what Thomas Blom Hansen (2001) has called some of the most powerful registers of higher knowledge, authority and the sublime in India's contemporary political imaginary. Campaigning with the slogan *Prajala Kosam Pragathi Kosam* (For People and Progress), Chandrababu Naidu declared that states should become strong economic entities on their own, able to plan for their own economies and raise their own resources. 'No meaningful liberalisation without economic decentralisation,' he declared (*Business Weekly* 2002). This reformist agenda invoked a tradition of Indian statecraft and Naidu presented the state as an instrument of technocratic rationality that could achieve for Andhra Pradesh what India's central government had failed to do because of its commitments to the nation as a whole. This language and rhetoric echoed historic struggles for political autonomy by India's independence movement. As the Telugu commentator and activist K. Balagopal (1995: 2483) wrote, 'one may call this a process of the nation in the making, if there were a nation in the making'.

Reformatting Andhra Pradesh

At the end of the 1990s this Telugu nationalist project to re-imagine the cultural integrity, unity and identity of Andhra Pradesh found an ally in the discursive power of development planning to construct technical objects for intervention, delineated in terms of space and people, geography and demographics. As international financial organisations and development agencies lent their support to regional programmes of economic reform and growth in India they helped to re-imagine Andhra Pradesh as a discrete economic entity, a bounded, free-standing unit that could be mapped, measured, known, examined and compared against other units.

In 1998 the World Bank begin to experiment with a new type of lending operation in Andhra Pradesh, one that applied its regimen of structural adjustment policies to a more targeted area and population than that of a whole country. The 'Andhra Pradesh Economic Restructuring Project' (APERP) was one of the first times the World Bank had granted a loan to a regional rather than a national government, and it marked a major shift in World Bank strategy. In India the APERP signalled that the World Bank would now be directing resources towards state governments that could demonstrate their commitment to implementing economic reforms and their support for ongoing processes of decentralisation.

The challenge facing Andhra Pradesh, as the World Bank saw it, was that it had a population of more than 75 million people, the state was faced with the rising cost of public debt,[10] its per-person income was around US$385, nearly 22 per cent of its population was below the poverty line, and 40 per cent of its primary-school age children were out of school. The APERP provided the government of Andhra Pradesh with US$301.3 million in direct loans and a US$241.9 million credit facility aimed at restructuring public expenditure and encouraging private investment. The money was directed at six priority sectors (primary education, primary health, child development, road building, irrigation and public enterprise reform). Across each sector the World Bank advocated major cuts in public spending and changes in regulation aimed at expanding the role of the private sector in the provision of utilities, health care and education, and encouraging private investment.

This was the first of four economic restructuring and reform loans, totalling some US$695 million, that the World Bank made to Andhra Pradesh over the following decade to further the state's economic restructuring. Just under half of this amount – US$300 million – was financed by the British government under its commitments to international aid. The UK's DFID provided technical assistance in several areas, including departmental reviews, public enterprise and health sector reforms, and good governance. The money was also closely tied to a set of recommendations for specific spending reforms and represented a binding agreement that the government of Andhra Pradesh would accept the World Bank's fiscal discipline, committing it to end populist spending measures and to make wide reductions in spending.

The influence of the World Bank's financial support and its 'rule of experts' (Mitchell 2002) was immediately apparent in Andhra Pradesh. The World Bank's analyses and appraisals directly shaped the government's financial management, defining budget ceilings and spending targets. Many of its prescriptions were adopted verbatim, forming the basis for decisions on spending priorities and development strategies. Meanwhile, the idea of government shifted to that of a managerial or entrepreneurial entity (Harvey 1990b: 12; Peck and Tickell 2002) whose role was reduced to creating new incentive structures for private enterprise. The language of paternalism, of donations, hand-outs, charity and welfare provided by a benevolent ruler that had marked the policies of N.T. Rama Rao were gone. In its place came the technocratic language that surrounds the planning of market reforms, with keywords like growth, delivery, performance, transparency and good governance, and in which administrative or technical measures were the solutions to inefficiency, corruption or stagnation. At a time of intense competition between South India's state governments for inflows of foreign direct investment, this new language was not just aimed at powerful electoral constituencies but also at an international audience of investors and lenders.

Vision 2020

The full implications of these shifts were exemplified in a major new vision for the state's social and economic development. In 1997 Chandrababu Naidu created a series of 14 committees or 'task forces' to develop strategy papers for different sectors of the Andhra economy. Press releases noted the contributions of 119 people, including high-ranking civil servants and academic subject specialists. Two years later Naidu commissioned one of the world's largest management consultancy companies, the US-based firm McKinsey, to convert and format these strategy papers into a singular, unitary vision for the future of the state, *Vision 2020* (Government of Andhra Pradesh 1999). Like similar documents, *Vision 2020* exemplified the importance of the very far distant or indefinite future in projects of economic reform, and it imagined a long-term vista of growth reaching 20 years into the future and beyond.

Written and designed by McKinsey at a reported cost of 9.8 billion rupees (approximately US$2.3 million), this document presented a series of targets, time-frames and benchmarks for Andhra Pradesh's social and economic transformation. The course set by *Vision 2020* adhered closely to the spending regime prescribed under the terms of the World Bank's structural adjustment loan. Its roadmap for fiscal obedience, good governance, decentralisation and the expansion of markets drew heavily upon the dominant models and paradigms of development that were being disseminated by an array of international organisations in India, including the ADB and the UK's DFID. At its launch Naidu said that his government was directly 'drawing on the experiences of others' in an attempt to 'leapfrog over several stages of development' and 'telescope into one generation what took decades and, possible centuries, for other societies and other States to achieve' (Government of India 1999: 146–7).

While *Vision 2020* drew explicitly upon 'policy lessons' from Malaysia, South Korea and China, it also drew inspiration from a different kind of project, one that linked industrialisation, export-oriented development and economic growth to a politics of cultural revitalisation, linguistic identity and autonomy. One of its models was *Wawasan 2020* in which Malaysian president Mahathir Mohamad tied the re-imagination of an ethnic Malay nation to a technocratic vision of rapid export-led economic growth and envisaged a future in which Malaysia would be subservient to none (Greider 1997; Naidu 2000: 235). In Andhra Pradesh, *Vision 2020* similarly asserted the existence of a single, unified Telugu community with a common language and heritage, and also asserted the territorial integrity of Andhra Pradesh as a singular, united regional political entity: a state within the state. The *Vision 2020* document was Andhra Pradesh's coming into being as a technocratic state, a Telugu nation in modernity, that made it the equal of Delhi. 'My dream is to see my state as a Swarna Andhra, a golden state,' Chandrababu Naidu (2000) wrote. 'Once there is a vision, the rest falls into place.' As he also liked to tell journalists during his two terms in office, 'vision without action is a mere dream. Action without vision is a mere wastage of time.'

Vision 2020 was, as one Telugu observer noted, the 'document of a dream' (Bandyopadhyay 2001) and the future it portrayed was one in which the economy of Andhra Pradesh grew at an unprecedented and spectacular rate: 10 per cent, every year, for 20 years. It was a future in which poverty was eradicated, inequality eliminated and the education, health and wellbeing of all dramatically improved. Achieving this future required Andhra to witness a rapid epochal shift in its economy, away from agricultural to urban industry. Economic growth was to be driven by the rapid construction of an entirely new physical infrastructure for business and a 'quantum leap' in urban industries. Export manufacturing, in particular, was to be promoted as the solution to problems of unemployment and under-investment. By 2020, according to the roadmap *Vision 2020* laid out, export manufacturing would account for 21 per cent of the state's economy and would have created 43 per cent of new jobs.

The scale of new construction that this vision demanded was staggering: 350,000 km of new roads, double what already existed; 5000 km of additional railway tracks; two new international and six new domestic airports; between four and six new ports for container shipping; a 15-fold increase in telephone density; and a five-fold increase in the state's capacity to generate power from hydro-electric and thermal power plants. The costs were immense. Building the infrastructure of the future was estimated to cost the equivalent of US$32 billion, at least 70 to 80 per cent of which was to be privately financed.

Vision 2020 saw Andhra Pradesh reborn as India's friction-free or frictionless state (Mazzarella 2006): a state in which the mediations, frictions and blockages that comprise social life have been removed or effaced in order to allow the unmediated movement of capital and production of profit (2006: 485). By 2020, it imagined, the everyday work of government would be to create an enabling environment for business. This would be a state in which government was reduced to the rational and technical work of facilitation, attracting inflows of private capital and directing them towards the creation of infrastructure, health services and education. It would be a state in which the principal role of government would be to remove all impediments to competition or trade, and to facilitate the smooth flow of private capital; a state into and out of which investment could flow without resistance; and a state in which the market operated without any distortions or blockages.

No space appeared to better realise this fantasy than the economic zone, and *Vision 2020* made planned capitalist enclaves the pillars of the state's new economy. The zone was deemed to be as essential to Andhra's future industrial infrastructure as power plants, ports, airports, roads, and electricity or telecommunications networks. Andhra Pradesh *Vision 2020* declared, needed a series of 'world-class economic zones' that would encourage manufacturing activity in key industries, boost exports and become the state's new engines of growth (Government of Andhra Pradesh 1999: 247). By 2020, it was envisaged, 'Andhra Pradesh would be home to a large, thriving base of labour-intensive, export-oriented industries' that would 'provide large-scale employment for all' thereby 'increasing incomes and prosperity across the state' (1999: 245). These zones would be projects of the state government, planned and partially financed by the APIIC in partnership with private real estate developers.

This vision for the future of Andhra Pradesh was a work of considerable rhetorical power, 'equal parts management discourse and advertising spectacle' (Mazzerella 2010: 482), and on its publication *Vision 2020* became one of the most notorious and influential artefacts of development planning in contemporary India. Chandrababu Naidu described his desire to see Andhra Pradesh as a 'role model' that India's other chief ministers would begin to follow:

> I am confident that our success in transforming Andhra Pradesh will motivate other states to emulate our policies and programs. Once we achieve success in Andhra Pradesh, pressures will build up in other parts of the country to achieve higher levels of efficiency and performance. (Ghosh 1999)

Andhra Pradesh can become, he announced, 'the benchmark state'. Such calls won Naidu acclaim from political supporters eager to cement Andhra's influence in the ruling BJP coalition government in Delhi and were echoed in the international media, with *The Economist* (2000) magazine calling Andhra Pradesh 'the state that would reform India'.

Vision 2020's many critics, meanwhile, set out to reveal the disconnections between dream and reality, subjecting the document's claims and prescriptions to nuanced, empirical analysis. Political researchers and commentators challenged its vision by summoning different data sets on poverty, gender and literacy to expose the remoteness of this vision from current realities and an ignorance of social, economic and historical processes. For many journalists and activists on the left, *Vision 2020* became a powerful tool to mobilise opposition to the policies and programmes of liberalisation. *Vision 2020* was presented as a quasi-imperial formulation imposed on India by Bretton Woods institutions and international consultancy firms and an ideological smokescreen that conceals the vested interests of Indian elites, politicians and real estate developers.

Like the critics of *Vision 2020*, anthropologists have often chosen to focus on the rational, techno-scientific character of development plans and visions, and their combination with a market-oriented logic of government. But if these development imaginaries or visions have a 'make-believe' quality it is also because as Begoña Aretxega (2003) and Yael Navaro-Yashin (2007a, 2007b) have put it, fiction and fantasy are vital to the fabric of political reality.

Vision documents and development blueprints – like constitutions, white papers and passports – are central to the ritual performances of modern states, powerful symbols through which modern states make themselves real and tangible. They belong to a genre of texts that we might call techno-fiction, a documentary mode of anticipation that incorporates forms of modern technical expertise and modes of knowledge to envision the future and grant this projection the quality of an achievable goal. These written artefacts of planning and policy are not sterile, inert or passive documents. On the contrary, they make dreams of development authoritative and precise, legitimate and useful. Like other kinds of texts we might describe these vision documents as 'affective': they are 'charged phenomena' that give dreams of development a particular potency, engendering and provoking irony, cynicism, contempt and wit (Navaro-Yashin 2007a: 94). Indeed, we might say that the cynicism and disdain that *Vision 2020* produced among its critics is evidence for precisely such 'affectiveness'.[11]

In India, *Vision 2020* had another kind of effect, compelling Indian states to produce their own vision documents. Indeed the symbolic power of a long-term vision for development was so self-evident to India's Planning Commission that in 2000 it established a committee of 30 experts to draw up its own national vision document. After protracted consultation this was finally published in 2002. 'Every country needs a vision statement which stirs the imagination and motivates all segments of society to greater effort,' the Commission's Deputy Chairman wrote in his introduction, adding that such a statement should be understood as an expression of the possible rather than the literal. 'This vision statement is neither a prediction of what will actually occur, nor simply a wish list of desirable but unattainable ends. Rather, it is a statement of what we believe is possible for our nation to achieve' (Gupta 2002).

The Mediated Dream

Vision 2020 far outlasted Chandrababu Naidu's tenure as chief minister, and has remained a major reference point and guide for development policies, plans, policies and interventions across Andhra Pradesh. In 2004 the TDP was ousted from office by the Indian Congress Party, led by Y.S. Rajshekhara Reddy. The new government reiterated its commitment to programmes for reform, growth and development and continued to promote economic zones as critical infrastructure projects.[12] With the Congress Party's return to office after 20 years, proposals for SEZ projects in Andhra Pradesh gained momentum and became a centrepiece of master plans for the development of districts and urban development regions, including Visakhapatnam.

In the wake of the 2005 SEZ Act the number of projects in Andhra Pradesh dramatically increased. Between 2005 and 2010 planning permissions and government approvals for the acquisition of land were accelerated in order to facilitate a number of new projects. These included some of India's largest SEZs: the 13,000 acre Lepakshi SEZ planned for Anantapur, in south-western Andhra Pradesh, the 12,000 acre Sri City SEZ, in the south-east of the state, close to the city of Chennai, and the 12,000 acre SEZ, planned for the port city of Kakinada. New projects also included private SEZ projects proposed by private companies. One of the most high profile of these was the Apache SEZ, a footwear manufacturing complex owned and operated by a supplier to the Adidas Corporation, that was eventually built over 300 acres in the southern district of Nellore.

In Visakhapatnam district alone, the 2000s saw planning permission approved for six new SEZ projects. Three new zones were dedicated to the production of pharmaceuticals, two were dedicated to IT and software services, and one was planned as a massive multi-product zone (see chapter 3). Reiterating the state's support for zones that replicated the Chinese model, the director of the state's infrastructure development corporation told journalists, 'if all our projects materialise we are confident that even Visakhapatnam can become another Shanghai' (*The Hindu* 2008).

On paper these economic zones were the foundational infrastructure projects that gave form to visions of Andhra Pradesh as a friction-free environment for business. They were to be spaces in which capital could flow without brakes, impediments or limitations, unencumbered by history, politics or culture. Yet creating the conditions for capital to flow without impediment always involves sticky relationships between people, middlemen, mediators, and brokers. As the political economy of neoliberalism shows, the everyday work of realising this fantasy has hinged on elaborate forms of brokerage and mediation, from the pro-active interventions of state governments and legislatures, to the bodies of technocratic expertise marshalled and circulated by international NGOs, to the vested interests that stand to benefit from the planning and construction of a material infrastructure for capitalism. Indeed, far from creating unmediated spaces – or spaces of immediation (Mazzarella 2006) – India's SEZs have rendered the work of mediation ever more apparent.

India's SEZ projects stand as a reminder of the continued centrality of the state to supporting, organising and subsidising the market. In India, as elsewhere in South Asia, the production of these zones has required a complex set of parliamentary procedures, including the design and approval of dedicated parliamentary bills, as well as accompanying pieces of secondary legislation. In this regard economic zones exemplify one of the paradoxes of neoliberalism: that the freeing up of the market involves the extension of the state rather than its rolling back.

As I explored in this chapter the post-liberalisation era in India has seen a plethora of new actors incorporated into the work of development planning. In 2000 the government of Andhra Pradesh commissioned one of the world's largest management, risk and restructuring consultancy firms, KPMG, to act as a strategic adviser for the development of its economic zones. They were given a mandate to make the state more competitive by designing zones that were attractive in terms of their location and their fiscal incentives. The firm had previously advised a number of governments, including those of China and Bangladesh, on the creation of economic enclaves and this was their first such contract in India. In Andhra Pradesh they played a pivotal role in developing the state's policy framework for SEZs, advising the state government on the location of SEZ sites, building strategies, legal reforms and the selection of private partners. Eventually they also provided auditing and management services to zone investors.

In 2002 the government of Andhra Pradesh employed another global management consultancy firm, Price Waterhouse Coopers, to advise on the restructuring of rules and regulations for its SEZs. The firm developed a set of streamlined procedures, and outlined new incentives and concessions for investors, which were eventually written into a new piece of dedicated legislation – the first time a state government had announced an exclusive state-level SEZ policy. These state-level contracts proved lucrative. On the basis of their work in Andhra Pradesh management consultancy firms like KPMG and Price Waterhouse Coopers have gone on to advise the governments of Gujarat and Maharashtra on their state-level SEZ strategies.

The rapid proliferation of economic zone projects in India shows how visions of social and economic transformation can create and align with particular interest groups. Far from the frictionless enclaves imagined by technical experts, economic zones have proven to be contentious sites of speculation, investment and inter-caste competition. Attempts to realise visions of growth have blurred the line between the 'sublime' and the 'profane' dimensions of state-making (Hansen 2001). If India's economic zones promised to realise the technocratic fantasy of a frictionless state, then the SEZ, perhaps more than any other space, reveals the profane aspect of this dream, showing how the sanctity of 'expert rule' is everywhere violated by the brutal and partial everyday work of the state and the pursuit of unabashed self-interest. As Laura Bear (2011) has put it, neoliberal planning in contemporary India is not only sustained by rule-governed rationales of government but also by the forms of charismatic power and speculation that are deployed alongside them. Indeed, as she has shown, the bureaucratic work of liberalisation comes to hinge on the stimulation of informal ties, personal relationships and friendships between politicians, bureaucrats and entrepreneurs.

By enabling India's state governments to compulsorily acquire agricultural land and transfer its ownership into private hands, for example, India's SEZs have frequently become instruments of real estate speculation operated to the benefit of transnational property developers, as well as India's industrial corporations, industrial capitalists and rich farmers. During the 1990s the ascendancy in India's political sphere of a neoliberal economic orthodoxy coincided with competition between Andhra Pradesh's two largest caste communities, Kammas and Reddys, for control of the state assembly, public contracts, real estate and urban space. In their visions of development Kamma and Reddy political leaders combined 'global registers of governance' and 'local languages of stateness' (Hansen and Stepputat 2001: 9). They enlisted and were enrolled by globally circulating paradigms, language and models of neoliberalism. At the same time they drew upon meanings, genealogies, trajectories and mythologies of state power and planning which are specific to India. In doing so they added legitimacy and authority to their regimes as modern, technically competent and pro-market, while using the state to strengthen the position of their respective political parties and to enrich individuals (Mooij 2003).

Large-scale infrastructure development projects in Andhra Pradesh frequently reveal the nexus of politics with caste, with the contracts for public-purpose projects – ports, roads, power plants – invariably won by Kamma and Reddy contractors loyal to either the ruling TDP or the Congress Party. Special economic zones have proven to be a particularly lucrative investment vehicle for these two dominant caste communities, allowing Kamma and Reddy industrialists and property developers to transfer surplus capital from the state's rich and fertile coastal plains into its poorer agricultural interior, acquiring new real estate with the assistance of the state's government, and driving up land values with the promise of new industries and jobs. The proliferation of economic zones across the state since 2005 has reflected these localised flows of capital and agricultural surpluses as much as transnational or global flows. For critics, the state's SEZs have created a new mechanism through which a nexus of Kamma and Reddy politicians and capitalists, linked by caste, kinship and community to the districts of coastal Andhra Pradesh, have laid claim to urban space and land in and around the state capital, Hyderabad, while championing the idea of a single, unitary Telugu land and people.

Claims for the linguistic, cultural and territorial integrity of Andhra Pradesh have been deeply contested. Since its emergence as a state in 1947, Andhra Pradesh has been riven by breakaway movements in the landlocked interior regions of Telangana and Rayalaseema, and by mobilisations in its coastal belt for a *samaiyka* (united) Andhra. In the late 2000s Andhra Pradesh was paralysed by a resurgent campaign for the state's dissolution and mass mobilisations for a separate state, called Telangana. In October 2013 this campaign was transformed by the Indian government's decision to bifurcate Andhra Pradesh, setting in motion a process that will eventually lead to the creation of India's 29th state, Telangana.

These struggles for the dissolution of Andhra Pradesh and independence for Telangana were catalysed by the increasing importance of Hyderabad city and its surrounding lands to Kamma and Reddy industrialists, evident in the proliferation of SEZs in the early 2000s. By the middle of the decade an extraordinary concentration of 31 economic zones (54 per cent of all zones in the state) had appeared around the periphery of Hyderabad, the state's commercial and political capital, driving up land prices and leading to a dramatic real estate boom (Seethalakshmi 2009: 62–4). Land for these zone projects (virtually all of them established as hi-tech, biotech or information technology SEZs) was acquired by the Andhra Pradesh Industrial Infrastructure Corporation and transferred to the ownership of private property developers, on condition that a minimum portion be used for industrial/economic purposes. At the end of the decade, however, several property developers asked the Ministry of Commerce to 'de-notify' portions of this land, citing the impact of the global financial crisis on investment flows in the IT sector.

Across India private SEZ developers have repeatedly shown themselves to be interested primarily in building up a portfolio of assets that can be sold for a profit to other investors in the future (Searle 2010; Seminarist 2008). In the wake of the 2008 global financial crisis, for example, many private SEZ developers and promoters put projects on hold, claiming that the economic downturn had negatively affected their investment flows and outlook. Over the next five years India's central government was asked to 'de-notify' or re-draw the borders demarcating 54 SEZ projects and by the end of 2012 only 166 of the 577 SEZs granted formal planning approval across the country were actually operational. Yet this process also allowed developers to retain ownership of land originally acquired for SEZ projects, and to sell it to third parties or use it for purposes other than that originally intended.[13] In some cases the financial crisis created new opportunities, allowing real estate developers to sell land acquired for SEZ projects at a much higher value than they originally acquired it for.

In Andhra Pradesh, for example, property developers discovered that it is just as lucrative to imagine infrastructure as it is to actually build it and many planned economic zones only exist on paper. Across the state, land acquired for zones lies vacant and empty, either because zone developers have found themselves without access to credit and unable to finance its construction, or because property developers are waiting for the land to accrue value before they seek to have it de-notified and sold. As of 2013, only 38 of the 115 economic zones in Andhra Pradesh for which land had been formally acquired were operational and large areas of land that had been bought up below the market rate – ostensibly for the creation of public-purpose industrial infrastructure projects – lay vacant and empty.

*   *   *

While India's political elites, wealthy rural landowners and large corporations may have stood to benefit from the planning, building or operation of SEZs this does not mean that they are the sole architects or agents in their construction. Instead, in and around India's SEZs the schemes and dreams of regional politicians and transnational corporate executives rub up against, and sometimes articulate, the dreams and desires of rural communities and under-employed young people, as well as inspiring and interacting with the dystopian imaginaries of social movement activists. As I explore in the following chapters of this book, it is in the convergence and contradictions between these diverse futures that zones are made.

3

The Land of Speculation

In February 2002 the Chief Minister of Andhra Pradesh, Chandrababu Naidu, unveiled plans for what was to be the largest economic zone yet built in India to delegates at the World Economic Forum in New York. This was Naidu's third visit to the forum and he saw the event as an important opportunity. 'What I set out to do,' he wrote in his autobiography (Naidu 2000: 134), 'was to go out and market the state, by going to every investors forum, domestic or foreign, and making power-point presentations on what Andhra Pradesh has to offer …'

Accompanied by an entourage of officials and cabinet members in New York Naidu pursued this strategy with vigour. Two blocks away from the forum's main event in the Radisson Hotel he held a series of closed-door meetings with the representatives of US-based biotechnology companies. In addition he found time for an official visit to the New York Stock Exchange. By the time he left the US he had signed six memorandums of understanding, including one with US giant Monsanto to guarantee the continued support of Andhra Pradesh for genetically modified cotton, and had negotiated an agreement with the Stock Exchange for technical assistance to help establish Hyderabad as a centre of financial trading. Naidu's government is often remembered for championing inflows of capital from biotechnology and information technology industries, but his visit to the 2002 World Economic Forum offers a reminder that political visions for growth and development in India have also hinged on the attraction of capital investment in export-oriented manufacturing projects.

One of the highlights of Naidu's visit to New York was the unveiling of plans for an ambitious new infrastructure project in Andhra Pradesh. At a special lunchtime event for 70 invited guests and forum delegates he launched the blueprint for a 'Shenzen style economic zone' that he claimed would help 'transform the state into an economic hub for the Asia Pacific region'. On the dais Naidu was joined by an associate director of KPMG India, the international consultancy firm whose office had prepared the plans. The project they unveiled – the Andhra Pradesh Special Economic

Zone (APSEZ) – was to be a massive enclave encompassing 5.1 square miles (9200 acres) of land. Naidu told the audience that a site had already been selected for the zone close to the industrial port of Visakhapatnam, and promised that his government was ready to offer 'all necessary support' in order to make the economic zone a 'commercially attractive proposition'.

The initial phase of the project, including the acquisition of land, was anticipated to cost US$400 million. This included the capital costs of connecting the site to roads, power, water and waste facilities, as well as the creation of designated plots for manufacturing and housing. The state was looking for a private partner who would invest two-thirds of the total cost for the site's development, and would take responsibility for designing, financing, marketing and operating the zone. Selling this public–private partnership to prospective investors also required Naidu to conjure up the 'possibility of future profit' and he suggested that the up-front costs of the project would be quickly offset by the phenomenal US$7 billion worth of investment that the zone was projected to attract during its first decade of operations. In doing so he reiterated the modernist fantasy of the economic zone as an isolated and autonomous space free from the frictions of politics and culture that I explored in the previous chapter. For all practical purposes, he said, the zone would be excluded from the jurisdiction of the central government. 'It will,' he said, 'be an economy by itself.'

The launch party in New York was the first in a series of roadshows held by the government of Andhra Pradesh across the US, Europe and the Middle East as it set out to find a private developer for their flagship SEZ. Over the following year ministers and secretaries in the Andhra Pradesh government presented the project at business forums across North America and western Europe, once inviting journalists and investors to meet them over breakfast in London's Dorchester hotel. This global roadshow was accompanied by advertisements in the international and domestic media, with a full-page spread appearing in *The Economist* magazine and sponsored pull-out sections appearing in India's weekly news magazines.

*   *   *

The vast tract of land that had been earmarked for the APSEZ lay across a densely populated tract of heavily farmed land on a coastal plain some 60 km south of Visakhapatnam city. Neither the blueprints that were unveiled in New York nor the publicity brochures designed to market the zone made any mention of the people living on or working this land, or gave any account of how the government proposed to acquire it from them. Yet the proposed zone was carved out of two rural sub-districts (*mandals*), Atchutapuram and Rambilli, that recorded a population of 108,956 people in the 2001 Indian census. The proposed zone would directly affect the residents of 27 villages that lay within its planned perimeter and indirectly affect thousands more who owned or cultivated land within the zone's boundary.

At the same time that the blueprints for the APSEZ were being unveiled in New York the state government placed a full-page notice of the project in the Visakhapatnam district rural news supplement of two Telugu daily newspapers, *Eenadu* and *Andhra Jyoti*. The notice gave what it called 'preliminary notification' of the state's intentions to acquire land for an economic zone in Atchutapuram and Rambilli and announced that the formal process would begin in 15 days. The notice also declared the government of Andhra Pradesh's intention to pay a price of 80,000 rupees per acre to people holding private titles (*pattas*) for land within the zone's perimeter and to resettle those who currently lived on the site.

The notice was followed by a public meeting in the small market town of Atchutapuram. At the meeting Visakhapatnam's Collector, head of district-level government, announced the appointment of a team of special deputy collectors to supervise the land acquisition process. He reassured landowners that they would be paid a fair price for their land and explained that those who were forced to move would be provided with a package of compensation.

The meeting ended in uproar.

In the previous chapter I showed how India's economic zones have been shaped by the dreams of politicians, planners and international organisations, and I explored planning as mode of anticipation. In this chapter I turn my attention to the development imaginaries attached to these projects by those they displace, and explore how grand visions for the industrial future are translated, opposed and appropriated. Places like Atchutapuram and Rambilli constitute the frontiers of rural industrialisation in India and here technologies of anticipation associated with modes of planning or government are brought into a productive engagement with other kinds of anticipatory practice, as diverse communities of people work towards futures that improve upon the present.

Figure 4   Old fields, new road: inside the Andhra Pradesh special economic zone

Tracing the acquisition of land for the APSEZ over a decade, this chapter explores the wider landscape of speculation created by large-scale infrastructure projects in India. As a mechanism for acquiring tracts of real estate and as a space for private enterprise liberated from the frictions of government, India's SEZ policy has encouraged what Timothy Mitchell (1999: 455) called 'exuberant dreams of private accumulation', inviting industrial corporations, property developers and industrial capitalists to fulfil their fantasies of personal enrichment. Yet economic zones also encourage modest dreams of profit among those who are most affected by their construction, interweaving and overlapping with other projects of personal and social transformation. As a consequence, attempts to realise blueprints for SEZ projects in India rarely produce clean-cut narratives of resistance or opposition to market futures. Instead they bring visions of economic growth, industrialisation and employment into conflict or messy alignment with the dreams and desires of wealthy high-caste landlords, small-scale farmers and Dalit communities as they pursue political power and projects of upward social mobility. As Steven Gregory (2007: 215) put it in his account of the tensions and conflicts surrounding the Caucedo Multimodal Free Trade Zone in the Dominican Republic, the interpretations and responses to these massive infrastructure projects reveal the 'peculiar, context-specific manner in which material and discursive global flows congeal as they are realised in place and in a historical context'.

The pattern of public opposition and resistance to India's SEZ projects has been deeply localised, differing widely from state to state and frequently from district to district within a state (Mody 2010). As I show in this chapter, understanding popular political responses to these projects and the willingness of people to accept the loss of land and livelihoods demands attention to the particularities of place: not just to local social histories of agrarian change, land reform and inter-caste conflict but also to the place-specific ways in which people imagine possible futures.

In some parts of India, in places like Nandigram in West Bengal (chapter 1) or Raigad in Maharashtra (chapter 6), people have appeared to oppose zones outright, in apparent defence of agricultural livelihoods or in opposition to the destruction of the environment by industrialisation. In other places, political mobilisations around SEZs have been driven squarely by demands for better land prices and compensation packages (Vijayabaskar 2010). As close attention to context reveals, in places where agricultural livelihoods have been materially affected by policies that privilege urban industries or where local histories of industrialisation have shaped expectations, landowners have proven themselves inclined to accept SEZ projects but have actively lobbied the state for increased compensation (ibid.). Meanwhile, in places with long histories of caste oppression and land grabbing by dominant castes, the rural poor and ex-Untouchable, Dalit or Scheduled Caste communities have had powerful incentives to accept the terms of their displacement, or to invest SEZs with hope that processes of industrialisation will have a liberating effect at the bottom of social and symbolic hierarchies (Levein 2011: 469). In these cases we might speak of a structural 'willingness to be displaced' (Baviskar 2009: 60).

As I explore the particular context in which land was acquired for the APSEZ in north coastal Andhra Pradesh I examine how the politics of land acquisition in India is underpinned by an economy of anticipation. Commitments to land and property among people threatened with eviction by economic zones are not just commitments to custom or history but commitments to particular futures. Farmed agricultural land and lived-in homes are inscribed with ideas and norms about how future generations should live, about future personhood and social relationships, as much as they are with the past. Moreover, when families look to borrow money against their future incomes to meet the costs of marriages or education, land becomes a pivotal source of collateral.

When people seek to negotiate the future they do so by harnessing the material and symbolic resources that have historically accrued to them and their families. The respective assets, networks and influence of rich, high-caste landowners, former tenant farmers and Scheduled Castes living in the segregated villages of Atchutapuram and Rambilli presented vastly differential affordances with which to fashion their future. Their attempts to do so shaped not just how the SEZ was perceived but also how it was constituted as a space. Alongside spectacular fantasies of short-term profits on the sale of land, the project encouraged modest dreams of improvement in ways of living among those displaced by its construction and was incorporated into diverse projects for social and material transformation. These dreams become intrinsic to the zone's material texture: part of the roads leading into and out of the zone; part of the walls erected around them; and part of the housing colonies into which people are resettled.

In Andhra Pradesh – as elsewhere – to exchange land for industrial infrastructure projects is to exchange these futures. It is to trade the future inscribed in fields and homes, in existing livelihoods and agricultural labour relationships for the futures inscribed in urban spaces, in factories, roads and new forms of waged labour. The politics of displacement around the APSEZ were struggles over the terms of this exchange, with people seeking to acquire material gain and private advantage just as they sought to reproduce or challenge the social order.

The First Infrastructure

'The first infrastructure is land,' Mr B (a pseudonym) told me with a smile, from behind his desk in the district collector's office, built on the grounds of Visakhapatnam's old British colonial fort. His phrase was well chosen. In India large-scale industrial development projects hinge on a piece of colonial-era legislation, the Land Acquisition Act (1894), that granted the colonial state power to compulsorily acquire land for public purpose. In the postcolonial era successive Indian governments have invoked the principle of 'eminent domain' to acquire privately held land in the interests of what Nehru called a 'greater common good'. Mr B's office in the Visakhapatnam District Collectorate was built on the ruins of a British fort, overlooking the Bay of Bengal, offering a reminder of the colonial technologies of government upon which India's modern state is built.

Since 1947 the Indian state's power of eminent domain has been used to appropriate vast swathes of land for large-scale industrial infrastructure projects, including steel plants, dams, mines and roads. In 1984 the law was amended to allow the state to acquire land for private parties and this amendment, originally intended to facilitate small-scale local development projects like schools and roads, became the basis for the large-scale acquisition of land for industrialists and manufacturers under the SEZ policy (Balagopal 2007).

In their opposition to India's SEZ projects social activists often represent the state as a coherent, unified entity. But the micro-politics of land acquisition processes in places like Visakhapatnam reveal that the everyday state in India is as anthropologists have long described it to be: that is, a congress of institutions, agencies and agendas that are not necessarily well connected and that are represented to the majority of people through unsystematic bureaucratic practices by a cast of individual functionaries who constitute the human face of the Indian state and to whom the everyday work of enacting its decrees is delegated (Gupta 2012: 55–58; Fuller and Bénéï 2001; Hansen 2001).

Mr B was one of a team of 'special deputy collectors' appointed to oversee the acquisition of land for the APSEZ project. The special deputy collectors assigned the task of acquiring land for the APSEZ were all men. Like Mr B they were born and educated in north coastal Andhra, and had reached middling civil service positions in local government. Mr B himself had grown up and been educated in the neighbouring town of Vijayanagram and had spent years as a provincial revenue officer before he was reassigned. Like his colleagues he viewed this assignment as something of a hardship posting: an arduous and unpleasant duty performed with the anticipation of a future promotion, that would take him away from the comfort and cool of his office desk into the hot countryside of north coastal Andhra Pradesh and into complex interactions with communities whom the APSEZ would directly affect.

Mr B's work took him to the countryside of Atchutapuram and Rambilli, across low granite hills covered in thorn bushes and scrub, that local folklore associates with Rama's wanderings in search of Sita in the epic Hindu poem the Ramayana, and over a flat coastal plain that geologists describe as a mix of sandy loam and silty clay. At the turn of the century thousands of acres of this land were used to grow cash crops, principally millets (*jowar* and *bajra*), rice and sugar cane, commercial quantities of pulses (greengram, blackgram, horsegram, cowgram), sesame, chillies and groundnuts. In the mid 1990s increased demand for raw material in local paper mills and scaffolding in Visakhapatnam's construction industry had seen farmers plant forests of silver trees (*saravedi chetlu*) and at the turn of the century a considerable area was given over to non-food cash crops, including tobacco. In addition the area was scattered with copses of cashew and coconut trees, harvested largely for domestic consumption, and heavily grazed by herds of sheep and cattle, whose milk was sold to the district dairy cooperative.

Until the late 1940s three-quarters of north coastal Andhra Pradesh was controlled by *Zamindars*, hereditary landlords who acted as tax collectors for the British. Their estates were comprised of several villages and the *Zamindars* took rent from their tenant farmers and paid land revenue directly to the colonial administration. At independence in 1947 the *Zamindari* system was abolished and a series of land reforms saw tenant farmers issued with title deeds, or 'private *pattas*', to land.

The principal beneficiaries of these post-independence land reforms were two caste communities, Gavaras and Kapus, who comprised the majority of tenant farmers and numerically dominated the population. The villages of Atchutapuram and Rambilli are home to multiple caste communities and Gavaras and Kapus lived alongside those who had come to be identified with some occupational niche in the agrarian economy. They included the Chakalis (washermen), Sales (weavers), Telkas (oil pressers), Bagurus (Barbers), Yadavas (dairy farmers) and Settibalijas (distillers). Meanwhile the region's ex-Untouchable or Dalit communities, Mallas and Madigas, lived in distinct and separate colonies, historically separated by a kilometre or more from caste villages.

The first generation of post-independence land reforms in Andhra Pradesh removed gross differences between the old 'landed gentry' and this 'peasantry' but they also created new distinctions between those who now constituted a 'rural propertied class' and those who continued to live without legal title to land (Srinivasalu 2002). In 1971 a second wave of land reforms in Andhra Pradesh saw a ceiling imposed on land ownership. New legislation reassigned areas of surplus land held above this ceiling to the rural poor: landless cultivators and ex-Untouchable or Scheduled Castes. In Atchutapuram alone around 2400 acres of land held by the state and surplus land were assigned in this way. Beneficiaries included small communities of Dordekalar Muslims and Adivasis, only a few hundred in number, who had resettled in the area.

However, in Atchutapuram and Rambilli, like elsewhere in Andhra Pradesh, the reallocation of surplus land was met with stiff opposition. Many higher-caste farmers devised ways of ensuring that the best land remained in their hands. Some paid off local revenue officials to keep the title deeds of reassigned lands registered in their names. Others ensured that the worst land in their possession was reassigned, only giving up plots with rocky or poor-quality soils.

Many ex-Untouchable families opted to sell the land they had been assigned and used the money to migrate out of the area altogether, moving into new colonies on the periphery of Visakhapatnam. In the late 1970s the government of Andhra Pradesh passed new legislation – the Assigned Lands (Prohibition of Transfers) Act, 1977 – that prohibited the sale or transfer of assigned lands. The new law assumed that land assigned to Scheduled Castes would only be sold or given away under very pressing circumstances. The law allowed transfers and sales of this land to be cancelled retroactively but it also allowed the state to take back or 'resume' this land (colloquially known, after the name of the assignment document, as 'D. Form *patta* land') at any future point in the name of a higher, public purpose.

These systems for documenting and recording land ownership and usage, as historians remind us, have their origins in the imperatives of the colonial state to 'discover and to order' (Agrawal and Sivaramakrishnan 2000). In the postcolonial nation-state the power of land survey, census and mapping activities to act as instruments of visibility and legibility made them 'technologies of rule' that de-contextualised and standardised complex patterns of land use and agrarian practices, disadvantaging the customary claims made by Scheduled Castes and tribes in India's forests and hills (Gupta 1998). Yet technologies of government never entirely realise bureaucratic fantasies of total visibility or legibility and in other places their failure has created opportunities for landowning families to reassert control of agricultural land.

During the 1980s and 1990s in Atchutapuram and Rambilli the systems that were supposed to record precisely who owned and cultivated land fell into deliberate disuse. Here, as elsewhere in India, the illegal occupation and accumulation of land once distributed to the poor became the subject of what we might call a wilful bureaucratic ignorance (McGoey 2007, 2012). Village secretaries (*tahsildars*), who held the power to cancel or check the sale of assigned land, frequently chose not to implement the law. Substantial tracts of land once assigned to Dalits were illegally transferred to new owners or were gradually encroached upon by neighbouring farmers. Many land records are not properly updated and many have never carried the names of tenants or cultivators. One consequence of this bureaucratic ignorance has been that, since the 1980s, former *Zamindari* families in Atchutapuram and Rambilli have been able to reassert control over prime agricultural land while former tenant farmers – Kapus and Gavaras – have been able to steadily extend theirs.

At the end of the 1990s, when the APSEZ project was announced, the largest landowners in Atchutapuram and Rambilli remained the descendants of former *Zamindari* landlords, high-caste Kshatriya Rajus and Velamas. Eleven large landowning families farmed plantations of between 25 and 50 acres in size, while 200 farmers claimed ownership of between 4 and 10 acres of land. Much of the remaining land was a complex patchwork of small, fragmented plots, between 3 and 6 acres in size, controlled and farmed by Gavara and Kapu farmers. Some 1500 farmers laid claim to between 2 and 4 acres of land but the vast majority, some 20,000 households, farmed smallholdings of less than 2.5 acres. In the 2001 census ex-Untouchable Malla and Madiga families constituted a minority 6.5 per cent of the area's population and they invariably farmed the worst quality plots.

The Politics of the Displaced

This agrarian political economy lay at the heart of political mobilisations around the APSEZ. In 2002, within weeks of a public meeting to announce the acquisition of land for the APSEZ, local farmers established a 'Welfare Association for the Displaced', the Nirvaasitulu Shanksema Sangham. The association was formed with the specific purpose of increasing the price to be paid per acre of land by the government and to extract guarantees of employment. One of its key demands was that the state promise formal sector employment inside the zone to at least one member of each family. The association also lobbied for additional compensation to be paid for trees and structures planted or built upon the land. At its peak the association claimed to have 200 members, with representatives from at least 22 of the affected villages. Over the following three years the association organised *dharnas*, or relay-hunger strikes, outside the district administrators' office in Visakhapatnam. But there were no active Dalit participants in the Welfare Association for the Displaced. 'We are not fighting', Malla and Madiga villagers frequently explained to me. 'The fights are happening in places where the land is good.'

The language used by the association was marked by a total absence of anti-SEZ rhetoric. Its members expressed no direct opposition to the zone or to India's SEZ policy. They did not object in principal to the potential inflow of transnational capital nor did they object to the potential environment impact of the zone on the landscape. Indeed, their demands did nothing to contest the idea of an economic zone as an engine of growth or a vehicle of social mobility, and made no attempt to 'dislodge the possibility of development' (Redfield 2002: 810) that the zone promised.

On the contrary the association's politics implicitly supported the project and its activities focused squarely on securing improved terms of compensation for those landowning higher-caste Hindu farmers who constituted its membership base. Its repeated demand, made in pamphlets, public meetings and on demonstrations, was for 'encroachers upon private land' and people farming 'D. Form *patta* land' to be properly identified and paid compensation on a par with those holding legal titles. This was a concern that aimed at ensuring reparations for those farmers whose families had expropriated, illegally occupied and farmed lands once given to the poor.

As they were deployed in the land acquisition process, survey and mapping instruments became technologies of anticipation as much as technologies of government. By making assets visible and legible, in ways intended to help planners and policy-makers calculate the costs of future compensation payouts and manage future conflicts, they attempted to bring the future into view. It was precisely the power of these bureaucratic tools to materially affect the future that made them the object of considerable attention for landowners.[1]

As Mr B and the team of special deputy collectors began to survey and verify land holdings in the area as part of the land acquisition process they began to uncover these deliberate inaccuracies in local land revenue documents. In around 5 per cent of cases, they reported that one person's name appeared in land records and another person could be found cultivating the land on the ground. In many more cases 'land losers' claimed ownership of more land than they had the records to support.

Despite their international roadshows and launch parties, two years after plans for the APSEZ had first been launched in New York the government of Andhra Pradesh had yet to receive any expressions of interest from prospective investors. At the beginning of the 2000s, as Chandrababu Naidu was setting out to make his state attractive to investors through the creation of a purpose-built infrastructure for investment, other Indian states, notably those of Maharastra, Gujarat and Haryana, were doing the same thing. Other massive SEZ projects, including Mumbai's massive Navi SEZ project, proved to be more attractive to potential investors, and securing investment for Andhra Pradesh's flagship project proved to be a very hard sell. A deadline for the submission of bids was extended three times but, by December 2003, the very final date, the government of Andhra Pradesh had not received a single one.

This lack of interest from private investors and the competition from other Indian states had important implications for the land acquisition process then taking place in Visakhapatnam. Concerns in Hyderabad that a delay in the land acquisition process would scare off potential developers saw the deputy collectors put under intense pressure to complete the verification exercise as quickly as possible. 'We were supposed to check the ownership records of each claim,' Mr B told me. 'But the people from whom I took my orders, insisted that we had to accept claims without any enquiry to speed up the process.'

As the acquisition of land for the APSEZ became a matter of political expediency, landowning farmers worked to shape the outcomes of the process. Mandal revenue officials were paid off to forge or amend local land records, falsify title deeds and tenancy documents; ramshackle buildings were hurriedly erected on land in order to claim compensation on built structures; fictive cultivators or tenants were added to documents by landowners claiming compensation on their behalf. An army of brokers (*taragarilu*) or middlemen (*tikaadu*) arose to intervene in family disputes over land ownership. Village-level political leaders, village secretaries and elders all stepped up to act as mediators in the land census, calculating and measuring land, arbitrating in disputes between relatives, issuing passbooks and verifying title deeds – all in return for a cut of future compensation payments. On their visits to small hamlets and villages, negotiations between the special deputy collectors and farmers were frequently heavy-handed as groups of men deliberately outnumbered, harangued and roughed up these neat and tidy city officials in an attempt to scare them into cutting a better deal.

In coastal Andhra Pradesh, as elsewhere in India, the land acquisition process created a new stage on which Andhra Pradesh's political parties could manoeuvre for advantage and rhetorical positioning in order to extend their power and influence. In other parts of the state claims that farmers were being forcibly evicted from their land provided a potent tool for political mobilisation (Jenkins 2011). Plans for the APSEZ galvanised all of the state's political parties. Inflows of campaign money transformed the local political landscape, shifting the centre of constituency politics in this part of Andhra Pradesh away from the market town of Elamanchili to the rural *mandals* of Atchutapuram and Rambilli. The state's main opposition party, the Congress Party of India, zeroed in on these *mandals*, gambling organisational resources on constituencies that had been supporting the TDP for over 20 years in pursuit of electoral dividends. Meanwhile the Communist Party of India (Marxist) lent its financial support to the Welfare Association for the Displaced.

The run-up to the 2004 state assembly elections saw furious campaigning as Congress Party candidates channelled dissatisfaction among landed farmers at the terms of the compensation offered to them. The Congress Party's nominee for the Elamanchili constituency, was a local landowner named Uppalapati Venkata Ramanamurty Raju (also known as Kanna Babu). Kanna Babu's family of former *Zamindars* traced their lineage to a dynasty that ruled the Vijanagara Empire in the seventeenth century and his collected assets made him the fifth richest contestant in that year's assembly elections. On the campaign trail he promised to raise the price of land acquired by the state to 295,000 rupees if elected. Meanwhile, Konatal Ramakrishna, another Congress Party nominee standing for the nearby constituency of Annakapalle, told voters in Rambilli and Atchutapuram that he would go to jail to secure a price of 500,000 rupees per acre.

In response, the Chandrababu Naidu government twice increased the price at which they would compensate people for land inside the zone, first to 245,000 rupees per acre and then to 275,000 rupees per acre. In May 2004, however, Naidu's ruling TDP was swept out of government by the Indian Congress Party. Those candidates who had actively campaigned on behalf of 'land losers' around the APSEZ were now voted into office. At the end of that year representatives of the newly elected Congress government announced details of a new compensation package at a public meeting held in Atchutapuram town.

The price of land they offered to those with legal title was set at three and a half times what had originally been offered, 295,000 rupees per acre, with separate valuations for built structures and trees. For every residential structure that was demolished the government offered to grant the right to 250 square yards in a purpose-built resettlement colony, and proposed to pay 40,000 rupees towards the cost of constructing a new house on this plot. In addition, families were offered 5000 rupees towards the cost of transporting their building materials, 10,000 rupees towards the cost of two milk cattle, and 3000 rupees towards the cost of building a livestock shed on their new plot. Scheduled Caste families living on land that had been assigned to them and who could show their 'D. Form *patta*' documents were to be offered the same sized plots in the resettlement colony and 100 per cent subsidised housing. In addition each family was to receive two lump sums. The first of these was intended to compensate families for lost wages. The second was a subsistence allowance of 19,200 rupees, intended to carry families over until they secured new sources of income, and again calculated on the basis of a minimum agricultural wage (240 days at 80 rupees day).

The announcement marked the climax of the campaign by landowning farmers to increase the price of their land and expand the compensation package offered to them.[2] Soon after the announcement the richest Velama and Raju farmers formally accepted the package offered to them by the state government. In doing so they brought a de facto end to negotiations and forced smaller landowners to follow their lead.

At the end of 2004 the special deputy collectors announced the completion of their enumeration exercise. In Atchutapuram town they took over a room in the land revenue office, and added digital photographs of households and individual family members into a database. Their records listed the members of 4958 households whose homes fell within the borders of the proposed zone and who stood to be resettled. They also identified some 6922 acres – two-thirds of the total area of the site – as privately owned, meaning that its owners were eligible for compensation. Here as elsewhere across Andhra Pradesh, however, these final figures obfuscated historic patterns of land use and ownership. The records concealed the diversity of land use by classifying as non-agricultural all land that had been set aside to rejuvenate its soil, or land that was used for grazing, for fodder or for firewood.[3] Meanwhile the database listed plots of land that had once been redistributed to Scheduled Castes and the rural poor as publicly owned, and so ineligible for compensation. Higher-caste farmers who had captured this land from Dalits continued to lobby state officials and politicians to compensate them for its loss, and the Welfare Association for the Displaced continued to represent their interests.

Cultivating Futures

Just as politicians like Chandrababu Naidu must conjure up the 'possibility of future profit' to attract prospective investors in infrastructure projects, so too government officials like Mr B must conjure up the prospect of material improvement and social transformation in order to convince people to accept the acquisition of the land or their forced displacement with the minimum of resistance. It is a task that sees government bureaucrats ally themselves with myriad other actors. As Mr B put it, 'the responsibility to persuade people to leave their land is not mine alone. Everyone has a part to play, including political parties, political activists and their associations.'

In the countryside across Atchutapuram and Rambilli teams of government surveyors and special deputy collectors, political candidates on the campaign trail, and elected members of the Legislative Assembly constructed the zone as a future-oriented space. They attached and adapted visions of development, economic security and upward social mobility to the space of the zone and cultivated expectations of what its future might hold. In village after village people heard a similar story:

> If you stay here you might not have a good future. But if you move then your future and your children's future will definitely be better. If you are living in thatched houses now, then afterwards you will be living in slab houses with metal roofs. Your children will have big colleges and hospitals. Your lives will improve.

Many critics of displacement in India attach considerable power and agency to the promises of bureaucrats and politicians. Travelling around Andhra Pradesh to meet communities displaced by the construction of its economic zones the late Telugu lawyer and human rights activist K. Balagopal (2007) argued, for example, that people were being 'persuaded by promises of jobs, alternative lands, rehabilitation in a properly constructed colony'. If people ever doubted these promises, he wrote, 'they were not un-amenable to persuasion by smooth talking officers'.

If people find these promises seductive, I would argue however, it is not because they are inherently persuasive or convincing, or because people attach credible or plausible futures to development projects. Rather, it is because they invoke local registers of aspiration and tap into vernacular dreams for social and material transformation that are assembled from globally circulating media forms and out of local social histories. These stories opened up new possibilities for rich and poor alike to think about and envisage good lives for themselves and their families. Sometimes they did so in reference to people living in far-off places, in Hyderabad or Delhi, in the United States or Australia. More often, however, this meant in reference to people living closer to home: upwardly mobile commodity traders in the rural market towns of Atchutapuram, Annakappale and Elamanchili, Visakhapatnam's agrarian nouveau riche (Upadhya 1988, 1997), or labour aristocrats like the public sector employees living in the nearby Steel Township of Ukkunagaram. Rich and poor alike were very specific about the kinds of housing they expected to be provided with if they had to leave their existing homes: namely larger, more permanent, electrified, homes made with new materials; not apartment blocks that had no room for expansion but 'houses that you can build on top of' or 'houses that you can build up from'.

For many people, however, it was the promise of stable, secure, employment that lay at the heart of their hopes for the future. Government bureaucrats – from the district collector to municipal revenue officers – assured villagers that they could expect at least one of their children to have a job in the zone's upcoming industries. Local politicians like K. Ramakrishna, a cabinet minister in the state assembly, told public meetings of farmers that the 'the main intention of the government is to provide employment to the land losers'. 'You can't convince people to leave their land for payment only,' one of the six special deputy collectors assigned to manage the land acquisition process told me frankly. 'The price of the land works to convince them 50 per cent and the hope of employment works to convince them 50 per cent. They think that industries are going to appear and they will be given preferential employment.' In the hinterland of Visakhapatnam these promises of employment invoked specific local histories of public sector-led industrialisation.

Since the 1950s a succession of large-scale industrial projects, including the Visakha steel plant (see chapter 2) and a thermal power plant built by the National Thermal Power Corporation, had transformed the region's socio-economic geography by creating permanent public sector jobs for 'sons of the soil'. These projects had become dominant features in the local landscape, shaping ideas and expectations of displacement and resettlement as well as hopes and aspirations for employment. These projects were visible across Atchutapuram and Rambilli: the smoke stacks from the steel plant's chimneys could be seen rising into the sky from rooftops and high ground, while the distinctive red- and white-painted towers of the 1000-MW Simhadri thermal power plant rose up on the horizon.

During the 1970s and the 1980s the construction of these two plants had involved large-scale programmes of land acquisition that had shaped local expectations of compensation and resettlement packages. Families whose homes had fallen within the boundaries of each project had been issued with rehabilitation cards – 'R Cards' – providing them with a state guarantee of formal sector employment for at least one family member. Those families whose homes fell on the other side of the boundary received none. The residents of Atchutapuram and Rambilli *mandals* were acutely aware of having missed out on the opportunities for compensation and employment that these projects created, offering a constant reminder that development is geographically inflected, unevenly mapped onto the landscape, creating new contours of proximity and distance.

These two programmes set important precedents and stories about the fortunes of farmers whose land had once been acquired for the steel plant or the thermal power plant, which circulated widely around Atchutapuram and Rambilli. People told me, for example, how in neighbouring Parawada government revenue officials had gone from village to village handing out cash payments to those people whose land was being taken, of how they had distributed money to people regardless of whether they held legal documents to land, or whether they were owners or tenant occupiers. Such stories coloured the expectations of those who would be displaced and acquired a new potency with the wave of new infrastructure projects announced for Visakhapatnam's hinterland as part of the TDP's 20-year vision for the state's development (see chapter 2).

The extent to which ideas about labour lie at the heart of forced displacement and resettlement (Li 2010, 2011) was made vividly apparent to me one day in December 2004, during a month spent cycling around Atchutapuram interviewing farmers. One afternoon I stopped in Madigaurupalam, a Dalit colony on the outskirts of the village of Dipturo. The outer boundary of the zone had been drawn diagonally through the colony and one of the villagers, Appa Rao, drew a line in the ground diagonally through the village to show me where a wall was due to be built, cutting the settlement in half. A cot was pulled into the shade for us to sit down on and for a couple of hours I asked and fielded questions. It was the prospect of permanent, public sector employment, jobs that come with a raft of attendant benefits and social protections, that most animated men like Appa Rao. Over the past four years numerous government surveyors and special collectors had passed through Madigaurupalam – meaning literally, the place of Madigas – in connection with the APSEZ. 'Whenever people come,' Appa Rao said, 'they tell us that there is a chance we will get jobs. But we want government jobs. That's compulsory. There must be government jobs. We won't accept private jobs. If there are no government jobs we won't leave.' In Madigaurupalam, like other villages inside the boundaries of the proposed SEZ, the promise of stable, secure, employment lay at the heart of hopes and anxieties about the future.

As they worked to enumerate land losers and negotiate settlements, the government surveyors and special collectors fostered fantasies of the zone as a 'state space' rather than as an enclave or estate for private enterprise. Nowhere in the land acquisition process did state officials use the zone as a platform to make arguments for economic liberalisation or present the zone as a site of liberalised regulations built to encourage private sector investment. Instead the zone was represented as a space of state activity and intervention in which people were invited to imagine they would be protected from economic precariousness. Answers to questions about what the zone was were arrived at locally, in ways that reflected hopes and aspirations, as much as being imposed from outside. If fantasies of employment in the zone proved attractive this is because, for many people in this corner of Andhra Pradesh, the promise of a steady income leading to a predictable life cycle of births, marriages and families is the dream of the good life. In my interviews with young people – the children of high-caste, landowning farmers and Dalits alike – people constantly returned to these everyday aspirations. In Atchutapuram and Rambilli these are the futures that people seek to bring about on an everyday basis by correctly observing rites and *pujas* to reduce the malevolent power of local village goddesses – Nokalamma or Pedamma – and bring about prosperity and fertility. As I explore later in this chapter, these rituals proved particularly important as people struggled to adjust and adapt to the experience of displacement.

For some people the promise of future employment was also the promise of a transformation in political subjectivity. As sites of formal employment, India's SEZs are not sites of exception from citizenship but gateways to citizenship from which the working poor can imagine themselves as new kinds of political and economic subjects, who can make new claims upon the state for protection, rights and entitlements (Cross 2009). For Dalits – Mallas and Madigas – it was also the possibility that processes of industrisalisation and urbanisation might transform village social relationships that made the zone a space of promise and hope. For many young Dalit men, the zone was imagined as a potential catalyst for social reform, a moment of rupture that would create an unparalleled opportunity to rebuild and recreate new kinds of inter-caste relationships. This same possibility provoked the ire of some farmers. In Kapu and Gavara villages people complained bitterly that the SEZ would erode caste distinctions. 'The Scheduled Castes are going to benefit most', I was told again and again, 'because now they are going to be provided with the same facilities as us.'

Just as the social geography of Atchutapuram and Rambilli has been shaped by local histories of industrialisation, this landscape too has been materially shaped. The agricultural economy of north coastal Andhra Pradesh has been systematically neglected and overlooked by both the colonial and the postcolonial state. Over the second half of the twentieth century changing patterns of cultivation and intensive cash cropping dramatically increased the demand for water here. Yet despite the intensi-fication of agriculture, the fields of Atchutapuram and Rambilli remained largely rain fed. Against a backdrop of urbanisation and industrialisation, public investments in water storage and transportation have been directed towards Visakhapatnam city. Further south, at the confluence of the Krishna and Godavari rivers, green revolution agricultural fortunes hinged on the extensive irrigation system built by colonial engineer Arthur Cotton. But in Visakhapatnam district the construction of the Yeluru reservoir and the Samalkota and Polavaram canals in the 1980s and 1990s were primarily directed towards meeting the demands of urban petrochemical and heavy metal industries, as well as the needs of its growing urban population. At the end of the 1990s less than one-third of farmed agricultural land in Atchutapuram and Rambilli was irrigated. There were a few canal systems, a small number of tanks (bunds) and a limited number of tube wells.

By the early 2000s a combination of liberalising social and economic policies coupled with a decline in net rainfall and repeated failures of the South Indian monsoon created the perfect storm in Andhra Pradesh, and precipitated a crisis in agriculture. The rising costs of agricultural livelihoods coupled with low or negative returns pushed many who had invested heavily in expensive seed varieties or fertilisers into debt. In Andhra Pradesh the 2000s saw a significant rise in farmer suicides attributed to indebtedness and agrarian distress. Between May and June 2004, as negotiations over compensation packages for those to be displaced around the APSEZ reached their climax, there were 400 recorded suicides by farmers across the state (Rao and Suri 2006; Sridhar 2006b).

Against this background, it is perhaps unsurprising that farming families had come to see their land as increasingly dry or low-yielding and to see the long-term future of agricultural livelihoods as deeply insecure. Under the terms and conditions of resettlement all displaced families were promised plots in a dedicated colony on which to build new homes but there was no provision to allocate them with land for farming, cultivating or grazing. Families whose agricultural lands were to be incorporated within the zone were confronted with the choice between using their compensation money to purchase land elsewhere or leaving agricultural livelihoods altogether. For diverse communities of people across Atchutapuram and Rambilli, the coming of the zone promised to rehydrate the landscape, bringing access to formal sector employment and new kinds of non-agricultural livelihoods. By contrast, a future without the zone looked dry.

Speculative Exuberance

At the end of the 1990s the price of one acre of land in Atchutapuram and Rambilli averaged 40,000 rupees. Following the announcement of the APSEZ in 2002, local land prices rose rapidly. Amid rampant speculation about the future of the region the price per acre at which the government of Andhra Pradesh acquired land for the zone at the end of 2004 was soon just a fraction of the rate at which parcels of land around the proposed site were being traded. After the formal land acquisition process concluded prices continued to rise. By the end of the decade when (as I explain below) the zone eventually became operational, the price of land here had increased 250-fold, so that one-third of an acre of land was changing hands for up to 2 million rupees. This spectacular escalation in land prices was acutely felt in the countryside around Atchutapuram and Rambilli. Here questions of whose fortunes were made or lost, and how much money had been saved or spent in real estate purchases around the periphery of the zone have become prominent subjects of conversation.

In September and October 2009 I spent several weeks travelling around the countryside in Atchutapuram and Rambilli collecting local accounts and stories of the land acquisition process. In interviews, old and young farmers alike repeatedly took me through in often painstaking detail the precise amount of money offered to them by the government for their land at specific moments in time, vis-à-vis the changing values of land outside the zone. I frequently tried to twist these narratives, searching for what I imagined might be more personalised accounts of change, and asking people to describe how the process had made them feel. But talk constantly returned to numbers – numbers of acres and rupees per acre – until it became apparent that these numbers were central to how the coming of the zone had been experienced. Personal stories about the coming of the zone were stories of calculation and calculated decision making, stories of profit and loss, of how much money had been made by selling at the right time and how much had been lost by selling too early, or too late.

Those with access to privileged information had been the first to act. As elsewhere in India, a small number of politicians traded on their insider knowledge about a forthcoming SEZ in the countryside around Atchutapuram and Rambilli.[4] In 2001 there was a small flurry in *benami* transactions (transactions under false or third-party names) as people quietly acquired parcels of land inside and around the site of the planned zone in advance of any public announcement. Those who did so stood to profit handsomely, either from the compensation package that the state government would eventually pay to landowners or from the rise in real estate prices.

After the zone had been publicly announced, landed Raju and Velama farmers became real estate speculators, buying up and selling on plots of land adjacent to the zone as hopes about the economic prospects of the area sent land prices skyrocketing. Those to benefit from these speculative investments in real estate were not only the region's upper castes or members of an entrenched political elite. Middle-class teachers and bankers in the nearby market town of Atchutapuram made hundreds of thousands of rupees by joining together to buy up small plots of land outside the zone and quickly selling them on to the region's property developers. 'The farmers looked at us like we were fools,' I was told, 'they knew the SEZ was coming but they didn't understand why we wanted land that was miles away from it. They sold it to us to pay off their debts, to get their children married, or because it wasn't profitable.' Often their aspirations were modest. One Gavara caste primary school teacher from Anakappalle made enough money buying up and selling on plots of land around the zone to build a two-storey marble residence for his parents. 'I always thought about what I could get if I sold the land for a profit', he told me:

I didn't have big dreams. I just wanted a better life. I wanted a big house, air-conditioning, and I thought about buying a car, I didn't care which model, I just wanted a car – if you drive a car around here then you're rich – and I thought about my family, it was my father's dream, to live in a good house like this one, with a lawn, with balconies and a terrace.

Other beneficiaries were the enterprising young men who found themselves serendipitously drawn into the game by acting as mediators between parties in small land deals. 'It's just like marriage,' a young Yadav man named Shankar told me. 'You have to get someone to tell about you. To say that you're good. And people around here will trust you to close the deal because you're local.' In 1999 Shanker had been a wispy 19-year-old Yadav boy who used to pass his days cycling around the countryside, hanging out at a ready-made garment shop in Atchutapuram town chatting to tailors, collecting gossip and, by his own account, not doing very much. Until, that is, he overheard his brother-in-law talking about the sale of an acre of land and mentioned the conversation to the owner of a ready-made clothes shop. When the shopkeeper expressed interest in the land Shanker brokered his first deal.

'Transactions won't happen if you approach a person directly,' he explained to me. 'Then people will just think you are planning to sell it at a higher price. You always need someone to go in-between.' As a go-between Shankar operated on low margins, making 200 rupees on every tenth of an acre that was bought and sold. With the coming of the SEZ Shanker found himself in an enviable position as a go-to broker and he profited from the flourishing real estate market. By 2006 he had made enough to delegate the day-to-day operation of his brokerage business to a friend and invest the proceeds of his deals in a political career.[5]

Meanwhile middling farmers without ready access to capital – like the Kapu and Gavara landowners who stood to lose plots of land inside the zone – borrowed money against their future compensation payments in order to purchase land. These deals hinged on a written agreement (*puroni*) to purchase a plot of land at an agreed price, accompanied by a token advance payment. In coastal Andhra the parties to *puroni* transactions agree to close the deal within a fixed period of time, conventionally three months for agricultural land. Brokering *puroni* deals emerged as an immensely lucrative business, with political leaders at village and *mandal* level taking 2 per cent commission in return for negotiating between sellers and buyers. Those farmers who settled their claims sooner and secured their compensation faster found themselves able to buy up these plots of land while it was still available and affordable.

Many discovered, however, that their compensation payments were not immediately forthcoming. Figures at every level of local government – from elected members of the legislative assembly to junior clerks in the land registry office – worked to siphon compensation money into their own pockets. In the small market town of Atchutapuram, sub-district or *mandal* revenue officers demanded a cut of the compensation before they agreed to sign the order releasing cash payments to claimants. Richer and more powerful claimants paid them off quickly or threatened them with violence. But those who could not, who refused or who attempted to report their misconduct, were held to ransom. Revenue officers threatened to deposit compensation payments in court and ensure that a claimant's access to it would be endlessly delayed on a technicality if they were not guaranteed a cut. Landowners without validated title deeds or who were caught up in a wave of domestic disputes as extended family members quarrelled over their respective claims to inherited property found their compensation payments delayed indefinitely. Scheduled Castes living on *patta* land that the state had redistributed in the 1970s frequently found their cases relegated to the bottom of the pile by officials. Meanwhile the families of agricultural labourers, who had long since lived on and cultivated fields belonging to rich Velama and Raju landlords, found themselves further disadvantaged. Revenue officials asked them to bring the '*patta* landowner' with them to the revenue office if they wanted to claim compensation. Such demands rarely worked out as farmers frequently refused outright to enter negotiations or demanded half of any compensation.

Unable to settle these claims or unwilling to pay off land registry officials, many farmers now found that they were unable to meet the terms of their advance purchase agreements. Without assets to guarantee their loans they were unable to complete the transaction and compelled to sell it on. An informal market in *puroni* agreements sprang up around Atchutapuram town as buyers lost their advances and were forced to sell on their purchase agreements. People spoke from experience when they described a *puroni* exchanging hands as many as 30 or 40 times over a six-year period, leaving the original buyer with little idea of how much the plot was now worth and even less idea who had now agreed to buy it. *Benami* transactions – in which a third-party or a false name is used as a 'front' for the real seller, purchaser or owner – became ubiquitous.

While larger landowners quickly accepted the terms of the compensation package offered to them by the government many smaller farmers had hesitated, holding out for a better deal. When they eventually accepted the inevitable many found that they had acted too late. As local land prices rapidly escalated many of those who were set to lose land to the zone found it virtually impossible to buy new plots within a 40 km radius of the zone and many eventually found themselves shut out of the local land market altogether.

The evidence of a real estate bubble around the APSEZ was visibly apparent between Atchutapuram town, gateway to the zone, and the neighbouring town of Parawada, gateway to the National Thermal Power Corporation plant. At the end of the 2000s there were over 50 private residential developments along a 15 km stretch of road. Plans for housing layouts were advertised along the roadside, the fantasy images of gated compounds and luxury properties incongruous next to the paddy fields, villages and hillsides around them. These advertising signboards either associated themselves directly with the SEZ or borrowed from the repertoire of terms used to market it. 'Suchir's Grand Bay: Enter into Elite Zone' read one, 'Vishaka Residency Deluxe: Shape of Your Dreams' read another.

The property developers were not global players or even large Indian industrial houses but small regional firms owned by Kamma and Reddy industrialists (see chapter 2) from Hyderabad and Vijayawada. These were companies that lacked the political capital and high-level government connections required to purchase lucrative land inside Visakhapatnam's municipal boundaries and instead had looked to coastal plains and hillsides outside the city's limits. The dream homes they promised were not marketed to people displaced by the zone but to outsiders, middle-class Indians to whom they promised an escape from urban poverty, pollution and poor governance, and to a global diaspora, like the non-resident Indians living in Maryland or Dallas, whose parents had migrated from Andhra Pradesh to the United States in the 1970s and who were now looking to return.

On internet chat rooms dedicated to Indian real estate these prospective buyers can be found tracking news from Visakhapatnam. Discussion groups track auctions of land by the city's municipal authorities and new housing projects. Among the online avatars are speculators who have no interest in living on the land they purchase but are looking to buy low and sell high. But there are also those who describe desires to relocate to Visakhapatnam and imagine themselves building new lives in a small community of returned expatriates. Between February 2007 and August 2009 some 36,000 people had viewed an online discussion forum about real estate in Visakhapatnam in one online discussion forum called the 'Return to India Club'. Looking to recruit other families to their dream they pitched ideas about exclusive gated compounds with facilities to 'rival anything found in the USA'.

In Atchutapuram and Rambilli stories of land deals being conducted over the phone or internet by people who have never visited the place were relayed with a mixture of amazement and derision. 'Some of these people don't even know where they are buying houses,' Shankar, a local stringer for the *Eenadu* newspaper told me:

> It's 50 kilometres from here to Visakhapatnam but on the map they look like they are side by side. People see the advertisement on the internet. Then they pick up their cell phone and they buy a house. But they have no idea what they are buying or where it is.

Sure enough, stories of fictitious developments abound and disappointed buyers frequently post their personal accounts of unscrupulous deals online: 'I visited this place 2 months back when i was in India and this place is completely abandoned after that grand entrance construction,' somebody calling themselves 'rgudapat' posted on the Return to India Club forum in 2008 after a trip to Atchurapuram. 'No watchman as well. So use caution if u put in more money. Btw, i heard that their golf project is also on hold.'

Making a Place for Resettlement

In June 2006 the team of special deputy collectors finalised arrangements for the resettlement. They planted signboards in 27 affected villages and pasted up printed lists of households that would be resettled along with the names of all family members. Villagers were given one month to register objections and errors. Five months later, in November, the collectors called village assemblies (*grama sabhas*) and read out a final list of those whose homes would be demolished. These families were eligible to receive a fixed plot of land on which to build a home within a planned resettlement colony. Each village was to locate in a particular section of the colony and – against popular opinion – plots within each section would be decided through a lottery process, with names for each plot drawn at random from a list.

The first families began to move to the resettlement colony in late 2007 – many of them hiring auto-rickshaws to transport their belongings. If those displaced by the APSEZ had once imagined that they might be resettled in a less rural location – like one of the townships along the main highway leading to Visakhapatnam city or to the small market town of Atchutapuram – then they were to be sadly disappointed. They did not travel far. The resettlement colony was located on the very edge of the zone, on an expanse of flat, unsheltered scrub-land once used to graze cattle and goats. In a bitter irony the colony's creation had itself demanded the resettlement of a small community of Christian converts (formerly Yadavs) already settled on this land. These residents lobbied furiously to be able to retain their homes but their efforts proved futile and they were resettled several hundred meters away, to new plots elsewhere within the new colony.

Two years after the first families had moved here the colony boasted none of the amenities promised by government officials. Residents enjoyed connections to electricity, water and waste disposal but there were no schools or hospitals. The colony's centrepiece was a squat, concrete office that had been designated the *panchayat* or village headquarters but there were no clearly defined public spaces or trees. The only shade or shelter from the heat of the midday sun lay in the shadow of towering electricity pylons that bifurcated the colony and which emitted a constant buzz. Despite these limitations, however, the colony's new residents worked to inhabit it and, as they made it into a place for living, they re-coded its space, inscribing it with symbolic and spatial markers of caste, class and the divine.

To the unknowing eye there were no obvious memorials to the villages that the colony's new residents had left behind. To visiting anti-SEZ activists this was interpreted as a deliberate oversight and evidence that India's state governments intended to make the acquisition of land for projects like this harder to track and trace. In the 1970s and 1980s, by contrast, the resettlement colonies built to house those displaced by the construction of other large-scale infrastructure development projects in this part of coastal Andhra Pradesh – like the steel plant – had been memorialised in public signboards that displayed the names of former villages. But while they were not publicly marked the villages of the displaced were made an intimate part of the SEZ resettlement colony. Roads and junctions around the colony were informally named after abandoned villages and residents could point to rows of houses and name with precision the settlements in which their occupants had once lived.[6]

Figure 5   Resettlement colony: Main Street

On the inside and outside of these new homes the lives of improvement and betterment that people had imagined for themselves materialised. Most new residents had invested substantial portions of their compensation payments in the construction of new houses for themselves and their families. In the choice of building materials and designs these were aspirational constructions, built as improvements upon former dwellings. Yet they also continued to reflect the disparities in wealth and land ownership that differentiate high- and low-caste communities in the region's villages. Families who had lost additional lands and property to the zone received additional compensation, in line with the final negotiated settlement. Wealthy, high-caste Velama and Raju families were able to build large permanent structures with ostentatious features, marble porches, wrought iron gates and heavy wooden doors. Meanwhile, ex-Untouchable Malla and Madiga families built low, clay-walled structures that imitated the style and materials of their old homes, though now topped with corrugated iron roofs. Meanwhile, on the inside of these homes people placed on prominent display the new domestic appliances and household consumer goods – things like televisions, gas stoves and refrigerators – that had also been acquired with compensation money.

All of the colony's new residents experienced the resettlement as a social-spatial rupture but their accounts of the process are not univocal. Upper-caste Hindu farmers and their families, for example, voiced anxieties at the erosion of barriers between castes, describing their discomfort and – sometimes – outrage at being forced to live in such close proximity to castes who were beneath them in a ritual hierarchy. 'I'd prefer to be living with my caste beside me,' one *panchyat* vice-president, a wealthy Velama landowner, told me. 'But,' he said, gesturing to the buildings on either side of his, 'this one is Satya Baliga and this one is Kapu and there is nothing I can do.' On another occasion a Kapu farmer pointed at the houses that lay opposite him on the other side of the road. 'When we used to live in the village the Scheduled Caste community was about a kilometre away from us,' he said. 'Now the only boundary between us is this road and we can't do anything about it.'

One day in the colony I was accosted by a particularly angry old Kapu woman who asked me to record her frustrations, shouting at me:

In this place everything has been turned upside down; Kapus are eating from the Malla's plate and Mallas are eating from the Kapu's plate. The poor are being treated well, while the rich are treated shabbily. The ones who lost our lands are now being treated the same as these people who never had any? How is it possible? This government doesn't care who we are. The officials and politicians who did this to us are fit for nothing, they should be thrown on the funeral pyre and turned into ashes.

For these higher-caste families the move to the colony and their new proximity to other castes created new kinds of moral and spiritual danger. The elderly widows of farmers lamented the loss of ancestral connections to the land and the loss of places associated with the dead. Some saw the uncertainties and tension that accompanied their resettlement as the result of an inauspicious move. 'You shouldn't move from west to east,' they told me, correlating their shift with the onset of new ailments and sicknesses, fatigue and tiredness. For others the space of the colony – a space outside old village boundaries and beyond the protection of its deities – presented new kinds of moral dangers. Some families who had been allocated plots in the south-east corner of the resettlement colony found themselves forced to live beside a small temple to Nokalamma, one of the region's seven prominent village goddesses, to whom is ascribed a malevolent power. Once this temple had marked the outer boundary of the village of Mathuru, and was half a kilometre away from the nearest homes. Now the temple stood in the midst of whitewashed family homes, provoking fear and anxiety among those who lived close by.

As higher-caste farmers and their families adjusted to life in an uncertain, dangerous and inauspicious place they paid heightened attention to the correct observance of everyday Hindu rites and *pujas* aimed at reducing the malevolent power of gods, unloading misfortune, bringing about prosperity and fertility, or ensuring immunity from danger. For many families these included a repertoire of rituals associated with the worship of snake goddesses, and some of their concerns were played out on the occasion of Nagula Chauvithi, when farmers entreat snakes, cobras and serpents for protection and fertility. Across this part of coastal Andhra Pradesh village temples and anthills, favoured nesting grounds for snakes, are important sites of worship to snake goddesses. With their move to the SEZ colony many farming families sought out new sites of worship closer to their new homes. Newly resettled Kapu families from the village of Dippturo, for example, had scoured the colony for anthills and, once a year, could be found pruning bushes and clearing away trees around its eastern perimeter so that these snake pits (*valmeekam*) could be decorated with vermillion paste and flowers, milk poured into the holes and eggs left at the entrances. When I joined them in 2009 they described how, in years past, this had been a family feast when large extended families (*anta kutumbam ganta*) had celebrated together. 'We all used to go together and we'd even wait for anybody who was late,' they remembered. 'We used to plan it and all go together, some years to the fields and some years to the temple. Now,' they complained, 'The joy is not there, we are doing this just because it has to be done.'

For ex-Untouchable communities of Mallas and Madigas, however, the rupturing of village relations was unequivocally positive and as they adjusted to life in the new colony they worked to erase social, spatial and symbolic markers of caste. Young Dalit men, in particular, saw the move to the colony as prefacing a radical transformation in inter-caste relationships and they were charged with a powerful, reformist urge to make their displacement a catalyst for change. 'Our forefathers used to stand up when the Kapus passed by and in return they would get nothing but abuse. Even Kapu children would shout at our old men without any respect' they complained.

> But things are different now. Our generation have studied, we have passed tenth class or completed ITIs [Industrial Training Institutes] , and now we are living side by side, why should we have to stand up before them?

For these young men the move to the colony was experienced as socially liberating. Their descriptions of everyday life in the new settlement were of opportunities for interactions and friendships that reconfigured long-standing inter-caste relations. 'Some of the other boys come and eat with us now, they share food with us. Not all, but some,' young Malla and Madiga men informed me, reporting how Kapu and Yadav young men sometimes visited their homes, breaking village prohibitions on inter-caste relationships that their parents still observed. For these young Dalit men, the SEZ had also brought about a shift in generational power, which they saw as a catalyst for the reorganisation of village social structures. Like many young men across this hinterland of Visakhapatnam they frequently used the Telugu word *corrullu* to describe themselves. Literally 'people who roam', it had come to stand as an epithet for youth and masculinity; those with the freedom to move about. 'The *corrollu* want to organise things differently around here,' I was repeatedly told. 'In the colony the *corrollu* are different.'

Of course, the question of whether or not displacement and resettlement can substantively transform village-level relationships over time is a matter of considerable debate, not just for social scientists (e.g. Levien 2011) but also for those most affected by the experience. Jaded with age and experience the fathers of young Dalit men were sceptical that their move to the resettlement colony could overcome entrenched caste prejudices. Muppaddi Appa Rao, the father of four young Malla men, was a retired railway employee. Over the course of his career he had worked in the states of Madhya Pradesh and Assam but his family home had always remained in the countryside of Atchutapuram, in a Scheduled Caste colony surrounded by villages of Kapu farmers. 'The way that the Kapus and us used to live over there, the way that we used to address them and call them, well that's the same way that we have to address them and call them now that we live over here. The situation hasn't changed,' he told me.

The SEZ Air

While the coming of the SEZ was experienced as a moment of rupture, higher-caste farmers also described how it brought with it an 'SEZ *uppu*' or an 'SEZ *hawa*', an SEZ air or wind, that gave them a temporary lift or propulsion, carrying them a little higher and a little forwards. Alongside their investments in homes and houses many families used their compensation payments to settle unpaid debts, including medical expenses and groom-price payments. Others invested portions of their compensation money in vehicles of small town private enterprise, auto-rickshaws and small family stores. Four kilometres away, the town of Atchutapuram became flooded with auto-rickshaws. In 2009 my brief survey recorded around 400 of them. Meanwhile many new homes across the resettlement colony boasted a metal shuttered room on the front porch, as families looked to the future by building small family-owned shops or trade stores into their properties.

The market town of Atchutapuram saw a boom in commerce. Velama, Kapu and Gavara businessmen opened up jewellery shops and motorbike showrooms, hoping to tap a local population flush with cash from compensation payments and to capitalise on new labour migrants looking for work inside the zone. Families who owned prime real estate around the town's crossroads now commanded exorbitant rents, demanding between 100,000 and 300,000 rupees in up-front deposits on a three-year lease for commercial space. In 2009 I was given a tour of the town by part-time journalists writing for the Telugu-language dailies *Eenadu* and *Sakshi*. They counted 22 new hotels, 3 petrol pumps, 7 jewellers and 2 motorbike showrooms opened in the previous two years. A nihilistic billboard for one of them – advertising Hero Honda motorcycles with the slogan 'Don't live on the edge, live over it' – now towered over the crossroads, catching the tone of salespeople as they encouraged young men to blow their share of compensation payouts.

In the resettlement colony, however, by the end of the decade the 'SEZ air' had begun to disperse. The few shops that had once opened up in the SEZ resettlement colony had now closed down for lack of business and there was no longer any weekly market. The travelling salesmen who continued to set up stalls here acted as a barometer for the changing economic fortunes of its families. One Wednesday in late September 2009 a local dealer in imported Japanese branded televisions set up a tent outside the zone's main administrative building. A large banner proclaimed a *Dasara* Special Mela but nobody was taking advantage of his special offers. 'If you look around here the place looks good,' he said. 'The houses look good, there is water. Everything seems nice. But the money situation has reached a climax. The money's exhausted now and everyone is looking for work.' The dealer looked over an array of cardboard boxes stacked up behind him and emblazoned with the outlines of television sets, music systems, gas stoves and electric rice cookers. 'If we had come here two years ago we could have sold all of this and gone back to town to bring more.' When people first began moving to the colony, he explained, it was flush with compensation money, attracting insurance dealers, money-lenders and salesmen to the area. Now the business had dried up and he had begun to offer credit to potential customers. 'We're telling people that they don't need to find a big amount. They only need to find a basic instalment. Look, understand one thing. When we say people here don't have money it doesn't mean they can't buy a TV or a stereo … The rice might be hot but it won't stop you from eating.'

While wealthy Velama and Raju families had successfully used their compensation payments to convert land and property into new assets, investing in real estate around the zone or in businesses ventures in the market towns of Atchutapuram and Anakapalle, less wealthy Kapu families now struggled to find alternative sources of household income to replace that portion which had previously been derived from the agricultural economy. In their accounts of displacement and resettlement upper-caste farmers and Dalits alike described their belief in these promises and their conviction that the coming of the SEZ presaged secure factory jobs for them or their children. 'Until we left those old houses, got in auto-rickshaws and moved to these new plots, we believed them,' I was frequently told by residents in the SEZ resettlement colony.

In 2010 the perimeter of the original zone could still be seen marked out across the countryside in a line of whitewashed concrete markers inscribed with the initials of the Andhra Pradesh Industrial Infrastructure Corporation. But Chandrababu Naidu's vision of the APSEZ as a single manufacturing enclave run by a single developer had long since fragmented. Even before the final package of compensation had been agreed with the displaced, the government of Andhra Pradesh had begun to rethink and restructure its grand designs for the swathe of land around Atchapuram and Rambilli.

In the absence of any bids from a single developer, the Andhra Pradesh Industrial Infrastructure Corporation had parcelled up and re-marketed this land to investors in different ways, enlisting the help of international development organisations and consultancy firms. Under the terms of a bilateral agreement on development cooperation the German Development Agency (GTZ) provided technical assistance to the state government and developed a new blueprint for a series of smaller industrial parks on the site. Half of the land (5479 acres) formerly acquired for the original zone was re-classified as a 'multi-product SEZ', with a Danish engineering consultancy (L&T Rambøll) appointed to develop a plan for attracting investors. The remaining half was incorporated into new visions for the development of this region, with 1000 acres integrated into a proposal for a massive 'Petroleum, Chemical and Petrochemical Investment Region' that was envisaged to stretch for some 600 square km across Andhra Pradesh's coastline.

In July 2005 the state government signed a public–private partnership agreement with a Sri Lankan garment company, Brandix, to develop a purpose-built apparel park on 1000 acres of land originally acquired for the zone. The company opened its massive dying, cutting and stitching complex in 2007, and began manufacturing ladies underwear and lingerie for major US brands. By the end of the decade, Brandix was the zone's largest employer, with some 3000 workers, only a fraction of whom were drawn from the countryside around the zone or its resettlement colony.

In common with garment manufacturing companies in economic zones across South Asia the company sought to control its workforce and pre-empt future labour conflicts by hiring from outside the local labour market. Young male managers were recruited through a network of regional employment agencies, while the largely female machine operators were recruited through government-sponsored skill development centres, set up during the early 2000s in Visakhapatnam's highway townships to prepare young women for work in garment manufacturing industries by teaching them how to sew at speed. This strategy saw the preferential hiring of workers who lived far from the zone and whose families or communities were less well placed to hold an employer accountable than workers who had been displaced by its construction and who now lived in its immediate vicinity.

The majority of these new factory workers travelled to work inside the APSEZ from Visakhapatnam city and the new towns on its periphery, and three times a day – at 5.30 am, 1.30 pm and 10 pm – the small market town of Atchutapuram was shaken by the roar of 35 buses carrying them to and from their shifts. This convoy of buses created an impressive spectacle, fixing the attention of bystanders as it roared through town, kicking up dust and grit. Around the town speculation was rife about the impact of the Brandix factory. The number of employees was wildly inflated in a local imagination and, as I explore in chapter 6, women workers inside this company quickly became the object of both fascination and disgust among the countryside's unemployed young men.

Similar experiences were repeated in the zone's other new manufacturing units. Invariably, when people from the SEZ colony approached companies for work, they were told either that they did not have the necessary qualifications for the work or, if they could present evidence of their post-secondary level education, that they were too old. The managerial logic was not lost on high-caste farmers. 'These things are just excuses,' one Velama landlord complained, as he described his inability to secure employment in the zone for his sons. 'Education and age are just excuses not to recruit local people. Maybe it is because these companies have their own people that they want to employ or maybe they are afraid that local people will do something if they employ them.'

Excluded from the zone's nascent industrial labour force those people who had been displaced by its construction now found themselves competing against each other for work in the zone's informal economy. Rather than the promised formal factory jobs, residents of the resettlement colony worked for casual day wages in the zone's loading bays, on its construction sites, or as gardeners or cleaners. Faced with their exclusion from waged employment opportunities and competition in the zone's informal economy, some former farmers established themselves as informal labour contractors and divided up a share of the limited spoils between them. At the end of the 2000s Kapu farmers who had been resettled from the villages of Dippturo and Muturopalem organised lower-caste and Scheduled Caste men from their villages into four labour gangs and devised a rotating schedule so that irregular work loading or unloading delivery vehicles at the Brandix manufacturing units could be shared between them.

Former landowning families – whose farms and fields had once provided a major source of household income – felt these new insecurities most acutely. Reflecting on the failure of the zone to deliver promises of employment farmers presented themselves as the victims of unscrupulous government bureaucrats and fraudulent officials, and described the land acquisition process as a kind of alchemy in reverse. 'We gave them gold and they gave us silver,' went the proverbial expression. Others voiced their anger at having been played by politicians on the electoral campaign trail. One Velama farmer, whose family continued to own tens of acres of land in the area, complained:

> We trusted the collector, the ministers and the members of the legislative assembly but nobody comes to ask us how we are living now. Now they tell us that if we don't vote for them in the elections they won't help. How can they link the elections to our lost land? I belong to the ruling party [Congress] but even I can't do anything. We are looked upon very cheaply these days, completely ignored.

The economic insecurities facing these higher castes now affected those who had once provided them with caste-based occupational services. Chakali caste families who had once eked out a living by cleaning and mending clothes for higher castes now lamented the loss of patronage and mutual dependency. 'In the old village all the Kapus were at one end of the village and other castes were at the other end of the village,' one old Chakali man from the village of Dipputuro, told me 'but we always had the right to demand certain things from them'. His father and grandfather had washed and ironed clothes for the village's Kapu families and, in exchange, they had been entitled to a share of the harvest. 'If I had a daughter who was getting married then I would have the right to ask people for things. We used to be able to rely on two *putus* of rice ever year.'

The destruction of the village had injected ambiguity into these relationships. 'Now,' he said, 'the farmers tell us, "We used to feed you in the village, so if you need something just come here and eat," but how can I demand anything from them?'

Yet challenged to reflect on their past enthusiasm for the APSEZ, people also acknowledged how structural conditions in the agrarian economy had once made the zone and its futures so appealing. 'What else could we have done?', an old Kapu man asked me rhetorically during a walk around the colony one day. He gestured into the distance, towards the home and smallholding that was now enclosed within the zone's boundary wall.

> We were getting older, and people came and said these things to us. Of course, now people think they made a mistake. We have given away all our strengths [*ayupettu*], our documents, everything to them. All the money they gave us has been spent on constructing a new house. Now

our only hope is that someone will come here and give some job to our children. We wanted companies to come to the zone and run profitably so that we can get secure and stable jobs. People from outside don't care like we do.

The Future is Here

A decade after the APSEZ was first announced in New York, a massive, two-lane highway had been built to connect the small market town of Atchutapuram to the zone's new manufacturing units and its resettlement colony. This long, black line of tarmac blazed a straight line through the countryside, resembling an airport runway as much as a road, and the row of blue, green and white signboards planted along the central reservation read: 'APSEZ: The Future is Here'.

Figure 6   The future is here

Inside the zone the road streaked past the low, circular clay buildings and thatched structures of displaced villages, abandoned but not yet demolished. In 2010 the final portion of this road – connecting the zone to the resettlement colony – was still incomplete. Construction work had been stalled by a dispute between the state government and a private contractor, amid accusations about the mismanagement of funds, and the line of black tarmac stopped abruptly in the middle of the countryside, half a kilometre short.

Rather than present the large-scale industrial infrastructure projects that are transforming them as cohesive economic and political projects – as complete, finished, predictable, let alone as coherent and knowable – this book shows them as spaces that are constantly under construction. To this end the incomplete and unfinished road between the APSEZ and its resettlement colony offered itself as a powerful metaphor for the development imaginaries attached to large-scale infrastructure projects in India. Even when these projects fail to realise the hopes and expectations invested in them, their built structures – roads, boundary walls and resettlement colonies – continue to resonate with dreamed-of and desired futures. Even as they fail to attract investors or to generate employment, India's economic zones continue to relay past promises into the present, producing new dreams, desires and aspirations.

In 2008 the government of Andhra Pradesh scaled down its ambitions for the APSEZ still further, blaming the global economic downturn and the fall-out from the financial crisis. In 2012 the state government faced a major energy crisis, as demand for electricity across the state outstripped supply. In the middle of that year the government imposed an 'energy holiday' on all industries, leaving SEZ factories without access to electricity for twelve days each month and further diminishing the attractiveness of these spaces for investors. In the absence of interest from investors the state government successfully appealed to have more of the land that had originally been acquired for the APSEZ re-classified. At the end of 2012 a further 2236 acres of land was formally 'de-notified', meaning that it could now be leased or purchased by non-export-oriented industries.

Similar stories – of land that is acquired for SEZs and is re-classified after a small coterie of landowners or real estate speculators has profited from its rise in value – have become legion in contemporary India. Across the country journalists, activists and independent researchers have revealed discrepancies between the area of required land that appears in early project proposals and the area of land that is eventually 'notified' as an economic zone, with this excess or surplus land eventually used for purposes other than that for which it was originally acquired. Such investigations also reveal instances where people with political connections have been able to acquire land around the site of an SEZ far in advance of any public announcement and before the accompanying escalation of real estate values. For many critics, these studies offer clear evidence of collusion between elected representatives or public officials and private business interests, and reveal zones as the outcome of rational and calculating interests.

Yet while the creation of SEZs in states like Andhra Pradesh has rarely run counter to the interests of powerful constituencies, this is not to say that land acquisition processes are directed solely by knowing agents of the state or capital, shaped primarily by the blueprints of planners, architects and management consultants or the demands of investors and industrialists. Indeed, our understanding of the social and material politics of these spaces is impoverished if we imagine them as driven by a singular logic of accumulation or rule, materialising over-accumulated capital's search for a spatio-temporal fix (Harvey 2005; Levien 2011) or a regime of dispossession aimed at capturing and enclosing previously unexploited territory.

On the contrary, close ethnographic attention to the politics of land acquisition, displacement and resettlement in India shows how these processes are equally shaped by speculative investments, the everyday dreams that animate ordinary lives, the hopes of farmers and the rural poor. At India's frontiers of rural industrialisation we find people adapting to market futures and re-working trajectories for the transformation of space, just as we do in the mega-cities where slum communities are displaced by projects of gentrification (Ghertner 2010) or in the isolated hill tracts where communities of Adivasis are displaced by mining or big dams (Baviskar 2004; Shah 2010). At times these efforts may constitute a subaltern or reformist challenge to the social order, but they may also constitute a conservative attempt to reproduce or re-establish old hierarchies. And, just as the compulsory acquisition of land for development sometimes compels those threatened with eviction to imagine impoverished and insecure futures, so too it creates arenas in which people re-imagine themselves, their lives and their livelihoods as better.

In Atchutapuram and Rambilli the coming of an economic zone fostered dreams of profit, gain and political power, and communities of farmers sought to harness and manipulate the land acquisition process in ways that concealed their illegal occupation of land redistributed to the poor or guaranteed higher compensation payouts for their families. For some the process was managed in extraordinarily advantageous and lucrative ways and higher-caste farmers, Velamas and Rajus, converted their assets into new forms of social and political capital or accumulated new property. Of course, not all farmers benefited equally from the coming of the zone, but rather than seeing 'accumulation by dispossession' as an external project driven by the interests of corporations and capitalists, we might also see this as a bottom-up process that overlaps with inter-caste struggles over land that have characterised India's agrarian political economy.

As I have tried to show, living towards the future involves not just the structural resources bestowed upon people by history but also the 'quotidian energy' to imagine or dream of a better life beyond the conditions of past or present possibility (Appadurai 2013: 287). In this respect the coming of the APSEZ appeared to be a great leveller. While the poor and socially marginalised were not able to profit in similar ways, the zone opened up a new arena in which Dalit communities could imagine for themselves new kinds of economic and social subjectivities. The land acquisition process allowed young men from Malla and Madiga communities to imagine a future of caste equality, lending credence to arguments that projects and policies associated with India's economic liberalisation create spaces of liberatory potential for Dalits (e.g. Omvedt 1995).

As they take shape on the landscape of rural India special economic zones emerge out of this economy of anticipation. These projects are shaped by the diversity of futures invested in them and the articulation of these different futures with each other. Over the coming chapters I look inside these spaces to show how – even when economic zones fail to realise the expectations of those they displace, attract or employ – dreamed-of and desired futures continue to shape how they are imagined, perceived and encountered.

4

The Factory of the Future

Sometime in 1996 a middle aged Israeli man with business interests and directorships in the international diamond industry travelled to India to identify an appropriate location for a new processing facility. He was travelling in his capacity as the CEO of a financial holding company registered in Luxembourg called the Millennium Group. The Millennium Group was set up as an investment vehicle for two major corporate players in the European diamond industry: Bettonville, one of the world's largest manufacturers of diamond cutting tools and Hennig, a UK-based diamond brokerage firm for the world's largest diamond mining company, De Beers. Through the Millennium Group these investors were looking to build a new low-cost, diamond cutting and polishing facility in India and they had hired a management consultancy firm to propose suitable locations. Their shortlist proposed five sites, all of them first-generation economic zones built by India's central government (see chapter 1). Over several weeks the businessman and his colleague visited each of these zones, inspecting their facilities and meeting with the zone authorities. At the end of their visit they settled on the Madras Export Processing Zone, located outside the city of Chennai in Tamil Nadu.

As they were wrapping up negotiations in Chennai, however, the consultants suggested that the Millennium Group might like to consider another option, an economic zone further along India's east coast, outside the city of Visakhapatnam in Andhra Pradesh. The Visakhapatnam special economic zone (VSEZ) is one of India's oldest (see chapter 2). Arrangements were made for the Millennium Group's representatives to fly there and back in a day. They were met at Visakhapatnam's airport and were driven directly to the zone where they were introduced to its development commissioner, a high-ranking woman officer in the Indian Administrative Service and given a tour of the facilities.

The meeting continued into the afternoon. At some point, the development commissioner made a telephone call to the city's airport and arranged for her visitors' return flight to be delayed by two hours. This bravura display of executive authority, demonstrating a willingness and ability to accommodate the needs of foreign investors, proved decisive. By the end of their visit the Millennium Group's representatives had decided to build a factory in the zone, at a reported cost of just under £1 million. As a senior executive later reflected:

> When they decided to come here there was no serious study. They came, met with Ratna Prabha and were convinced. She delayed their flight by two hours so that they could stay and they decided to build the factory. She was one of the main reasons they decided to come to Visakhapatnam.

The factory they founded here, Worldwide Diamonds, was to become the Millennium Group's flagship. Over the next decade it pioneered the large-scale mass production of consumer diamonds, transforming what industry old timers call 'the art of diamond cutting and polishing' into what a new generation of factory managers call 'the art of manufacturing'. In doing so it transformed a corner of India with no indigenous tradition of gemstone cutting and little modern history of trade in precious stones into a hub for the global diamond industry.

In the previous chapter I explored how the acquisition of land for special economic zones in India brings grand visions of social and economic development into conflict and alignment with the dreams and desires of landlords, farmers and the rural poor as they pursue diverse projects for personal gain, political power and social mobility. In this chapter I focus on the pursuit of profit inside India's special economic zones and explore how the aspirations of transnational corporations are brought to life here. In doing so I explore how management – as a mode of knowing about and living towards the future – is central to the economy of anticipation.

The diamond manufacturing industry offers a unique window onto the anticipatory politics of management and labour in contemporary India. In 2008, before the global financial crisis led to a crash in world markets for consumer diamonds, an estimated 1.3 million people were employed in India to cut and polish what was, in terms of volume, 92 per cent of all diamonds traded on world markets.

The coming of the global diamond industry to the north-east coast of Andhra Pradesh is a classic story of globalisation's 'race to the bottom'. Between the mid 1800s and the 1970s the city of Antwerp in Belgium was the largest global centre of trade in rough diamonds and the world's major site of diamond cutting and polishing. In the 1970s rising costs of production and an increase in demand for diamonds saw manufacturers shift their operations from long-established cutting and polishing workshops to global locations with cheaper labour costs and more relaxed state regulation. Gemstone dealers in the Indian states of Gujarat and Maharashtra began to capture an increasingly high volume of this new trade. In the 1980s small, unregulated diamond cutting and polishing workshops flourished in the cities of Surat, Ahmedabad, Baroda and Saurashtra. By the late 1990s they had cornered a majority share of the global trade in cut and polished diamonds.

As Belgian and Israeli diamond manufacturers struggled to remain competitive they began to open small and medium-sized manufacturing operations in export processing zones in Thailand and China. As the costs of manufacturing in Thailand and China began to rise a small group of European diamond industrialists began to investigate the scope for building their own manufacturing units in India. With their extensive exemptions on import taxes, corporate profits and labour laws, as well as the promise of 'favourable industrial relations', India's export processing zones promised the perfect location. As diamond manufacturers in India sought new economies of scale, factories like Worldwide Diamonds became spaces in which to realise corporate ambitions of growth, profit and control.

Seeing Like a Global Subcontractor

The Worldwide Diamonds factory was an Anglo-Belgian joint venture, owned and operated by the Millennium Group, on behalf of two corporate shareholders. The first, Bettonville, is one of the largest global manufacturers of machines and tools for the diamond industry. The second, I. Hennig & Co., is the UK's largest diamond broker and the principal dealer for De Beers Consolidated Mines, the company that continues to dominate the production of rough diamonds worldwide. These investors were represented on the Millennium Group's board of directors. While Bettonville would use the factory as a showcase to promote its machine tools and new laser cutting technology, Hennig promoted the facility as a reputable, trusted and low-cost diamond processing facility for De Beers' 'Sightholders', traders who have priority access to rough stones mined by De Beers. Their joint venture represented a wider consolidation across the global diamond industry, as manufacturers, traders and retailers sought to cut costs by integrating their business operations.

Worldwide Diamonds was built across two floors of one of the zone's standard design factories and, from the outset, its organisation systematically broke the work of diamond cutting and polishing into a series of highly specialised and repetitive manual tasks. While craftsmen on the floor of an Antwerp workshop had once been trained to transform a stone from its rough uncut state into a finished diamond, here the process was divided into a series of specific manual tasks that were easier to learn and more amenable to control.

Worldwide Diamonds specialised in the low-cost, high-volume processing of small-sized medium-quality diamonds. Clients were offered a range of services, from the sorting of roughs to the sawing, smoothing and laser cutting of stones into fancy heart or oval shapes. The company charged its clients by the carat. In 2005 a basic polishing service for consignments of rough diamonds ranged from US$18 dollars per carat for stones weighing more than 2 carats to US$2.70 dollars per carat for the smallest of stones weighing less than a quarter of a carat each. Clients were also offered the opportunity to build their own, custom-designed 'factory within a factory' to ensure that stones were processed to their specifications.

At the end of the 1990s large-scale export manufacturing units like Worldwide Diamonds were exactly the kind of foreign investment that India's state governments were looking to attract, and over which they were becoming increasingly competitive. The factory opened in 1997 and in its first year of operations it exported cut diamonds with a market value of just over £1 million. In the second year the value of its exports increased six-fold to around £7.5 million. In Andhra Pradesh politicians presented the factory as evidence of the state's ability to attract 'world-class' investors. The company was garlanded with accolades, winning several awards for 'exporter of the year' from the government of Andhra Pradesh, who celebrated it as a glittering example of the state's economic transition.

By 2000 Worldwide Diamonds had become one of coastal Andhra Pradesh's largest private sector employers, employing around 1100 young Telugu-speaking men and women to cut and polish diamonds. Yet Worldwide Diamonds was a classic global subcontractor and waged labour here was comparatively low-paid and chronically insecure. New recruits were hired on a trainee basis for a two-year period on an annual contract that the company could renew or revoke as they saw fit. At its lowest the factory's monthly wage was akin to the monthly income of a day-labourer in the local construction industry. At its highest they were still less than the earnings of a successful, self-employed auto-rickshaw driver. The zone offered no residential facilities and every day the factory's workforce left the zone for their rented rooms or family homes in industrial highway townships and villages across Visakhapatnam's hinterland.

The mass production of consumer diamonds is a complex, ugly business. Cutting and polishing thousands of carats of rough diamond every month into finished luxury commodities requires a sophisticated industrial apparatus: the systematic organisation of time, space, machine tools and tasks, as well as a political infrastructure that can maintain control over a large labour force. For the first seven years of its operations, day-to-day control of the Worldwide Diamonds factory rested with a chain smoking, moustachioed Belgian man in his mid 50s whom I will call Ruben.

Ruben was born and brought up in a large Belgian city where his father had been a diamond polisher. Ruben left school at 16 and, after a year in a garage repairing cars, he was taken on as an apprentice in a diamond workshop. Over the following 30 years he worked his way off the workshop floor, taking a college course in management, and eventually managing factories in Africa and South East Asia. Ruben called himself a 'diamond man'. He had a practical knowledge of the diamond manufacturing process and a strong identification with diamond polishing as a craft. Like a handful of other Belgians and a couple of Israelis who were employed in this factory to train workers how to sort, saw, cut and polish diamonds, he was an industry old timer who regarded himself as an ex-worker, 'a diamond man, through and through', rather than a manager. By all accounts Ruben was a draconian factory manager. He gained notoriety among workers for shouting and screaming at people on the factory floor when they made mistakes and imposing punitive financial penalties on those who over-polished, cracked or lost stones in the manufacturing process.

On the 9th of January 2002 350 of Worldwide Diamonds' workers went on strike to protest at management practices and to demand improvements in working conditions inside the factory. A rally outside the zone's administrative building was broken up by police and at least 35 people were jailed without charge for several days. In the aftermath, the state government suspended freedoms of movement and association within a 20 km radius of the zone and the company is alleged to have dismissed two workers for trade union activism and imposed arbitrary fines of between one day's and one week's wages on 22 others.

This strike was one of the largest yet to have taken place inside India's special economic zones and briefly made Worldwide Diamonds a *cause célèbre* for India's leftist labour movement. The Centre for Indian Trade Unions (CITU) – a nation-wide labour federation aligned to the Communist Party of India – used the case as an important focus for their opposition to policies of economic liberalisation and to draw critical attention to the labour regimes emerging in India's offshore economy. As one CITU leader put it, proudly inflating the significance of their efforts, 'at that time nobody knew what a SEZ was. But we exposed it with our struggles.' Labour activists from the CITU presented evidence for the brutality of the company's managers and the suppression of organised labour in pamphlets, news magazines and reports to international labour solidarity networks. They organised a national convention of free trade zone workers in Visakhapatnam and dispatched an activist to share their experiences at an international workshop held in Bangkok by the Washington-based Solidarity Centre. Finally, in a test case, they submitted a complaint about the infringement of trade union rights in the zone to the UN International Labour Organization (ILO) in Geneva, setting in motion a legalistic process of investigation, as the ILO's resident experts and external academics attempted to establish whether the labour rights that it identifies as universal had been contravened. At the 2004 World Social Forum in Mumbai the CITU's general-secretary presented the story from Visakhapatnam as a graphic illustration of the conditions facing industrial labourers in a globalising India.

Under this management regime Worldwide Diamonds hit new peaks in production and profit. By 2004 the factory had 15 established clients, all of whom sourced their stones from De Beers', and processed an average 14,000 carats of rough diamonds, with an export value of approximately US$4 million, per month. The factory had established a reputation as one of the world's premier low-cost, high-volume processors of small-sized, medium-quality diamonds and it was able to undercut some of its major competitors by up to 30 per cent.

For its owners and corporate shareholders, however, the growth of their flagship factory appeared to have stalled and projected future rates of return on their investment failed to meet their expectations. Moreover, the factory's success saw its clients and competitors attempt to replicate their model. In 2003 the government of Andhra Pradesh invested 6 billion rupees in the construction of a purpose-built diamond polishing and jewellery manufacturing facility inside the VSEZ, under a public–

private partnership agreement with one of Worldwide Diamonds' former clients, LID, an Israeli-owned diamond company.[1] Meanwhile Indian diamond manufacturers began to open their own manufacturing facilities inside other economic zones being opened in Mumbai and Surat. As a labour-intensive, export-oriented business that depends on the import of high-value raw materials the diamond industry has been particularly well suited to the preferential tax and labour regimes created by India's economic zones. Between 2002 and 2007 exports of gemstones and jewellery from SEZs established by India's central government grew faster than textiles, garments and micro-electronic components.

As the Millennium Group looked to take their flagship factory into the future by sustaining its growth and remaining globally competitive it enlisted an executive recruitment agency in Brussels to find a new general manager. 'We wanted to bring in an outsider,' the group's senior executives told me. 'We wanted to think outside the box, to try and introduce new elements into the factory and to start thinking more carefully about human relations.'

The man they recruited, whom I shall call George, brought to Worldwide Diamonds a particular kind of technical expertise and a specific vision for the factory's transformation. George was a non-smoking, non-drinking, British man who had no previous experience in the diamond industry and no interest in the crafts of diamond cutting and polishing. He had grown up in a small town on the edge of one of the UK's old industrial port cities and, after leaving school, had studied electronic engineering at the town's polytechnic college. He began his professional career managing electricians in a local glass factory and over the next 20 years he worked his way up a managerial ladder through a diverse array of industries – from glass, to beer to paper, cardboard and packaging – before completing an MBA at a Scottish University. He arrived at Worldwide Diamonds having never before travelled to India, on a mission to transform the factory into what he called a 'world-class manufacturing unit'. 'I've worked in world-class factories and I've worked in very bad factories that wanted to be world class,' he said. 'This place will be completely different by the time I'm done with it.' He brought with him a vision of the factory of the future. 'In my head I can visualise it, I can see the utopian manufacturing plant,' he told me a few months after he had arrived, 'It's not going to happen here. But it's gonna come close.'

Attempts to realise corporate dreams of profit and growth, order and control, make India's SEZs into laboratories where managers attempt to replicate experiments with forms of industrial organisation and to reproduce particular kinds of working subjects. As I explore in this chapter, attempts to realise visions of the world-class factory have real material effects (cf. Miller and O'Leary 2008: 470). As they worked to build the factory of the future, Worldwide Diamonds' shareholders and managers forged new realities in the present, creating new work spaces, new forms of work organisations and new practices for controlling labour.

Managing Hope and Fear

At the end of 2004 I was granted a meeting with George, Worldwide Diamonds' new general manager. Looking to emulate a long tradition in the anthropology of industrial work this was the moment I hoped to gain access to the factory's shop floor as a participant observer. The factory's ground floor entrance hall presented an anodyne corporate face: a female receptionist operated a telephone switchboard, a glass of flowers reflected off a table surface, white blossom hung from the wall; the last month's export figures were carefully pinned in place on a green felt notice board. But behind this slick facade – considered so photogenic that it appeared in all of the factory's publicity materials, including colour brochures and corporate films – could be glimpsed the concern with control and labour discipline that defines the factory as a modern institution. On one side of

Figure 7   'Do not bite the hand that feeds you'

the foyer was a motivational message of the week, drawn in careful script on a whiteboard. 'Do not bite the hand that feeds you,' it read.[2]

Ushered into an air-conditioned office, I presented George with a letter of introduction, handed over a proposal that explained my research as a study of 'workplace culture' and explained my methodological interest in becoming an unpaid participant in the factory's work processes. To my amazement he was amenable to my request and, after checking my references, agreed that I could begin work as an unpaid apprentice in one of the factory's manufacturing departments. George had no interest in the written products of my research and made no demand that I conceal the factory's identity. Like the early pioneers of industrial ethnography he imagined that the presence of an interested outsider might have some kind of positive effect on the social and political dynamics of the workspace. 'It'll be like having a shrink on site,' he told me. What began as a provisional arrangement for 3 months was gradually extended to 12 and, over the next year, for as many six-day weeks as I could muster, I joined more than 600 people as they arrived at Worldwide Diamonds' entrance for the 6 am A shift and left with them as another 600 people arrived for the 2 pm B shift.

Over the course of a year I watched George and his Indian management team as they set out to remake Worldwide Diamonds into a world-class manufacturing unit and recorded hours of unstructured interviews with them as they spoke frankly about their work. As I explore in this chapter, the everyday work of factory management is a complex of anticipatory technologies and practices that involves diverse ways of knowing about and living towards the future.

The utopian factory of George's imagination was more than a private vision or individual fantasy. It was a globally mobile vision that is generated in and moves around what Nigel Thrift has called the 'cultural circuit of capital' (1996: 6–7). This is a vision that is assembled from and disseminated in the myriad case studies taught in international business schools and which coheres around a body of technical expertise, systems and practices for organising space, time and people that has come to be described as post-Fordist (Amin 1994). It is a vision that fuses the lessons of F.W. Taylor with the Japanese principle of *Kaizen* or 'continuous improvement' to imagine a 'lean manufacturing unit', in which all inefficiencies in the organisation of production have been eliminated.

Post-Fordist visions of the factory anticipate the production of new kinds of managerial and labouring subjects. As George worked to restructure the factory he singled out managers for pastoral care and appealed to the emotions, feelings and sentiments of workers. The first managers of Worldwide Diamonds had built the factory around the relatively simplistic industrial psychology of the early and mid twentieth century. They sought to impose control over workers by constituting them as docile bodies, the tools or instruments of managerial design, and they understood the behaviour or motivations of individual workers in terms of their basic needs or wants.[3] By contrast, George's post-Fordist reorganisation of workspaces and systems was aimed at bringing people into a more active and engaged relationship with the company; producing workers who managed themselves through feelings of responsibility, autonomy and ownership, and whose dreams and desires were more closely allied with the goal of profit making (see Miller and O'Leary 2008: 477; Miller and Rose 1995: 477–8; Rose 1989; Weeks 2011: 69).

For managers like George twentieth-century post-Fordist management systems and practices have the qualities of scientific fact. 'The model's universal,' George liked to lecture me. 'You can't argue with it: Lean manufacturing means identifying waste and eradicating it.' Yet all forms of techno-scientific knowledge are 'adapted and reconfigured' (Mol and Law 1994) as they travel and, as George's globally circulating vision of the world-class factory touched down in north coastal Andhra Pradesh, it was adapted to the particularities of place. Like managers elsewhere (e.g. Rudnyckyj 2009), George and his managers worked to make the model 'fit' the local context by drawing on multiple influences, ideas and sources. Their exertions of authority and control incorporated localised registers of social difference and hierarchy, paternal and pastoral care. While George and other European managers invoked the history of European colonialism in South Asia and established differences based on ideas of race, their Indian counterparts invoked class and caste. As they worked to bring workers into a closer relationship with the company by engineering feelings of attachment and obligation, they drew on localised idioms of kinship and desires for upward social mobility to cast waged labour as a filial duty or a pathway to self-improvement. The management regime that emerged did not correspond to the neat typology imagined by terms like 'Fordism' or 'post-Fordism', but rather involved a hybrid combination of disciplinary and pastoral modes of power.

As I explore in this chapter our understanding of what takes place on the floor of the global factory is impoverished if we think about managerial decisions as characterised by pure calculation. What constitutes management is both a body of technical expertise and a corpus of felt or embodied know-how. As Worldwide Diamonds' European and Indian managers worked to impose order and control on the workplace they drew on anecdotal or intuitive social knowledge derived from their own observations, analyses and uncorrected biases; they boasted of their 'feel' for the workforce, their 'grasp' of its social demographics, and their 'deep' understanding of worker motivations and interests.[4] 'They say management is a science', George would sometimes tell me:

> Bullshit! The principles might be scientific. But as for how you apply them, well that's all down to you! All the best managers use their intuition. They say, 'I know it sounds sensible. But something doesn't look right. Something doesn't feel right.'

Social theorists are increasingly alert to the feelings and emotions, sensations and sentiments that are produced by and within spaces of capitalism. As I explore in this chapter, just as India's SEZs give rise to desires for profit, order and control, so too they give rise to fears and anxieties that anticipate a future in which order and control has been lost. The global factory is an elaborate apparatus for controlling space, time and people in order to produce things. Like other modern institutions, the factory stands as an architectural, technological and relational monument to control. Yet this apparatus of control also stands as a reminder that control is never permanent or given, that it is always a temporary achievement, an incomplete and unsteady accomplishment, which must be worked towards, asserted, maintained and renewed.[5] Control, the global factory constantly reminds its managers, is ephemeral, tentative and un-assured. As George and his managers worked to build a world-class factory they worked to assuage anxieties about the loss of control, either by carefully monitoring their own relationships with workers or by introducing innovations to systems of recruitment and surveillance. In what follows I show how the global factories built inside India's SEZs are oriented by and towards possible futures and the everyday work of management is an anticipatory practice that makes these spaces into particularly fertile places for capital.

Making Managers

George sat at his desk in the general managers' air-conditioned office. The office was sparsely furnished, with little more than a computer, printer, scanner and a filing cabinet. The only decorative element was a row of *faux* antique wooden clocks fixed along one wall. These clocks showed the times in New York, Antwerp, Tel Aviv and Hong Kong and established this otherwise nondescript office as a global space connected to the diamond industry's international trading centres.

'I'm a capitalist,' George told me, clicking his pen nib back in and out on the desk:

Productivity equals profits. Efficiencies equal wealth. That's what I believe. I believe that what I am going to do here, the kind of stuff that I am going to do in this factory, works. It's a win-win situation. I really, truly, cannot see a loss in it anywhere! But I also know that it takes a lot of effort. It takes a hell of a lot of work by general managers and middle managers and lower-level managers to keep this seemingly effortless cycle going.

Until George's arrival the everyday management of the Worldwide Diamonds factory had fallen to ex-workers who had been promoted up the factory's internal hierarchy to become shop-floor supervisors. George's vision of the world-class factory, however, required managers to have only a very rudimentary knowledge of diamond cutting or polishing but an expert knowledge of management systems and production processes. One of his first changes was to replace the factory's old supervisors with a new cadre of management professionals and he recruited young Indian graduates with degrees in business, human relations and engineering. 'The old factory supervisors were dogged and determined and they knew the trade,' he said. 'But ask them to produce a spreadsheet or something and they didn't know where to start. What I needed was people who could understand my language.'

Management practices and regimes at European manufacturing units in India are always refracted through the history and legacy of European colonialism. In India men like Ruben and George enjoy a historical continuity with those white men once employed as 'factors' by the world's first multinational corporation, the British East India Company. Like their infamous predecessors, today's 'factors' are critical actors in the political economy of globalisation. Employed to take charge of a company's commercial and trading interests on the ground it falls to them to realise the capitalist futures of their shareholders and corporate investors. In the seventeenth and eighteenth centuries, the English word 'factory' came to be used to describe the places where company agents and merchants, or 'factors', conducted their business and had their residences.[6] The first 'factories' established in Visakhapatnam (then part of the Kingdom of Golconda) were trade depots in which European merchant vessels put in to buy long cloth and chintz, and around which the British eventually built a major settlement. As enclaves of global trade, India's SEZs enjoy a symbolic and temporal continuity with these earlier spaces of global trade. Just as the East India Company's factories were built specifically to meet the demands of foreign traders for speed and temporal efficiency, so that merchants could buy and sell goods immediately, so too India's SEZs are premised on the reduction of red tape and on the acceleration of customs procedures.

The language and idioms through which managers described their attempts to bring order, discipline and control to the factory's workforce and its spaces constantly invoked the relationships and policies of British colonial government. One of the few personal artefacts that George brought with him to India was a photograph of him and his wife. Taken in an English amusement park the photograph's aesthetic was what might be called imperial nostalgia: it was a sepia print that depicted a couple in mid-Victorian dress, she seated beneath a prominent parasol, he towering above her, in top hat and tails, a walking stick by his side. George put the photograph on prominent display in the penthouse apartment that he occupied in Visakhapatnam, overlooking the Bay of Bengal. It was a knowing and ironic gesture that both invoked a history of imperial commerce along this coastline and self-consciously acknowledged how his presence here reproduced elements of this history.

The recruitment of a dedicated Indian management team also invoked historical parallels. Just as European factors in colonial South Asia had once depended on a whole host of local intermediaries – from Hindu priests and merchants, to lawyers, judges and financiers – to elaborate and translate information about the nature of Indian society, culture and economy, so today's expatriate factory managers in India depend on new kinds of knowledge brokers and forms of expertise to help realise corporate dreams and visions. As they sought to establish control over their factory, Ruben and George felt themselves deeply reliant upon their Indian-born managers, men and women with postgraduate degrees in engineering, business administration or human resources from the country's higher educational institutions. They looked upon this managerial staff as agents of their rule, whose local knowledge was essential to the implementation of their grand designs. Ruben once told me:

> You can never rule an Indian with a foreigner. You will never understand them. The culture here is too different. You will never understand them like an Indian understands them. You will never understand what is in their minds.

The new management team George recruited were young men and women from Andhra Pradesh's upper-caste, middle-class Telugu families. Their parents were public servants, bankers or business people who had invested in their children's education. With salaries of 8000 rupees (approximately US$200) a month, these jobs represented the bottom of India's white collar, graduate labour market. Although none among them looked upon their employment in Worldwide Diamonds as a failure, none of them saw it as success and all of them dreamt of moving upwards into the higher ranks of business professionals or of travelling overseas to pursue further educational qualifications.

Global factories produce people as well as things, and managerial visions of the world-class factory demand that bodies, persons and selves be inscribed with new ethical formulations, feelings and sensations. As he worked to transform Worldwide Diamonds into the factory of the future George singled out this cohort of salaried, white-collar managers for pastoral care, coaching them to strive for self-improvement, to act autonomously, and to seek to realise themselves through work. These virtues, which correspond to notions of the liberated individual, lie at the heart of post-Fordist ideologies of management. Yet if George ever imagined that the pastoral care he lavished on new management trainees might produce managers after his own self-image he was mistaken. The projects of self-fashioning in which young management trainees were engaged on the factory floor were primarily concerned with local registers of caste and class distinction.

George's reorganisation of the factory created a new division of labour that placed technocratic expertise above the applied practical mastery of diamond cutting machines or tools. This separation and elevation of conceptual knowledge – a knowledge of procedures and systems – above a knowledge of machines, tools and materials and a practical dexterity lies at the heart of twentieth-century notions of scientific management and models of industrial organisation (Braverman 1974; Carrier 1992;

Sennett 2008). In Hindu India such ideas overlap neatly with the fourfold division of society into *varnas*, and the social symbolic relations of caste that distinguish between different categories of person, with religious or ritual practitioners elevated above the practitioners of manual trades. For many of Worldwide Diamonds' high-caste management trainees their expert knowledge and technical qualifications also indexed their social difference and distance from lower-caste workers. So, in the division of labour between managerial and manual work, the factory became a space that re-affirmed and reproduced the social and symbolic relations of caste.

On the factory floor caste and class coexisted as registers for expressing hierarchical social relations, with everyday descriptions of workers as uneducated, deficient in knowledge and analytical skills, intelligence and IQ, or lacking in maturity, enterprising spirit and morality, closely resembling rationalisations of ritual hierarchy. 'We can tell their level of ability from their level of education', the finance manager once told me over lunch in the executive boardroom. 'That's the only indicator we've got. People who haven't gone to good schools have a low IQ.' In an adjacent office the factory's long-standing assistant general manager, a Telugu Brahmin, complained, 'Workers here lack the capacity to think.' Managers invoked their own achievements in the field of education to establish a social and cultural distance from workers and assert their 'right' to occupy positions of relative power and earn differential incomes. '*They* are paying me to *manage*. *We* are paying them to *work*,' one management trainee told me, the slippage between pronouns asserting their identity with executive authority and their distance from a majority labour force.

You Can't Get Production with Sentiments

Tasked with implementing George's vision for the factory the new management trainees spent their first months in the factory immersed in an intensive training programme that promised to turn them into experts. They attended coaching seminars with George and were sent on problem-solving missions to the factory floor. They were also tasked with making the factory compliant with an international standards regime, and with the design of new work systems and spaces. These young managers prided themselves on their close, local knowledge of the workforce. 'People like us', one of them told me, 'we added the human factor. We understood the concerns of the people.' But, as they were coached to become future factory managers, these neophytes came to see their ability to 'detach' themselves from social relationships with workers as a precondition for the rational, market-oriented calculations and impartial decisions required of a global professional. Concerned with how to drive the future productivity of workers, they carefully bracketed their interpersonal relations, striving to purge themselves of sentiment and the affective ties of obligation or reciprocity.

As they saw it, the biggest everyday challenge of modern factory management was to avoid becoming embroiled in a web of close, binding, personal relationships with the people they were employed to manage and control. Being a successful manager, as they saw it, meant the ability to remain detached. They retreated from relationships with the factory's workforce, afraid that any intimation of closeness, friendship, or intimacy with individuals might offer them some kind of leverage in requests for a promotion, a wage increase, extra leave, extra overtime or a reduction in workload. Managers like Vikram, Jeet and Chiru put these problems succinctly to me. Their anxieties stood testament to the difficulties of imposing a high-intensity production regime on people with whom you enjoy close relations, and to the constant work or effort involved in successfully achieving a degree of 'distance' from workers.

> *Vikram*: Relations with workers can't be avoided. They're necessary; they're a must. Without them you can't get the required outputs on the shop floor. But at the same time you can't try to build good relations with workers here. You'll never be successful like that. If you want them to meet targets and to keep the quality up then you have to be strict, you have to be disciplined. You can't go with your sentiments. You can't get production with sentiments.

Understanding, finding and maintaining this fine line was a pre-eminent day-to-day concern and a repeated motif in my conversational interviews.

> *Jeet*: You can't be friends or enemies with the workers here ... There will be some situations when I have to compel workers to do certain things. And if I am maintaining a friendship with them I just won't be able to do that. But you also just can't get things done by being authoritative! I'm talking about being on the shop floor where you spend eight hours a day. When you're there you have to get personal with workers so that

you can create a good atmosphere for work. But there are always some limitations. Because when there is a managerial gap between you and them – and there should be a gap – you must not show it. You should not show the gap physically or allow others to feel it. But you have to maintain it. You have to maintain it for yourselves. How to maintain the line, though … well that varies from time to time … I can't draw the line straight away. If I immediately and stubbornly draw a line then it's sure that I'll lose the workers, and I don't want to lose them. These are the things that show our competences.

Reciprocal social ties are sometimes described in Telugu as *tapana*: actions that provoke a sense of compulsion in the recipient to do something in return. The accounts of young managers describe a keen aversion to *tapana* relations with workers, and to the obligations and responsibilities they bring. Chiru explained how these bonds worked in the context of his family.

Say I am at my house, with my two brothers. If I help my brother in one situation, he will help in another. If I do something for him then he will think to do something for me too. He will get some sense that he should help me. He will be feeling *tapana*. And some delay will be there. And that delay is useful. If I support someone at one time, later they will feel that they can come to me.

In the context of a manufacturing unit in which there was pressure to increase the quantity and quality of production, *tapana* relations and their expectations of delayed reciprocity were precisely what managers like Chiru sought to avoid.

I have not been touching the personal aspects up till now. No. I've just been going to a superficial level. If we go into the deep personal aspects it means touching a deep sensitive part of them. Am I right? If you go 20 to 30 per cent deep into personal aspects it won't affect them much. If I go deep it increases my responsibility also. I feel there would be some responsibility on my shoulders.

Such strategies of avoidance were tightly bound up with the creation and performance of a professional managerial self, a stable normative identity that was frequently associated with the figure of the engineer.

Vikram: When I came here, I learned from the workers. I used to be friendly with them so that I could manage problems that came up. But I maintained those relations in a smooth and cool manner. I behaved as an engineer.

While managers observed and profiled workers they worked to maintain a distance from them.

Jeet: The workers should not know me. I should only know them. They should not be able to guess me [to know what I am thinking], because they can use that. But I should be able to guess them. I should be able to know their strong points and their weak points. From the first, I didn't bring personal relations into the job. According to me, the job is entirely different and personal is entirely different. Managers are not interested in personal matters. So I won't allow people to ask me about myself. That is my way of living style. My father used to say 'Don't bring personals into job profile' because if you bring any one of the personal reasons into the job people will start to ask you: 'Sir, will you help me in this manner or that manner.'

For management trainees like Chiru, Jeet and Vikram, George was an inspirational figure. He epitomised the globally mobile professional they sought to become and they sought to emulate him, paying close attention to everything from his decision-making practices to his dress code. 'I really learned a lot from him,' Chiru told me, adding:

I have been observing him closely. I really like his management style. He has all these systems: Continuous improvement. ISO techniques. *Kaizan* and all. I like his systems ... his decision making ... the way he handles people. I also like his dress style. Very good. Smart. Professional. Formal.

Vikram agreed:

He never bends. That's the quality of a good leader. A bit harsh but a true leader should not be looking for support. A decision may hurt some people but afterwards people will see that it was a good decision ... Like that, a leader should make their own decision. He should not be sentimental. He should be a perfect decision maker. He should take a decision and keep it.

Anticipating Dissent

George spun around in his office chair. Behind him a mirror glass window looked out onto the factory forecourt, allowing him to see out, but preventing anyone from seeing in. The factory's first shift was about to end and a crowd of blue-uniformed workers milled around outside, waiting for the start of the second. He watched people coming and going. 'I don't know how to divide and rule here,' he said. 'I need to isolate the good workers from the bad. But I don't know how to separate the two. And then you have the grey... And I don't know who the grey are at all.'

'I was only here one week,' George told me soon after he arrived, 'and I could see what was needed.' Turning Worldwide Diamonds into a world-class factory, he explained, demanded a radical restructuring. 'I'm going to change everything,' he said. 'If you change everything even half a percentage point towards efficiency then you will become more efficient.' This vision of hyper-efficiency was to be accompanied by a dramatic intensification of the labour process. 'Ten or eleven thousand carats per month for a factory of eleven hundred people is roughly enough to break even,' he said.

> So if you make 12,000 carats that means the next 1000 are pure profit. So what I'm going to do here is make less than 1100 people turn out more than 15,000 carats. I can see it now. I'm not just saying I think it's possible. I know it's possible ... and it's going to be very, very profitable.

Achieving such levels of productivity, however, would introduce new demands on the factory's labour force. India's special economic zones were constructed precisely to make it easier for employers to hire and fire workers and the success of companies like Worldwide Diamonds is premised on the uncertainty of employment, leaving workers anxious and insecure. As transnational subcontracting companies like Worldwide Diamonds seek to remain globally competitive they do so by producing workers who feel or experience this precarity in ways explicitly intended to bring about gains in productivity and commitment. Under George's management, workers were constantly reminded of the ease with which global manufacturing companies can move from one location to another in search of low wages and less regulation, deliberately fostering a fear of capital flight.[7]

Precarious labour regimes always risk producing volatility or discontent and management regimes in the global factory always anticipate the possibility that control can be lost. Anxieties at the loss of control and concerns that managers produce the right kind of workers are perhaps nowhere more clearly manifested than in recruitment preferences and hiring strategies. When the Worldwide Diamonds factory first opened, government officials in the zone's administration acted as informal labour contractors. As they worked to realise a promise of 'peaceful industrial labour relations' for the zone's investors, administrators channelled groups of poor young women into its labour force, producing the docile or subservient factory worker as a gendered category. 'A lot of girls used to come to me for employment,' the zone's first development commissioner told me.

> They used to come with all kinds of stories. They would say 'My husband has beaten me' or 'My husband has deserted me' or 'I'm a widow.' So, I'd talk to the diamond company and tell them, 'Take this girl if you feel she is good.' Like that, I put so many girls in employment. And once the word spread, once people thought 'If you go to her she'll get you a job,' more people came.

As demand for labour increased Worldwide Diamonds managers were encouraged to 'bring in their own people'. The strategy gave the company easy access to a pool of workers who could be quickly called upon to fill gaps or boost numbers and it also created new opportunities for patronage and clientalism.

If the factory's first managers had hoped that by recruiting workers through these kinship and patronage networks they would have a more disciplined workforce they were eventually proved wrong. In the wake of the 2002 strike the company attracted considerable attention from trade union activists. A former diamond polisher, who had been sacked for his part in the strike action, was recruited by the CITU and he became a conduit for logistical support to the factory's workforce. Over the following two years production was frequently stopped or slowed by everyday acts of worker resistance, from the downing of tools to coordinated foot-dragging, and in 2005 (as Andhra Pradesh's political parties prepared for local elections) the CITU began an organising drive.

'I consider this the single biggest threat to the future viability of this factory,' George told me, brandishing a letter he had received from the CITU demanding improvements in working conditions. 'These people! They're the same people in Indonesia. The same people in the Philippines. They hate us. They hate these zones. They want the zones closed. And now they're targeting us.' He jabbed his finger at a hammer-and-sickle emblem on the letterhead:

Can you imagine what they're saying? 'Brothers and Sisters, we are going to strike until we get more salary … Until we double your salaries … Until the company gives you housing …' Can you imagine! There's a whole group of them and they come together, sit together, every night and talk and talk about this factory. They're very clever. They're much more clever than I imagined. But they're not cleverer than me.

Against the backdrop of these anxieties about the loss of managerial control over labour George turned his attention to the production of particular kinds of working subjects, and he introduced a formal face-to-face interview and a series of standardised tests into the factory's recruitment process. This was a strategy intended to anticipate future challenges to management and to predict the future responses of individual workers to disciplinary and decentralised modes of power.

In May 2005 I followed the company's personnel managers as they worked to recruit new diamond polishers from over one hundred applicants who had replied to an advertisement in a local newspaper. Some 90 people were invited to attend an interview – most of them aged between 18 and 20, with little or no previous history of work in formal sector factory employment – and I sat in on 17 of them. Here, as at other sites of global manufacturing, managers articulated a preference for young and in-experienced workers whose skills, ambitions and interests could be shaped around the production process. As the company's head of personnel put it, 'Young people are open…we can give them new inputs, we can give them new thoughts, we can mould them, they can be built from scratch.'

In the interviews the personnel managers tried to identify those candidates whom they deemed most likely to commit themselves to industrial work discipline. One of the personnel managers, Siva, explained how he tried to infer a candidate's likely commitment from their father's occupation.

> Suppose a candidate's father is a labourer. Suppose he is a rickshaw driver or or doing cultivation. Suppose nobody is working in his family. Or suppose the father is an old man and is aged or sick. Suppose this candidate is the only person who is going to feed his family. If we could find such kind of candidates, definitely they will work hard and they will stick to the job.

As he prepared to hire a new cohort of workers, one of the factory's personnel managers, Ravi, explained how he tried to gauge a candidate's commitment by paying close attention to their speech, appearance and self-presentation.

> I'm going to ask them directly whether or not they will come to work in times of struggle or strike. But I'm not only interested in their answers. I'll see the way they are sitting. The way they are talking. And the way they speak. If that person is looking around like this ... [Ravi looked quickly from side to side, craning his neck in every direction, demonstrating what a young man might look like who was attentive and alert to his surroundings] when a future problem arises, this kind of person might be active. That means they might be thinking about something other than their work. If a strike arises definitely he'll be one of those asking you questions and going against the management. In such cases we would normally reject him.

Yet just as they were taught to single out docile workers, managers also looked for people who could be trained to manage themselves. Framed by globally circulating models of the world-class factory and post-Fordist philosophies of control at a distance, managers looked for 'active' or 'agentive' workers who could shoulder increased responsibility for their own production, working autonomously and independently. The factory's personnel managers were taught to single out candidates who could 'think for themselves'. 'They should have logical thinking,' these managers told me. 'They should be very quick, very fast.' 'They should be active in speaking.' 'They should be someone who tries to know things.'

At the end of the interview the interviewers scrawled their comments on an assessment form. 'Can be trained,' they wrote, or, 'OK for next round.' Or: 'Thinking capacity is nil ... Blindly she will follow work without having any creative or logical thinking.'

Under his new regime George introduced a series of tests that were intended to select the most 'agentive' or 'enterprising' workers. Under the old system', he explained to me, recruitment decisions were left to the discretion of Indian managers. 'Now', he said, 'we've added problem-solving and spatial awareness tests. So that when we get about 180 applicants only 8 people actually get through.'

Lifted from schoolbook mathematics and geometry textbooks these tests included a diagrammatic puzzle and a written exam. The puzzle required applicants to draw a series of geometrical shapes – circles, squares, rectangles and triangles – and label the angles, and to answer a series of questions, like 'What is the algebraic formula for a + b squared?' or 'What is the formula for calculating the area of a circle?' The exam tested candidates on mathematics, general knowledge and language, through 50 multiple-choice questions that included sections on percentages and fractions, geometry, dimensions, capacity, series, reasoning and analogies. Out of a possible 90 marks the pass rate and cut-off point was 35. This was also the average score; the kind of score you might get if you had to guess the answers to questions you didn't fully understand or couldn't read.

The personnel managers talked me through the rationale:

In the first rounds we are looking at behaviour and attitude. We are looking at whether they are pessimistic or optimistic, what is their nature, what their response to situations and people. But in the tests we are checking their knowledge. See, it's not possible to check this in a personal interview ... If they don't possess basic knowledge then we don't want them.

Love the Company

At the heart of George's vision was a reorganisation of the factory's assembly line around the concept of cellular manufacturing. Workers were no longer to be organised along a single production line but teamed together in multi-skilled work cells focused on a single client. These work cells were to be offered collective rather than individualised incentive packages and given new responsibilities for quality control. Embedded in this rationalisation of space and the devolution of power was an explicit attempt to re-engineer the mechanics of control by harnessing feelings of attachment and connection, loyalty and commitment, to the goals of production.[8]

The new management trainees tasked with implementing George's restructuring project were told to judge, anticipate and micro-manage the emotional states of its workers. 'When you are implementing these changes', George coached them, 'you need to think psychologically. You have to try and understand how workers are thinking, what they are feeling.' 'If you want to be a general manager,' he told them, 'you have to be a psychologist. You have to be an anthropologist. You have to be a sociologist. You have to look at things from the worker's perspective.'

For George the factory was a microcosm of capitalist economy and society. As he saw it, post-Fordist strategies for industrial reorganisation materialised truths about human nature. 'Being free to express yourself and take control of your job – I believe in that. Communists don't,' he once told me. 'All these changes are actually about liberating people to work independently.' At the heart of the model of cellular manufacturing is a group of workers organised into a 'team'. These teams were central to George's project of reorganisation. 'What we need here are small groups. Teams. Teams that people can love. Teams that we can make love the company.' The team was to lie at the heart of the new work cells:

> George: When we put people in these cells it's not going to be one factory any more, it's going to be lots of little factories and workers here are going to love it. There hasn't been a factory yet where people didn't love it once it started. When they're in their cells, they'll really care about it.
>
> Team-working is what people do without thinking about it. We know how they are going to behave. That this is what people do naturally ... You put workers in a team and they get this feeling of belonging. Humans love it. They all like it. It bolsters their feeling of well-being. And then nothing can hold them back. The little half per cent improvements in efficiency only come like this. The team frees them. The team shrouds them. The team gives them comfort and protection. In the team people can say, 'What about this? Can I do this?' And the team leader will say, 'Yeah, I understand what you're talking about and it's a good idea. I agree with you. Just do it.'

In the aftermath of these briefing sessions the management trainees took to the project of emotional engineering with gusto. They summarised George's lessons for me:

Workers can be tuned. You just have to get into their minds. You have to try and explain what will be the costs if you don't do this or if you don't do that. You have to make them feel responsible for the work and the job.

One batch of management trainees were tasked with running 're-training classes for workers' that sought to bring these ideas and concepts to the shop floor. They attempted to translate these new management systems through the idiom of kinship in ways that sought to harness the affective power of family relationships to the organisation of production. These translations sometimes referenced agricultural labour practices. 'The cell will be like a family not a factory,' I once heard it explained, 'When a family owns some land and only family members work on that land, that is their duty.' In other instances they pointed to the significance of individual contributions to the household economy. 'It will be like a single family. A single person not working will affect the whole family. Each and everybody has a job.' In a letter written in Telugu to all company employees that set out to explain the company's restructuring, one of George's deputies addressed the workforce in similar terms, appealing to them as children with a filial duty to a corporate patriarch. 'Please listen to me, family members,' he began, 'I want to give you more information about our situation and future plans.'

George's planned reorganisation of the factory into work cells was intended to remove 'inefficiencies' in the flow of production. The factory's new management trainees had been tasked with producing a series of time-and-motion studies for the workplace and presented George with reports detailing the movements of workers between their seats over the course of a working day. In one reporting session a group of management trainees described, to the astonishment of their colleagues, that they had discovered how some polishers made an average of twelve trips from their seats to the 'checking window' where they collected new stones over the course of their eight-hour shift, collecting five stones each time. In another they described how stones in the Preparation Department move from a polisher to the monitor, who checks and clears it in the section, then back to the worker, who takes it to the window controller, where it goes to a quality checker from whom it might be sent via a runner back to the worker.

Like the classic time-and-motion studies popularised by F.W. Taylor at the beginning of the twentieth century these studies were intended to make the workplace visible in new ways and allow managers to calculate optimum or 'objective' rates of production without remaining dependent on the claims or assertions of workers themselves. In Worldwide Diamonds these reports were the basis for new spatial layouts designed to optimise time.

The new spatial layouts were months in preparation and were drawn up by teams of management trainees in the company boardroom. Two young management trainees, Sumant and Gopal, were given responsibility for testing the efficiency of different layouts. During their brainstorming sessions the cellular workspaces began to take virtual shape as their pencil sketches were converted into black, blue and red ink plans on a large whiteboard. Sumant and Gopal took into account the measurements of the open plan rooms in which the cells would be built and the dimensions of machines. They adjusted the interior layout of machines and workbenches based on their calculations of the optimum number of movements that rough diamonds needed to make as they were passed from polisher to polisher.

As Sumant and Gopal collaborated on these designs they became aware of the new kinds of power and authority being inscribed in them. The outcomes of their decisions would affect how much space a machine operator in the factory would have to manoeuvre over the course of their eight-hour shift, of their six-day working week. One day they stood in front of the whiteboard discussing the measurement of passages and doorways in the new cell. There was a moment of debate over whether the space for a doorway between a worktable and a side-wall should be 60 or 90 centimetres.

'What if the doorway opened this way?' said Sumant, pushing open an imaginary doorway with his hand. Gopal joined in the role-play with a grin, walking through the imaginary door that Sumant held open for him.

'So this would be the corridor?' Gopal said. 'That could work. Then there would be another door here, right?' He opened the real door to the boardroom with a flourish and jumped through it.

'Who is going to move through that door?' said Sumant.

'Only authorised persons,' said Gopal, and he touched Sumant's arm with a grin, 'Like us!'

They both collapsed in nervous giggles at speaking aloud what their design sessions left unsaid. In the factory of the future the difference between management and workers was no longer a question of degree but a question of kind. Unlike the managers of the past, who had worked their way off the factory floor, Sumant and Gopal belonged to a new community of technical experts, like George, who had no first-hand experience of the factory's labour processes, but who now exerted control over it.

The Factory of the Future

The company's first production cell was an impressive spectacle. Built into the far corner of a cavernous concrete room strewn with construction materials and dusty furniture, it had two back walls formed by the building's exterior and two front walls made from sheets of Perspex to create a totally transparent space. Looking at it from across the room, one of the managers told me proudly that it 'looked like it was made by NASA'.

At the entrance to the cell a conspicuously placed suggestions box invited workers to participate in a process of 'continuous improvement' by providing feedback on the layout of workspaces, the performance of machines or the design of production systems. Sumant, one of the management trainees, explained the logic behind the suggestions box to me by referring to a book that George had lent him to read, an autobiography of Jack Welch, the former CEO of the US multinational General Electric. 'Jack Welch accepted change, even if it came from the shop floor', he told me. 'He looked for and encouraged changes.'

In the old factory spaces workers had been allowed to decorate the areas around their seats with religious iconography and their work sections were adorned with images of Hindu deities and saints like Durga Devi and Sai Baba. The new space was purged of all such decoration. 'The place begins to look really messy if you have these things all over the place,' George told me, 'and if the factory starts to look untidy it starts to become untidy.' Instead the only decorations allowed in the cell were English-language posters that carried trite nuggets of management philosophy. These included a drawing of two white Caucasian hands holding onto two green-blue coloured hands above with the words, 'No-one can do everything. But everyone can do something', and a poster of Disney characters alongside a list of rules for achieving your goals through commitment and hard work. One day I came across a different kind of slogan, scrawled across a white pad where an anonymous worker had added a slogan of their own, a popular Telugu proverb, 'Success is like water through the rocks,' they had written, with ambiguous, perhaps sardonic mimicry.

Over a period of months two identical cells were built alongside this first one, carving up the empty factory floor into a series of futuristic work spaces. In the old factory wage levels had been calculated around piece rates that tied them to an individual's productivity and managers had attempted to instil an ethic of competition among their workers. George's restructuring project introduced awards for 'section of the month' and inter-section sports competitions pitted the cells against each other, as managers sought to incite what they called the 'competitive spirit' by fostering feelings of identification and solidarity within the teams. George once explained to me with excitement how the first team had surpassed their production targets:

> They just hit 120 per cent! The second team started just last week. And do you know how much they did? Do you know how much they did in their first week? One hundred and fifteen per cent! So you can imagine what happened next ... The first team got worried. Yesterday, they did 140 per cent! And today they did 147. You see ... [he paused] that's the point.

In the work cells responsibility for quality control was decentralised to machine operators and diamond polishers. Individuals were required to monitor the quality of their own work and they carried the full burden of responsibility for any mistakes, in ways that incorporated them more fully into a supervisory mesh. As one of the graduate trainees explained, 'It's a system where the worker feels more responsibility, where the quality of the product goes back to the worker, where the worker themselves has become a quality checker.' Another graduate manager put it more bluntly:

> We have to see to it that each worker is used to the maximum. In the new spaces each worker will be more responsible for their own work. They won't be able to blame anyone else for their mistakes and they will feel more inclined and committed to their work.

The layout of the new production cells was carefully planned in ways intended to keep the movement of people and diamonds to a minimum at the same time as increasing the visibility of the labour process to the observer. These new work spaces were planned with video surveillance in mind, designed to allow each person and work station to be seen. The simplification of work flows and the redesign of work spaces renovated the factory's physical infrastructure in ways that made the production processes and its products more visible to managers and more amenable to their control.[9] For George his reorganisation of the factory was self-evidently about control:

> I've read papers by some of those leftist academics who say that all this stuff about Teamwork and Cell Working is just another form of control … I mean, yeah … and? All this Continuous Improvement stuff. This stuff about belongingness. Everything. It's just fog. So we can squeeze as much extra production out of people as possible … The role of management in a factory like this is to make people feel happy as long as it can help production … But I'm not running a holiday camp.

Cellular manufacturing is premised on a flexible, multi-skilled workforce that can be moved between tasks or reallocated to specific jobs in line with the requirements of specific job lots or client demand. In the new production cells, workers were no longer to be specialised at only one task but were expected to be 'multifunctional', capable of taking on other tasks in the absence of a co-worker or as production demanded. Floor controllers and runners were expected to be able to operate bruting machines and to wield the handheld tangs with which diamonds were polished, and team leaders were expected to lead by example, contributing to the productivity of the group. 'Team leaders will also work alongside their team not just observing or checking but also contributing,' George told me 'not just seeing things, but getting down to things. It will bring a psychological change in workers.'

While George's programme of restructuring appeared to embrace decentralised power structures and emotional engineering, his plans for the day-to-day organisation of the company continued to hinge on centralised technologies of surveillance and supervision. Managers here were acutely aware that control was a temporary achievement, an incomplete and unsteady accomplishment that had to be maintained and renewed on a daily basis. In the same breath as he spoke of getting teams to love the company George described the need to maintain discipline:

You can get them to love the company but if you don't have a stick you won't get production. We need to make sure that if someone does something wrong everyone knows. And if we kick people out we need everyone else to say, 'What did they expect?'

The young Indian managers that he recruited to implement his vision agreed.

At the same time as his new factory managers sought to craft new kinds of working subjects by mobilising their hopes and dreams, they also sought to keep labour under control by manipulating feelings of precariousness and vulnerability, fear and anxiety. Visibility is key to the management of fear and across the factory floor a complex array of surveillance technologies was deployed to make workers feel under observation. Statistical tools, charts and databases for measuring performance, timekeeping devices, clocks and watches for monitoring productivity, work sections, cells and teams for organising production flows and glass partitions for increasing visibility all created an environment in which workers felt under surveillance and vulnerable to the whims of managers.

One of George's earliest interventions as general manager, for example, had been to dramatically upgrade the factory's closed circuit television surveillance system. The old factory was monitored by a rudimentary network of ten black and white cameras mounted outside the entrances and exits to each department, which could be viewed from a single TV screen in the general manager's office. Within months of his arrival he had recruited a new surveillance manager, and had installed a network of 72 colour, closed circuit televisions to create a constant visual record across the factory floor. The cameras recorded 24 hours a day at a frame rate of six frames a minute. Old footage was saved onto a hard disk drive for three and a half days – allowing it to be replayed and reviewed in the event of diamonds going missing or any incident on the factory floor. Meanwhile the live digital footage was compressed into small thumbnail images that were streamed onto a bank of television screens in the surveillance manager's office. From here the manager could control each camera, using a joystick to pan around or zoom in on specific work sections.

The new system was designed both to anticipate attempts by factory workers to disrupt the flow of production and to create fear and anxiety. 'When I came here I designed everything,' the surveillance manager told me. 'I identified where each camera should be positioned so that we could try and cover the total workspace.' Of course, as the man behind the camera he knew that this was not a perfect, flawless system. There were blind spots across the factory floor where the cameras couldn't see, like the space behind the water cooler in the Finishing Department or the corner immediately underneath the camera in the Preparation Department, or the toilets. As the manager knew, however, the power of the system lay in how people imagined its panoptic vision. 'First thing is,' he once explained from behind the bank of television screens in his office, 'to create an awareness in people that they are being watched.' The office itself was screened from view with thick grey shutters but the manager had arranged for one or two workers to see inside:

> No worker should know exactly what I can see from inside here. But I also have to make sure that they have some idea. So when we built this system I made sure that one or two senior workers came in here just to have a glance. I knew that they would go and tell ten people and that those ten people would tell another ten, like that the message would be passed on. Like that people will feel that they are being watched.

The Breeding Ground

The factory of the future is not just one in which ever greater value can be extracted from the labour process, it is also one in which new kinds of value can be created from systems of management and organisation, by turning expert knowledge into a commodity.

As young Indian managers and workers move between industries in search of promotions and career opportunities, their experiments travel. Managerial technologies and practices that are tested in one location move to others. As the Millennium Group looked to improve the profitability of their flagship factory they diversified their business beyond diamond cutting and polishing and began to 'package' their managerial knowledge and expertise into consultancy products that could be marketed and sold to other companies. As they did so, the experiments with management systems and practices, remuneration packages and strategies for labour control that had taken place in Worldwide Diamonds were rolled out, retried and tested at other locations. During the 2000s this small factory in north coastal Andhra Pradesh became, as one of its executives unwittingly put it, a 'breeding ground'.

In 2000 the Millennium Group expanded its interests by launching two further subcontracting units in the southern Chinese coastal city of Shenzen in a joint venture with a Hong Kong-based entrepreneur. The computer systems, management procedures, human resource strategies and accounting practices introduced into the factory in Visakhapatnam were sold as consultancy products through the Millennium Group to these new companies.

By 2005 the Millennium Group had began to package its management knowledge and expertise into 'upstream' consultancy services for the diamond industry. The systems quality management and cellular manufacturing that George had introduced, and the spatial layouts that the young Indian managers had built now became consultancy products that other companies could buy. 'We built these systems. We saw that other companies didn't have them. So we're selling them. And others are buying them gladly,' one of the company's executives told me. The group's finance manager explained the business logic to me:

> The diamond world is small. As soon as you start doing something successfully people will come and ask you, 'What are you doing? How did you do that?' So then you can sell it to them. You say: 'We have invested a lot in this. With the amount we have invested in it we can't just give it away. So if you want it, buy it.'

At the heart of this new consultancy business was the skilled expertise and labour of Worldwide Diamonds' IT specialists, production managers and shop-floor workers. Just as the Millennium Group sold its knowledge and expertise so too they began to hire out diamond polishers and production managers who had been recruited and trained at the Worldwide Diamond's factory as 'technical consultants', for whom they could charge substantial fees. Diamond processing companies in India or China, Botswana or South Africa, for example, could hire consultants from the Millennium Group to train their staff in flexible production strategies and human resources systems, or to supervise workers.

Between 2000 and 2005 Worldwide Diamonds sent one in ten of its workers to diamond factories operated by the Millennium Group's partners outside India, in China, South Africa, Botswana and, on one occasion, to Russia. These opportunities did not begin as incentives or rewards for productivity at the factory but, as they played into dreams of labour migration and social mobility among its workforce, this is what they became. When he took over George had been quick to recognise the significance of these aspirations. 'For the people who work here,' he said, 'getting a foreign job and sending money home is like the holy grail. Here they might earn X dollars a month, in an overseas factory they'd be on around $500.'

As they worked to build the factory of the future these dreams of overseas labour migration were allied to Worldwide Diamonds' profitability (see Chapter 5). The possibility of being picked to spend one or two years working at diamond manufacturing units on the edge of Zhuhai City, southern China, or in Gaborone, Botswana became a new incentive with which managers sought to encourage the productivity of workers. The factory's management were keenly aware of these dreams and worked strategically to fan the hopes of workers under their supervision. As the department manager, Subha Laxshmi, put it, looking around the Preparation Department and considering the people working there:

> everyone works here for those chances only … In the middle there are lots of smaller carrots. But going outside India to work is the biggest carrot of all. Foreign jobs are a major motivating factor here, the biggest factor. People come here thinking that they might get chances to go overseas.

Utopian Endpoints

Global factories like those built inside India's economic zones are an ensemble of ideas, practices and technologies, ways of thinking and ways of intervening that share a future orientation. As investors and factory managers strive to realise fantasies of growth, profit and control they look upon time and space as both risk and opportunity (Thrift 2006: 142). The factory of the present is a socio-technical apparatus built to materialise dreams of order, control and profit, and the factory of the future is a utopian endpoint in which all space and time has been perfectly coordinated around these goals, and in which the subjectivities of managers and labourers have been precisely tuned to them. Of course, as corporate investors and their managers attempt to realise this endpoint they also realise the limits of their fantasies.

At the beginning of 2006 George claimed that his restructuring of the factory had dramatically improved the efficiency of its cutting and polishing operations and had delivered new value through its management consultancy. But the factory's new work teams struggled to keep abreast of their production targets and the profitability of George's newly designed cross-functional manufacturing cells began to plummet. George urged the factory's corporate shareholders to wait for the downward curve to bottom out but it did not. After six months their faith in George's vision for the factory of the future and their patience ran out. George had failed to meet the Millennium Group's expectations. In June 2006, less than two years after he arrived to oversee the restructuring of their flagship unit, George and the Millennium Group parted company by mutual consent. George returned to the UK, where he took up a position as the manager of a packaging company.

As they reflected upon and evaluated why George had failed to sustain higher rates of growth, performance and profitability, the Millennium Group's executives blamed the failure of his universal models of management. For them, the failure of management was the failure to localise enough; the failure to adapt to or understand the socio-cultural particularities of place. 'He didn't try and adapt things to here, to India,' a senior manager told me. 'Everything should be adapted to the local environment. What works here might not even work in Anakappalle, or Hyderabad. Everywhere will be different and to operate in other places, you have to become like them.'

For some people, the particularities of place were defined by strategies for the organisation and control of labour. 'He was obsessed with the idea that the cell should only have eleven members in the team,' I was told. 'He'd done all the calculations, looked at different models and he'd come up with this number eleven and he insisted that there should be only eleven but he didn't understand the concept of the Indian team.' With only eleven members in each team these dedicated work groups collapsed on days when workers didn't show up for work or absented themselves. 'He didn't understand how to give people leave or to factor in absenteeism.' For others George's failure had been a failure to make the model fit the particularities of the diamond industry. One senior manager told me:

> George tried to impose his model of manufacturing. He was obsessed by it. He claimed that the model had to be followed and he just treated diamonds like any other product. He just thought that if something had worked in the glass industry or the paper industry it would work here too.

Today, the factory remains one of the most high-profile manufacturing units in Visakhapatnam. On the back of George's failure and their unrealised expectations of growth and profitability the Millennium Group invested their hopes in a new general manager, a member of the Indian management team, and appointed him to drive their flagship manufacturing unit into the future.

To think of capitalism as a practical order that is constantly in motion, as I seek to do in this book, means seeing how relationships of power and control are constantly made and re-made. As I show in this chapter, the everyday work of management is a social practice, constituted not just by forms of rational calculation, knowledge or skills but also by sentiments and desires (Yanagisako 2002: 13–21). To think about the factory through this economy of anticipation is to see management as a constellation of future-oriented practices that emerge as culturally mediated responses to problems, dreams and anxieties. Like the dreams of freedom (chapter 1) or planning (chapter 2) that I have discussed elsewhere in this book, managerial dreams of total efficiency, order and control have real effects, increasing the intensity of labour just as they shape innovations in labour control. Disciplinary and pastoral modes of power both involve an economy of anticipation, as managers set out to elicit hopes and fears for the future in workers and to direct them to profitable ends.[10] Meanwhile managerial fears and anxieties at a future loss of control are channelled into the factory's disciplinary apparatus, innovations in recruitment, surveillance and attempts to engineer relationships between managers and workers.

Ethnographic attention to management in the global factory rarely reveals the coherent totality of practices used to classify post-Fordist production regimes (Ngai 2005: 108) or the cohesive programmes aimed at securing domination or rule that labour activists ascribe to capital. Although the parameters within which managers act may remain fixed by the forces of global competition and shareholder demands for value, management models or paradigms are not 'total systems' and a considerable amount of ad hoc, tactical and bottom-up strategising is required to make them operational. While this strategising is always inflected by history it is also, always, oriented towards the future.

5

The Labour of Aspiration

10.30 am, 29th April, 2005 – the lag end of another eight-hour shift in the Worldwide Diamonds factory. In machine sections, a row of young men and women dressed in identical blue uniforms sit in front of electrically powered spindle machines where they grind the edges off angular fragments of dirty-looking rock. Fluorescent strip lights illuminate each person from above, and the white glare immerses them in an artificial brightness. This space is filled with the sound of machines in motion, an incessant background throb of mechanised wheels and spindles, and the chinking of rock on synthetic carbon. For the past four hours, the pace of production here has been frenetic but now, on their return from a half hour lunch break, people begin to apply their intimate knowledge of tools and materials in ways that gently slow their work rate and grant their bodies some respite from the endless repetitions. On the factory floor there is a perceptible shift. The soft hum of human voices mingles with the machine noise and short, snatched samples of conversation rise above the din.

'Mine has a light. Does yours have a light?' Madhu leans across the workbench to peer at a digital watch on the wrist of his friend and co-worker Sunil, comparing its qualities with his own timepiece, gifted to him by an uncle. 'Oooh! Yours has a light,' Madhu says, with mock jealousy. 'Come on! Give it to me! Let me crush it!'

Four yards away, Appalla Raju is teasing Kondal Rao about his birthday belt buckle, an enormous silver contraption on prominent display today beneath his paunch. At issue is who will have the greatest capacity for rice beer when they celebrate the onset of his twenty-third year at the end of the month. 'You'll never drink much wearing that belt,' says Raju. 'You'll need to open your trousers!'

Alongside him moustachioed Ramu is operating a double spindle machine while giving Sai advice about buying televisions. 'If you can buy a TV for 25,000 rupees and one shop offers you a three-year guarantee then you have to take it, you don't have any risk,' he says. 'Why would you buy

Figure 8   Kondal Rao with single spindle machine (2005)

the same TV from another shop without any guarantee? If I'm a customer, why should I take a risk if I don't get any benefit?'

In the adjacent work section Durga Rao, a lanky young apprentice with a wispy beard and a gangly gait, is flirting with Rama Laxshmi, a married mother of two with ankle bracelets and painted nails. They sit around the scaife, a rotating wheel laced with diamond dust, polishing the first facets into the surface of rough stones. As they push the stones backwards and forwards they sing. 'How about this tune,' says Durga, 'do you know how it goes? *For the first time / if you kissed me…*' Rama Laxshmi finishes the line, '*How might it be?*'

Standing at their bruting machines, sitting at the spindle machines or grouped around one of the hand blocking tables, the factory's blue-uniformed workforce pass the time, the subject matter veering from the mundane to the salacious: life, sex, television, money, marriage, death. 'This is how things are here,' Kondal Rao once told me. 'See! It's not so bad. We do the stones and we play with words (*maataladu*). We laugh and toil at the same time.'

Today, however, the staccato rhythm of the shift is suddenly broken. Individual workers begin to be called, by name not by number, out of their work sections and into the Perspex cabin where Subha, the department manager, appears to be interrogating them from the comfort of her soft, swivel chair. In the cornering section, where I sit cutting the corners of rough diamonds alongside Sai Rao, Appala Raju, Suresh and other young men, this unprecedented and extraordinary occurrence provokes a flurry of speculation.

After it is her turn to be called up, Lakshmi returns to her stool and is accosted by co-workers desperate for information. 'Madam is asking everyone what they want in the future, what their dream in the company is …' she struggles to explain, wiping her eyes with laughter and looking anxiously at the CCTV cameras in the corner of the room. Called from stool to stool, her words are repeated around the work section. In the cornering and blocking sections people put down their tools with incredulity to listen. Across the factory floor the chatter and conversation of workers across their machines and benches turns to the same subject. 'What is this about?' 'What does it mean?' And then, 'What should we say?'

From her desk the department manager, Subha, is oblivious to the furore that her questions have provoked on the floor of the work sections, only 20 feet away from her office space. It later transpired that the exercise was part of a 'competency mapping' initiative being undertaken by the factory's Human Resources Department. Subha had been asked to complete an assessment form for each employee, grading them on their technical ability, punctuality, team-work skills, and listing their career objectives, aims or targets as an indicator of 'a worker's interest in the company'.

'The problem,' she explained to me later, 'was that when we began asking workers about their aims or goals there was some confusion. People didn't seem to understand us, so we tried asking them in Telugu about their dreams (*kalalu*), and their aspirations (*karikalu* or *aakshalu*).' As she discovered, however, put on the spot like this, suddenly asked to reflect upon and represent their anticipated futures to their manager, many people struggled with what to say. 'In the end,' she explained:

> we also had to give people examples, otherwise their answers wouldn't be correct on the form. So, we asked them, do you want to be a monitor, a diamond supervisor, or do you want a chance to go to work in one of Worldwide Diamond's sister factories in China or Botswana. I had to say to them, you didn't just come here to be a worker did you? What do you want to become? Like that I tried to give them a correct picture in their minds.

As the manager's questions reverberated across the factory floor some people interpreted it as a managerial ploy aimed at spurring their productivity. 'That's their logic,' Sai explained to me. 'They'll ask us what we want, make us think there's something, and then we'll do more work.' He looked around and went on. 'Some people have been here for seven, even eight years running. They've heard everything this company has to say. They tell us, "There will be something, there will be something." But there's never anything.'

For others this moment presented itself as an opportunity for collective action to demand improvements in wages and working conditions. Naidu, the department's union organiser, slipped from his chair and began a call to arms. 'When you get called up to speak to Subha, you have to say that your dream is to earn more salary,' he told people, moving swiftly from table to table in the blocking section. 'Tell her that you want to sit in the same seat, doing the same work, being paid more salary.'

Speaking to each other over the waist-high piece of chipboard that separated the blocking section from the cornering section, people passed the message on.

> If everyone says that they desire more salary, instead of 'I want to be a monitor' or 'I want to be a checker' then there is more chance of getting something. Everyone should speak with one word.

As the flurry of activity continued, however, it became clear that there was going to be little unity among the young men employed in the Preparation Department. As they returned to their seats they were thoughtful and contemplative, as if mulling over her questions and their responses to it. And, when they spoke up, it appeared that if the young men employed in the Preparation Department spoke with one voice it was because the manager's question had elicited from each of them private dreams and aspirations rather than a spirit of collective action.

Returning to his double spindle machine Appala Raju said, 'I told the manager that I wanted to win an award for best worker and then to have a chance to go for a foreign posting.' A few minutes later his co-worker, Srinu with the big shoulders, returned to his seat and said, 'I told her if there is anything, that's good. Whatever comes I will take it but if a chance comes to go for a foreign position I will also take it.' Each of the young men in the cornering section returned to their seats with a similar story, of dreams for foreign labour migration.

Only one young man, Reddy, claimed to have said anything different. 'I said what everyone told me to say,' he said with a grin. 'I told the manager that I want to do this work and earn as much money as possible.' But behind his back the comments began. 'If there's one thing about Reddy that everyone knows, it's that he says one thing down here and another thing up there. That's why he's called "double Reddy".'

As it became apparent that few people on the A shift were prepared to 'speak with one word', the tone on the factory floor changed, and people's commentaries erupted with sarcasm and mirth. Shouting out above the machine noise Reddy called over to the young men in the cornering section, 'When I go up I'm going to tell her that my dream is to have her job and become department manager!' Ramu shouted back, across the section divide, 'I'm going to tell her that I want to be her boss and become the general manager.'

The joke caught on and travelled along the work sections. Giggling so much that there was spittle caught in his wispy beard, Durga Rao called over 'I'm going to tell her my dream is to be an engineering student and I want the company to pay for it.' Little Srinu pitched in, 'I'm going to tell her I want to have a car and I want her to be the driver.' Sai, the cornering section monitor with the endless romantic ambition, jumped in, 'I'm going to tell her my dream is to marry her, get 200,000 rupees in groomprice (*katnam*).' Patnaik, his counterpart in the blocking section parried, 'I'm going to tell her I don't have dreams anymore, working here gives me too many headaches.' Sidling over to Chinni's desk from the end of the blocking section the union representative Naidu had the biggest laugh: 'I'm going to tell her I don't need anything more. I'm full. My dream is to empty my belly and go for a shit.'

Consenting Dreams

In genres of activist writing and journalistic accounts of labour at new sites of global manufacturing in India we rarely hear the dreaming and desiring voices of a young industrial workforce. The stories they tell of work inside India's SEZs, for example, are stories of the everyday violence inflicted by capitalist work discipline, of the physical injuries and mental strains inflicted upon the bodies of individual workers as employers attempt to reduce costs or inefficiencies in production. Or they celebrate acts of organised resistance, the moments when waged industrial labourers put down their tools or refuse to work. In these dystopian portraits of industrial work and labour we often come across what the philosopher Jacques Rancière (2002: 248) called sepia snapshots of labour, full of nostalgic passion for traditional forms of labour organisation and tender-hearted curiosity for the practised movements of the craftsman. India's industrial workers, as Rancière might have put it, appear to be admired as long as they cleave to collective class identities, but they become suspect when they articulate identities based on caste, when they want to live as others, when they demand an individual wanderlust, or when they pursue the desires and passions that are associated with capitalism's ideological illusions (2002: 249).[1]

Of course, the proliferation of economic zones and enclave spaces has created a global labour force that is uniquely vulnerable. Workers in these spaces are frequently held hostage by the way that they facilitate the global mobility of capital, making it easy for employers to move from one zone to another to take advantage of cheaper labour costs or alternative incentive packages. The globalisation of production has also seen the reconfiguration of managerial power and authority. As I explored in the previous chapter, workers in global sites of mass manufacturing frequently find themselves subject to novel conjunctures of techno-scientific systems for discipline and control with place-based social hierarchies of gender, caste, ethnicity or race (see for example Salzinger 2000, 2004). Meanwhile they find themselves structurally disadvantaged by the legal frameworks for governing and administering these zones that curtail freedoms to organise or bargain collectively over the terms and conditions of work, restrict the jurisdiction of labour inspectors, or remove legal safeguards for workers who challenge unscrupulous and exploitative employers.

Yet, as ethnography of work and labour in the global factory always reminds us, even in global contexts of low-waged, hyper-intensive and precarious work these labour regimes cannot be reduced to despotic forms of coercion, control and domination. On the contrary, the more significant characteristic of labour regimes like those fostered by India's SEZs is not that young people must be physically coerced or cowed into low-waged, labour-intensive work but rather that they consent to it willingly. The decision to enter or accept these terms and conditions of employment is more than an economic calculation – as people weigh risks against necessity or need – it is a decision shaped by other ways of imagining and living towards the future (Cross 2010; Petryna 2003). As people move into and out of these spaces to exchange their time and capacities for a monetary wage, they bring with them personal projects for personal and social transformation, and it is in pursuit of these projects that people commit themselves or consent to terms and conditions of work that are often described as exploitative.

These projects and the relationships they engender lie at the surface of writing by feminist anthropologists and cultural geographers whose work contests the representation of workers at sites of export manufacturing in China, South and South East Asia, Mexico, Central America and the Caribbean as merely 'labour power' (Ngai 2003, 2005; see also Freeman 2000; Mills 1999). As they have shown, participation in the global labour force in these locations frequently creates new opportunities for young people to satisfy or challenge social ideals of what it means to be good or virtuous, masculine and feminine, as well as societal expectations about sexuality and marriage partnerships. Moreover, by creating access to financial resources it also creates opportunities for people to renegotiate their control over earnings, activities and behaviour in relationship to their families and wider society, and to participate in emerging patterns of mass consumption. As the anthropologist Carla Freeman put in the 1990s, people in the global labour force demand to be understood not simply as the labour for global commodities but also as the market for new kinds of consumer goods and services (Freeman 1998: 254).

The dreams and desires that young people carry into India's SEZs are part of an economy of anticipation that makes these spaces into particular places for capital, and in this chapter I focus on those of young men. Social commentaries on gender, work and labour in South Asia's economic zones have, to date, focused almost exclusively on the experience of women (see for example work by Chhachhi 1999; Hewamanne 2008; Lynch 2007; Kabeer 2000). Yet by the end of the 2000s between two-thirds and three-quarters of those people employed in India's SEZs were men. In Andhra Pradesh, for example, 74 per cent of all SEZ workers were men and the brief history of the Worldwide Diamonds factory, for example, had been accompanied by a gradual decline in the proportion of its women workers (see chapter 4). What had been a largely female workforce when the factory began production in 1997 was a predominantly male workforce eight years later, when only 21 per cent of workers were women.

These statistics – and the declining participation of women in India's industrial workforce – are sometimes attributed to the willingness of men to accept unfavourable conditions of work, or gender norms which deter women's participation in the labour force (e.g. Reddy et al. 2010). Yet they

Figure 9   Diamond boys at the end of another a shift (2005)

also reflect high rates of youth unemployment, the social and economic significance of formal sector industrial work in the imaginaries of young men, and the gendered politics of organised labour. In north coastal Andhra Pradesh, for example, the kinds of employment created by India's SEZs are immensely attractive for young men who see them not just as entry points to the formal industrial economy but also as entry points to citizenship, arenas in which to struggle for rights and recognition, as well as remuneration.

In post-liberalisation India, educated but unemployed or precariously employed young men occupy a particularly prominent social and political position, attracting increasing interest among scholars concerned with gender, class, communalism and political action (e.g. Jeffrey 2010; Osella and Osella 2006). Against the backdrop of rapid economic transformations they frequently emerge as key actors and brokers in political mobilisations.[2] Meanwhile, the struggles to realise prevailing ideas of masculine success and to gain access to secure salaried work has produced new preoccupations with time and the future, leaving many educated young Indian men beset with what Craig Jeffrey (2010) has called a kind of temporal anxiety.

As I explore in this chapter, when young men arrive for work on the floor of a factory like Worldwide Diamonds they carry with them aspirations for economic stability and security that are framed by family investments in education and their experiences of being educated; they carry desires to acquire, own and display material things that symbolically mark them out as young working men, and they carry normative heterosexual dreams of adult futures, of marriage and fatherhood. The cultural and political responses of these young men to the terms and conditions of precarious labour and their inability to realise dreams of economic security and stability have diverse effects, articulating and transforming historic relationships of caste and class, while shaping the everyday politics of work.

For some analysts the dreaming and desiring subjectivities of these young men demand to be understood as the product of a system that operates by 'ratcheting up' hopefulness and producing individuals who are optimised to seek for themselves the best possible futures (Adams et al. 2009). In critical Marxist traditions of cultural and social theory – that connect the work of Antonio Gramsci (1971) to that of Antonio Negri (Hardt and Negri 2000) – the aspiration for self-improvement and the pleasures of consumption are mechanisms of control that further interpolate people into the capitalist economy, engendering their consent to the terms and conditions of work. In a tradition of materialist psychiatry these dreams and desires sit in a collective subconscious (e.g Deleuze and Guattari 2004). As Pun Ngai (2005: 158) puts it in her ethnography of factory labourers in China, the question is not whether workers can realise hopes or aspirations through waged labour but rather how capitalism incites people to dream and desire in ways that engender their continued commitment to the relationships of its reproduction.

In this vein management practices and strategies appear as an ideological 'discourse of legitimation' (Boltanski and Chiapello 2007) that encourages people to project their dreams and desires into a capitalist future. In the fieldwork vignette above, for example, we might see how factory managers seek to ally the aspirations of workers to the goals of production, reflecting people's diverse ambitions and desires back to them in the form of individualised targets or promotional goals. And we might interpret the responses of young workers on the floor of the Preparation Department and their failure to speak collectively as the success of management technologies and practices in producing a particular kind of working subject, whose complex hopes and aspirations are neatly shoehorned into a logic of capital.

Yet if dreams and desires interpolate people into a capitalist economy this is not to say that the dreaming and desiring voices or actions of young people are 'engineered'. Persons, bodies and selves may be primed by discursive regimes or bio-political scripts of liberal capitalism to follow norms for self-conduct that emphasise choice, freedom, responsibility and a self-motivated, competitive individualism, but they can also deviate from them in inventive and original ways.[3] As I show, inside India's SEZs young people pursue personal projects of self-transformation, negotiate a wide array of kinship relations, establish collective identities and constitute themselves as gendered persons eligible for marriage. These projects have diverse genealogies, shaped not just in the school but also by the experience of being educated; shaped not just in the home but by feelings of love, care and obligation to mothers and fathers, brothers and sisters; and shaped by ideals and norms of male youth and adulthood that are both anchored in place and mediated by India's culture industries.

The dreams and desires of young men like those employed in the Worldwide Diamonds factory are what enable people to continue thinking about the future in an uncertain and precarious present (Berlant 2007: 299; Wacquant 2000). But that does not mean that we should assume that people know what they are working for. Dreams and desires can be sources of uncertainty and ambivalence as much as coherence and direction. This is an ambiguity that is materialised in the contradictory ways that young people may simultaneously contest and consent to the terms and conditions of labour. It is also reflected in the stories and jokes that young men tell about themselves. As young men reflect on conditions of economic uncertainty, instability and precariousness their anticipated and unrealised futures can also become objects of satire and a self-deprecating humour (cf. Hansen 2012: 16). Jokes like those in the fieldwork fragment above are funny to those who tell them because they recognise and mock the promises of education and the social expectations of adulthood, and because they acknowledge the structural conditions that mitigate against the collective realisation of dreams.

Technological Intimacy

Six days a week, in the hours before dawn, a somnambulant army of young men leaves their own or rented homes across Visakhapatnam's hinterland and travels along a vascular transportation network of dirt tracks and pot-holed roads onto National Highway Number Five and into the motley assortment of factories producing scrap metal, automobile parts, glass windows, contact lenses, potato chips, pet food, women's underwear, pharmaceuticals and diamonds inside one of India's oldest and largest SEZs. None of these zones offers accommodation or dormitory facilities to workers and people commute for up to four hours a day in order to join the waged labour force inside them. Some of them leave the caste-segregated farming and fishing villages along the flat coastal plains where their families have lived for several generations. Others leave the peri-urban colonies of rural-urban migrants that have grown up along the busy coastal highway where their parents once settled. These early morning journeys are all timed to converge, five or ten minutes before the first shift of the day begins at 6 am, on concrete forecourts outside the factories where workers will spend between eight and ten hours, depending on demands for overtime. At 2 pm these journeys begin all over again, as people employed on the B shift begin travel into the zones for work.

Among the people taking these early morning journeys in the mid 2000s were three unmarried youths – Madhu, Sai and Raju – who shared with a generation of young men the contours of their brief biographies. All three had been brought up by working families in the farming villages, market towns and peri-urban townships of north coastal Andhra Pradesh. Madhu, the child runaway who was adopted by charitable Brahmins in the highway township of Gajuwaka; proud Raju, the eldest of three brothers, born and brought up in the nearby fishing hamlet of Dippapalem; and love-crazy Sai, the adolescent labour migrant who had come to Visakhapatnam in search of his fortune from north coastal Andhra's poorest district, Srikakulum. As they made their daily journeys to and from the SEZ these young men carried with them the long-term investments of their families in their futures, as well as dreams and desires for personal transformation, material success and recognition. I first met Madhu, Sai and Raju on the floor of the Worldwide Diamonds factory, where we sat alongside each other for eight-hour shifts, sorting, cornering and blocking rough stones, and I have followed their stories into and out of this workplace over the course of several years. In this chapter I take their experiences of work, and labour as a window onto the experiences of many others.

In 2005 I spent twelve months learning to cut, polish and sort diamonds in the Worldwide Diamonds factory. Between January and December that year I lived in a rented room in the highway township of Gajuwaka, 4 km from the Visakhapatnam special economic zone and I joined more than

600 people as they arrived at Worldwide Diamonds' entrance for the 6 am A shift and left with them as another 600 people arrived for the 2 pm B shift. Over the course of a year, I was trained to use a variety of tools or machines, perform various sorting, cutting and polishing tasks inside the factory's manufacturing sections and was provided with consignments of stones to work on myself.

Some of my early interactions with young men on the factory floor were awkward and uncomfortable, suspicious and unfriendly. I had naively assumed it would be easy to form relationships here. I belonged to the same age group as the factory's majority workforce, I spoke good Telugu and I took great care to explain my interests as a researcher. Unsurprisingly, however, when I first arrived on the shop floor many workers assumed that I had been sent there as a management spy. Yet relationships between people in the industrial workplace are negotiated through their relationships with technology and, as I became part of the labour process, my relationships with the young men around me were transformed (Cross 2012a). Like any new entrant to the factory's labour force, over the course of a year I was rotated between the Preparation Department's three work sections – *cornering*, *bruting* and *blocking*. In each section I was trained to become a competent and productive machine operator, learning to handle single-spindle machines, semi-automatic bruting machines, rotating scaifes and hand-held tangs, and eventually able to cut and polish rough diamonds into a basic round shape, give them eight basic facets, a smooth, flat table and their sharp pointed *culet*.

As I discovered, for researchers and new workers alike, technical competence brings rapport, respect, trust, friendship, solidarity and complicity with co-workers. With a practical know-how of machines and raw materials came a social intimacy that did much to dispel the rumours and assumptions about my presence here and, as I became a participant in work groups inside the factory, so too I became a participant in people's lives off the factory floor, establishing lasting relationships that have endured over several years as we all aged, married and had children.

The Promise of Education

Like thousands of young men from north coastal Andhra Pradesh's non-elite caste communities Madhu, Sai and Raju were the first members of their families to be schooled up to the age of 16. Each had grown up in households that had been at one stage dependent on forms of casual waged labour in the rural and urban informal economy, as well as entrepreneurial forms of self-employment like home-based tailoring or the petty production of street food. Raju's family – like most others in the Palle caste community of Dippapalem – was largely dependent on the marine economy and his father's daily haul of seer, pomfret and prawns, sold to traders for eventual consumption in restaurants and hotels in Hyderabad.

Sai had been brought up in comparatively austere circumstances. His father died when he was young and he had been brought up on a small piece of land in a tiny Kapu caste village on the rural coastline of Srikakulum district. His mother raised him with financial support from her brother in law, and with income from the sale of cashews and coconuts grown on their small plot of land. Like the children of other fathers who were incapacitated, ill, aged, severely indebted or deceased, Sai understood from an early age that he was to become his household's primary wage earner.

By contrast Madhu had grown up in a comfortable housing colony in the urban highway township of Gajuwaka. His adopted father, who moved to the Visakhapatnam during its rapid growth in the 1970s from southern Orissa, began his working life in a restaurant selling tiffins and meals, before joining the city's industrial labour force in a large private fertiliser company, first as a casual day labourer in the loading bay and then as a salaried employee in the factory's bagging plant. The comparative security of his position in this unionised labour force was enough for Madhu's father to establish his family as members of the city's growing lower middle classes.

All of these families invested in the future security and upward mobility of their sons by supporting them through primary and post-primary education (Jeffrey et al. 2008). Here, as elsewhere in India, scholastic achievements have come to represent a powerful signifier of a household's financial standing and advancement, and diverse caste communities have pursued projects of social reform and upward mobility by making long-term investments in the education of their children.[4] All three attended Telugu medium government schools until they were 16, and all three had completed a two-year part-time course in a local, private industrial training institute, which represents the cheapest most accessible form of post-secondary level education in India.

Industrial Training Institutes (known across India as ITIs) represent the legacy of Nehruvian central planning and nationalist projects of industrial modernisation in education. Conceived by Jawaharlal Nehru in the 1950s under the slogan 'building the youth, building the nation', these institutes were originally intended to equip young men for specific jobs in public sector industries by training them in manual trades.[5] Until the 1990s ITIs remained largely state-run institutions with entry based on academic merit (though in line with national policies of positive discrimination there were reserved places for India's Scheduled Castes and tribes). In the 1990s, however, the lifting of barriers on the establishment of private sector educational institutions saw a dramatic increase in the number of fee-paying ITIs across India. In Visakhapatnam alone, the number of ITIs expanded from 2 in 1999 to 27 in 2005, dramatically increasing access to technical qualifications for the region's 'backward caste' and 'Scheduled Caste' families.

These family investments in education constitute a structural context within which young men like Madhu, Raju and Sai make sense of and navigate through India's provincial labour markets. The commitments of their parents to long-term strategies of social mobility through investments in education create a powerful incentive for young men, and they come of age carrying the burden of parental expectations as well as a deeply embodied feeling of kinship obligation and indebtedness. For many this debt is experienced both in feelings of filial love and respect and as a sense of moral duty or responsibility, which they struggle to repay through appropriate kinds of moral conduct and actions. Such tensions are acutely manifested in the choices and decisions confronting them on the labour market, where they frequently feel compelled to seek out and engage in forms of employment appropriate to their parents' investments.

In north coastal Andhra Pradesh the difference between desirable and undesirable employment for educated young men is the difference between the 'private' and the 'public' sector, between sites of precarious waged labour and shrinking arenas of permanent, secure and stable employment. For young men growing up in Visakhapatnam's hinterland, in the shadow of the public sector steel, iron ore and shipbuilding industries that catalysed the city's late-twentieth-century growth (see chapter 2), ideas of masculine success on the adult labour market continue to be measured against an image of the permanent government employee. This is the idealised image of a man living out the promise of a stable working life guaranteed by the reasonable certainty of continued employment, steadily rising wages, and a predictable life cycle of marriage and family. For many young men and their families this image is not just 'a means to family security' but 'the very foundation of the familial world' (Panjwani 1984:

291) and the Telugu words for full employment (*udyogamu, gujurani*) are reserved almost exclusively for full-time public sector employees.

Raju's future, for example, had been tied from an early age to the pursuit of secure and stable waged employment in the urban industrial economy. Neither his father nor his mother had attended primary school but they invested in the education of their eldest son. After completing the All India Secondary School Leaving Examination at a government school in the nearby township of Gajuwaka, Raju passed a couple of years in a variety of informal, low-paying jobs. He spent a few days every month at his uncle's telephone kiosk in a highway township, collecting coins from customers, and he sometimes joined his father to go night-fishing on a small boat up and down the coastline. When he was 18, he was enrolled at a private industrial training institute and began a two-year welding course. When he graduated he was the first member of his family to have acquired primary, secondary and post-secondary level school certificates. 'I think I have done well, my parents didn't have an education and now I have an ITI,' he once reflected. 'I think I can be happy with that. They were at one level and I reached this level. And as for my children ... well, who knows what they can do.'

At the same historic moment that access to education in India among formerly marginalised communities has increased, the economic value of this education has diminished. If families in Visakhapatnam's hinterland once hoped that investing in the education of a son was the passport to a secure salaried job in the city's steel plant, port or shipyard, then a decade of disinvestment and casualisation has seen these prospects fade and their investments in education turn out to be less profitable than anticipated. Against the backdrop of disinvestment in public industries, educated young men soon discovered that their qualifications led to precariousness rather than security.

In the 1990s, provincial urban labour markets witnessed decreasing opportunities for recruitment into the public sector and few prospects of anything other than insecure, flexible, temporary and poorly remunerated work (OECD 2008). Between 1997 and 2004 net increases in India's industrial employment occurred almost exclusively in the least productive, unorganised and informal parts of the economy, while recruitment into the public sector dried up. During this period, a figure of 6.5 per cent growth in annual employment disguised an average annual loss of employment in the organised sector of about 1 per cent per year (OECD 2008: 6–7). By the early 2000s local labour markets were saturated with un/under-employed young men holding technical qualifications but lacking both the opportunities and the resources to enter secure salaried employment. In 2002, only one-third of graduates from Andhra Pradesh's private ITIs were reported to be in waged employment. In 2005, Visakhapatnam's district employment exchange listed over 56,000 people seeking public sector jobs, 35,000 of whom held certificates from an ITI.

After they graduated, aged between 18 and 20, with diplomas in welding and diesel mechanics, Raju and Sai joined the ranks of educated but unemployed young men. Raju joined a bodybuilding gym and entered a local Mr Muscle competition before making an unsuccessful application to join the Indian army. After leaving school at age 16, Sai's maternal uncle had paid for him to pursue a two-year course in a provincial ITI. On completion, Sai propelled himself with other rural–urban migrants to Visakhapatnam, where he lived with a distant uncle, a permanent employee in the city's steel plant. Meanwhile Madhu was enrolled at the Visakhapatnam Defence Academy where his maternal grandfather had once worked as an English lecturer. His parents were able to negotiate a substantial reduction in the fees for one year but were unable to negotiate an extension. Madhu dropped out and began offering homework classes to school children in the residential colony where he lived.

Their search for work eventually brought them to Visakhapatnam's SEZ. Sai joined the company as a new trainee in 2000, recruited by a personnel officer who was a friend of his uncle. In time Sai would become a conduit for other young labour migrants from Srikakulum, with friends and friends of friends spending a night or five on the floor of the rented house that he shared with a group of other young factory workers in the highway township of Kurumanapalem. 'This is the circuit, ' he explained with pride. 'Some of them just turned up on one day and had an interview the next.'

Raju submitted an application to the factory one day in 2002, after seeing an advertisement in a local newspaper. Madhu applied for a position in 2004, on the recommendation of a friend of his elder brother, who was himself employed in one of the factory's polishing sections. They all projected their hopes and aspirations for the working future onto these sites of work and all of them entered the workplace in the hope that these jobs might be a 'channel' or 'source' of future stability and security. As Raju once put it to me, 'Every educated boy like me went to work in the SEZ with the dream of getting settled down in life.'

Fractured Expectations

On the floor of Worldwide Diamond Raju, Sai and Madhu found themselves amid a familiar demographic. In the mid 2000s, 68 per cent of the factory's blue-uniformed production workers were young men, aged between 18 and 22, who had been born and brought up in the highway townships and villages across Visakhapatnam district. This workplace was broadly representative of coastal Andhra's caste demographics. Recruited into the factory as entry-level workers and thrown together on the A shift were the sons of higher-caste Brahmin and Velama families, of Gavaras and Kapus, whose families owned and farmed small plots of land in the district's villages, as well as occupational castes like Palles and Vadabalijas, and the sons of ex-Untouchable or Dalit families, Mallas and Madigas. Only a fraction (around 1 per cent) were primary school drop-outs. The remainder had attended Telugu medium government schools until they were aged 16, often the first member of their family to have done so, and virtually all had gone on to complete a two-year part-time course in an ITI.

The terms and conditions of work here confronted everyone with a discrepancy between the promises and expectations of their education and their actual employment outcomes. In material terms, there was little to differentiate waged labour in the Worldwide Diamonds factory from insecure, precarious work in Visakhapatnam's informal economy, and their qualifications made no difference to their employment prospects or their earnings.[6] After three years of work in Worldwide Diamonds, Raju's daily earnings remained less than those of his two brothers who spent six nights a week on a small boat fishing up and down the nearby coast. 'One of them only finished tenth class and the other only finished class seven that's why they're fishing … it's small work. But now they're getting 100 rupees a day and I'm getting 70,' he once explained. 'So if they come here it's a waste. But if I go fishing it's also a waste. I'm educated! I went to an ITI! I've got a certificate!'

For some the perimeter walls and security gates that surround economic zones and conceal their working conditions from public scrutiny allowed them to hide the realities of work here from their families and communities. When Madhu first joined Worldwide Diamonds' workforce, for example, aged 18, he knew that his starting salary was far lower than what he might have earned by renting an auto-rickshaw and ferrying customers around the roads of Gajuwaka. But, like many other men whose family had invested in their post-primary level education, such work appeared to him as socially inappropriate. 'I needed to work,' Madhu once told me:

> But even if I could get more money by driving an auto-rickshaw I couldn't do that because of my father's position in society. Can you imagine, if his educated son suddenly started to drive an auto-rickshaw! We can't degrade the name of our father like that. Worldwide Diamonds wasn't a high-status job but it was closed. No-one knew what was happening inside. From the outside no-one knew if you were a manager or a worker there. That's the mentality of people around here. They think that working on the side of the road is not respectable but that working in a closed place, in a room, is professional. Here in my locality, nobody knew anything about that company. They just saw it as a good job.

As they sought to make their educational qualifications pay off in a context marked by high rates of youth un/under-employment, the diminished prospects of public sector employment and the comparatively high status afforded to factory work, young men like Raju Madhu and Sai had little alternative but to accept the terms and conditions of waged labour in the SEZ if they could get it, and to stick to it regardless. 'If I can find another source that offers me more money then I'll jump from here immediately,' Madhu once told me. But the lack of any suitable alternatives prevented him and many others from doing so. For many the SEZ become synonymous with the lack of opportunities to benefit economically from the investments of their family in schooling, with their inability to fulfil aspirations of post-educational employment and with their failure to fully achieve the kinds of long-term stability and security that would allow them to fashion themselves as successful male householders or providers.

The insecurity and vulnerability of waged labour in Worldwide Diamonds only served to impress upon the firm's young male employees their exclusion from secure salaried positions in local public sector industries, in ways that 'fractured' their relationship to dominant and idealised masculinities (cf. Osella and Osella 2006). For many young men, work here did not just fail to fulfil the aspirations of post-educational industrial employment, it also proved wholly insufficient for them to take on the householder responsibilities associated with male adulthood. For some young men the lived experience of low-waged and precarious labour was the feeling of being locked into perpetual immaturity and of being unable to realise dominant ideals of masculine success (see for example the work of Argenti 2007; Mains 2007; Osella and Osella 2006).[7] For these young men the factory floor was a space that crystallised feelings of disenfranchisement, discontent and failure, a waiting place to which they were temporally confined by the deferral of expected futures (cf. Jeffrey 2010). As Craig Jeffrey has observed, confronted with dominant visions and linear models of the life cycle that map periods of youth and maturity onto chronological time, many educated young men in provincial India have come to experience their exclusion from secure salaried work as a kind of temporal disorientation, and have come to experience the passing of time as a period of waiting, pause or perpetual deferral.

'In the government industries around here a new worker can dream and hope,' Raju once told me, in a reflection on the labour of aspiration:

> But in the SEZ factories you are dreaming without hope. In a place where the older workers are getting more or less the same salary as the new ones, there's no hope. For a guy like me that isn't a job, it's a hole. Of course I made good friends there, people I was happy working together with, people who could help me get information about things. Yes, I got experience. I got to know how to behave in the world of companies and organisations. But anything I got from that factory I got without any support and now I think that I made a mistake to ever go there. Guys who work there are like *gorotaka petalu*, sheep with tails: they can never grow up.

After his first week on the factory floor Sai had tried to quit. 'At that time I didn't like the work at all,' he remembered:

> The diamonds seemed so small, the work on the machines was hard and tiring. The money was very little. So after a week I went back to my uncle and said, 'I can't do this. I want to go back to the village.' But my uncle told me to stay with it.

Like many others he held onto the idea that factory labour was a time-bound, short-term solution until he could land a 'proper job' in one of the city's state-run industries. After three years Sai had become thoroughly disenchanted with his circumstances. In conversations with me he was often downbeat and hopeless: 'I know a friend in the village who got a government job. But not me. No, not me. I didn't progress. I'm just stuck. Stuck here in this private job,' he said:

This is the way of man. Everybody here is thinking about their future, about a long life. Nobody knows how long they will be here, or how long this job will be for. And if there is something better – a job for life that pays more money than this – we'd jump to it. But otherwise, we'll stay here, we'll stay on this train, the slowly moving life.

Men in the Making

Reflecting on the experience of work here few young men considered their education to have been a 'straightforwardly positive movement'. If they associated education with freedom from agricultural labour and rural poverty, they had also come to associate education with a compulsion to work, submission to industrial discipline, bodily suffering and class hierarchy (Osella and Osella 2006: 72). Yet many responded to the economic devaluation of their qualifications and the precariousness of their factory employment by re-affirming the cultural value of education. They were often deeply committed to the pursuit of further academic credentials; they stressed the cultural superiority of educated people; laid claim to their distinctiveness or social distance from 'less educated' peers; and had very specific ideas about what kind of work was appropriate for educated men (cf. Jeffrey et al. 2008: 73–6).

On the factory floor these shared experiences helped to erase or elide ideas about caste difference that remained locally pervasive. In the provincial market towns, highway colonies and villages of north coastal Andhra Pradesh caste difference continue to be spatially and symbolically marked (see, for example, chapter 2). Thrown together on the factory floor, however, young men studiously erased references to caste from their everyday relationships with each other. In everyday exchanges of cooked rice, curd, sweets and biscuits on the factory floor they broke historical restrictions on inter-caste exchanges (Cross 2012b). Many explicitly described the factory as a caste-less place that broke with social norms on inter-caste contact in the villages and peri-urban neighbourhoods where they had grown up.[8] People who had worked alongside each other for several years often claimed ignorance or disinterest when it came to the caste identities of their co-workers, and the factory gave rise to numerous inter-caste relationships between young men and women, including several elopements and marriages.

Yet just as common experiences of education and employment transformed ideas about caste so too they gave rise to class-based expressions of social distinction and difference. Once, during a lull in production, Raju took two, passport-sized photographs from a wallet under his blue uniform and passed them over to me. The grainy, black and white portraits showed his two younger brothers wearing open-necked shirts and looking uncomfortable. He pulled out a third photo from his wallet. This was a glossy colour portrait that showed Raju himself, smartly groomed in a slick suit and a red tie. 'Can you see the difference between us,' he asked, and waited pointedly for me to comment. Like his style of dress and his photo albums, Raju's ITI certificate was an important marker of difference; one that he used to establish social and cultural distance from his brothers and village peers.

Sai too, despite his disillusionment, remained committed to the cultural value of education in producing social differentiation. As I walked into Sai's home village of Amalapadu in Srikakulum district for the first time he introduced me to the collection of ramshackle brick-built and thatched buildings by describing changing investments in education. 'Now you can see where I came from,' he said:

> This is my village. Many people here are uneducated. When I was a small boy only a few people would send their kids to tenth class. Maximum people would have 6th class. Now everyone wants to have minimum tenth class, and other people are going for ITI or degree.

On the factory floor everyday relationships with machines, tools and technology transformed gendered bodies and persons, creating new arenas in which educated young men could achieve alternative forms of masculine success, recognition and personal authentication. Here, young men learned to look upon their practical know-how, technical skills and embodied knowledge of machines and tools as an end in itself. Cloistered together in the factory's machine sections, young men's experiences of education and intimate engagements with tools and machines outlined the contours of an alternative masculinity, one that valorised technical competence as a more desirable masculine attribute or quality than those intellectual and white-collar skills that command status and higher salaries. 'Look at them on their office chairs,' went the daily jibe from the section's young men. 'They don't even know how to start a machine, ' 'Do you want to know the difference between us and managers?' Raju once asked me. 'They're the people who just look at diamonds,' and he lifted his fingers up to his eyes, as if inspecting a stone with a magnifying loupe. 'But the people in here are workers' – and he rolled up his sleeve to clench his left bicep, wrapping his right hand around the muscle and gripping it tightly in emphasis.

As they learned to complete the sequence of operations necessary to cut and polish a diamond young men made their practical knowledge and technical mastery the grounds of status, agency and power. In their gendering of tasks and tools the work of using or making came to acquire a value in itself, generating its own rewards, pleasures and satisfactions. On countless occasions outside the factory, in a village or in a highway township, I listened as Raju, Madhu and Sai described their work to me, or friends and relatives. In public and private speech acts they asserted their technical knowledge and expertise as members of a unique occupational community, echoing a social division of labour between specialised castes. In this respect, diamond polishing generated its own prestige. The gendered satisfaction that could be derived from the knowledge of cornering was inseparable from their knowledge of the value of diamond as a commodity.

Through their intimate knowledge of and relationship to technology, young men performed a particular form of masculinity, one informed by lived experiences of education and caste, that celebrated toughness, endurance and mechanical skill as much as collaboration and solidarity and enabled them to achieve personal affirmation and recognition. In a world in which their ability to guarantee stable and secure economic futures often appeared negligible, tools and machines were also extensions of selves through which it was possible for young men to express and confirm their ability to act.

How to Spend it

In 2004 advertisements for the Telugu film *Mass* were plastered all over Visakhapatnam. Gigantic cardboard effigies of Nagajuna, the film's megastar, loomed over film theatres. Graffiti appeared along the harbour wall in the Old Town, screaming out the film's name in bold, black letters. Painted images of the hero in oversized denim trousers and big, bad sunglasses appeared on the back of auto-rickshaws spluttering through the highway townships in the city's hinterland, where the film posters remained in streets and public spaces for months before they faded away.

A quintessential example of high-budget, mainstream Telugu cinema, *Mass* was set and filmed on location in Visakhapatnam. The eponymous hero, Mass, arrived in the city apparently without parents or family, without caste or community, where he does battle with a cynical, unpleasant and very rich local businessman until he avenges a tragic past. The film's title is derived from the English word 'mass' which has entered vernacular Telugu both as a noun, as in 'the majority', but also as an adjective that describes a 'mass', majoritarian and non-elite culture. Some of this meaning is conveyed in the film's theme song, that could be reverberating across Visakhapatnam's hinterland for months after its release:

Anna nadichoste Mass. Anna niluchunte Mass. Anna 'look' este Mass!
[Brother, the walk is Mass. Brother, the stand is Mass. Brother, the look is Mass. Ma Ma Mass!]

Anna 'pant' este Mass, Anna 'shirt' este Mass, Anna madata edite Mass,
[Brother, the pants are mass. Brother, the shirt is mass. Brother, the cut is mass. Hey You! Mass!]

In this song *Mass* is an attitude – a walk (a swagger, a poise), a stand (he takes a stand, he stands firm, he stands up), a look (head lowered, eyes up, alert with controlled aggression) – and a style: a pair of pants (blue jeans, baggy cargos), a shirt (vibrant, loud), and a cut (not ironed and neat but creased and rugged).

Mass was a hit with audiences in coastal Andhra Pradesh. The hero's edgy, oppositional style appealed to young Telugu men and proved immensely popular among the Worldwide Diamonds workforce. Many of them joined the thronged cinema halls in Gajuwaka to watch it again and again, and they worked hard to fashion themselves after the film's hero.

One Sunday afternoon I accompanied Sai and other members of the Preparation Department to a local beauty spot, a hillside with an ancient Buddhist shrine 50 km outside Visakhapatnam city, for a factory picnic. Events like this are something of a social and cultural institution for the city's salaried classes and, during the warm dry months of November and December, parks, gardens and local beauty spots around the city are thronged with similar gatherings. In these annual rituals the city's public sector workers and their families reaffirm and perform the relationship between salaried employment and social reproduction. Like many of the people thronging Bojjana Konda that day, the group from Worldwide Diamonds had dressed up for the occasion and picked out their sharpest shirts. For young Indian men the question of what to wear is often a critical, everyday issue that lies at the heart of concerns and anxieties over public identities (Tarlo 1996: 19). On the outskirts of an industrial city like Visakhapatnam these concerns with appearance are fundamental to their self-definition as members of a waged or working class in the urban industrial economy (cf. Freeman 2000: 257). Being able to dress with the times costs money and the young men who could afford to fashion themselves after a cinematic role model like Mass marked themselves out as men with a disposable income.

We joined the crowd of picnic makers – families with children, husbands and mothers on a Sunday outing – and wound around the hillside to the caves that concealed large stone statues of Buddha. The climb was interspersed with pauses for breath and at the top I took a series of photos. The boys struck different poses for the camera. Shankar pushed his hands deep into his pockets, his thumbs hooked outside his trousers, his lips pursed, his jaw squared, his chin out. The others called over to him with admiration, 'Ooohhh Shankar you *Pulli*! Tiger!' Narasingha Rao sucked in his stomach. 'What about this? How do I look? And now. Here. Like this. See: this is *Mass*! Wait! Let me tighten my belt.' Caps, belts, shirts and sunglasses were handed around from person to person, so that everyone could use a combination of available objects to create, alter, check, and redefine their poses. Little Appa Rao and Sai stood together. 'Jimmie. Here. Just us. Together.' Appa Rao adjusted his hair. 'Wait. My hair is being blown by the wind. Wait! That's better. No, No. Not like that. Wait the sun is in the wrong place and my face will be in shadow. Here. Like this.' Sai fixed his costume, hesitated, looked up at me and asked with indecision, 'Jimmie? Shirt in or out?'

Little Suresh, the cornering section machinist, gave me particular instructions about the kind of photograph he wanted. 'Take it from here. Stand here. No, No. Not too close. Take it from there. Like that. So that you can see behind me ...!' For the first shot he positioned himself in front of a group of picnicking school girls who would appear to one side of the frame, unknowingly incorporated into his 'sweet memories' of the day. Then the sequence began again. 'Ok, Jimmie. Jimmie! Take another one. Wait. One more photo. Here. Me with Rajesh. Come here. Stand here. No. Not like that. Wait. Get my whole body, OK. Now, a bit closer. Not too far away. Wait. Wait! Let me get my cell.' He grabbed his mobile phone from a trouser pocket, held it up for the camera, tried to keep a straight face and froze.

Figure 10   Suresh with phone and friend

In the enthusiasm with which young working men fashion themselves on the latest style and acquire consumer goods, we can discern their commitment to consumption as an index of wealth and well being and the significance of consumer practice as a privileged site for the 'fabrication of self and society, of culture and identity' (Comaroff and Comaroff 2000: 294).[9] Of course, the role of consumption practices and consumer goods in strategies of self-representation is conditioned by social history as much as by financial resources (Bourdieu 1979; Osella and Osella 2000b), but the worlds of mass consumption and mass production remain tightly interlocked. For Raju, Madhu and Sai, the factory wage made it possible to buy clothes and things, the raw materials necessary for making selves and identities. For me, our photographic portraits threw into sharp relief the ways in which people consent to the terms and conditions of low-waged, exploitative labour in order to pursue material desires and projects of self-fashioning. On the floor of India's global factories young people – like their contemporaries in other parts of the world – navigate into the future while living between global capitalism's twin imperatives, 'to ceaselessly produce' and 'to ceaselessly consume' (Ngai 2003: 470).

The entangled worlds of mass consumption and mass production were revealed every day on the floor of the Worldwide Diamonds factory. The efforts of the factory's management to impose industrial discipline through dress could barely contain the commercial interests that flourish in India's contemporary fashion industry. Colours spilled out from beneath the bland, heavy, blue uniforms of production workers. The hems of women's saris or churidars flowed out from the bottom of the coats and the fat collars of men's loud shirts poked out from the top. In the Preparation Department, as the A shift began, male and female workers would parade their outside clothes before pulling the uniform over the top at the last minute. Major festivals become dressing up days in the factory and were accompanied by conspicuous spending on new outfits.

One day, as I stood with Raju alongside the four automatic bruting machines that he was simultaneously operating, cutting and polishing diamonds for a piece-rate wage, I asked him to explain the popularity of *Mass* to young cinema goers. He stood up straight to attention, heels together, posed smartly in the blue overalls of the production worker and said, 'this is Class.' He then unfastened his overalls, un-tucked the patterned, red skin-tight shirt he wore underneath and stuck up the fat starched collar until it rose above his neck. He lifted up one leg and rolled his skunk-striped jeans halfway to his knee, pulled out the loose end of his big buckled brown leather belt until it dangled from his waist, raised a foot (clad in a thick soled sports shoe), placed it onto the wooden box beneath his machine, rested his arm on his knee nonchalantly and pretended to chew chewing gum. He gave a broad grimace/sneer/smile and a knowing/ penetrating/lascivious look before announcing: 'And this is Mass.' The difference seemed obvious.

The Marrying Age

While young men like Raju, Sai and Madhu liked to emphasise their conspicuous spending on fashion, clothes and style, this was a partial account of their expenditure. Whether living at home or not these unmarried young men remained deeply committed to a larger family unit and contributed to a household economy by handing over a share of monthly wages directly to their mother or father. At home this money supplemented the incomes of parents or siblings, contributing to everyday domestic expenditures (like the costs of rent, food or electricity), as well as to the purchase of household consumer durables like televisions, fridges, music or VCD players. But factory wages were also invested in the long-term futures of households and families, contributing to the cost of school fees for a younger brother or sister, to refurbishments and extensions of the family house, to the correct observance of religious rites and festivals, as well as to life-cycle events, the costs of births, deaths and marriages. The household income from their factory wages often made important contributions to the repayment of debts incurred from the marriage of older siblings, or made vital contributions to the groomprice or *katnam* that could be paid to ensure a sister married 'well'.

For many of the young men employed in Worldwide Diamonds the factory wage played directly into dreams and aspirations for marriages of their own. But if their wage was deemed sufficient to meet the short-term or 'transient' consumer desires of unmarried, adolescent workers or to meet kinship obligations by making a contribution to a household economy, it was palpably insufficient to meet their longer-term aspirations to be householders, husbands and fathers. This fact became more sharply apparent to young men as they approached the marrying age.

Like India's middle-class college campus (Lukose 2005), hi-tech call centres (Poster 2002), brick kilns and construction sites (Shah 2006), its global manufacturing units are a stage on which young people's coming of age dramas unfold. Raju, Sai and Madhu reached the marrying age while they were on the Worldwide Diamonds payroll and for them – as for many other young men in provincial Andhra Pradesh – questions of sex, love and matrimony were a major preoccupation. In Visakhapatnam's telephone kiosks, on street corners, around *karim* boards, at cigarette stands, in tiffin parlours or (on the special occasions when they can afford it) in bars, over branded whisky or beer, groups of young men can be found regaling their friends with chronicles of romantic success and failure. These stories of lost loves, derailed elopements and future marriages are an essential accoutrement to their youth and masculinity, and they are told with a cinematic eye for detail, taking in the interests of other families in marrying off their daughters to eligible men, but lingering on the trials and tribulations of the male hero: the love-crazy man, the *prema pichadu*, who teeters on the edge because he follows his heart and not his head.

Yet many of these young men are also deeply realistic. They recognise that the status and income associated with being in waged employment is intimately connected to their marriage prospects and futures as husbands or fathers. Each month the distribution of factory wages and salary slips saw the young men employed in Worldwide Diamonds re-evaluate their earnings and savings against the future costs of marriage. After five years of full-time factory employment Sai, for example, claimed to have saved 30,000 rupees (US$750), putting a portion of his wage aside each month and, during festivals, taking it back home where his mother kept it hidden. Calculating the costs involved in establishing a new home he estimated that he needed another 20,000 rupees before he could afford to marry. 'How to manage?' he complained, recognising that on the urban market for marriage partners, his flexible contract in a low-waged, privately run, manufacturing industry could not compensate for his lack of family assets. 'I'm from Srikakulum. It's a poor district compared to this. My mother doesn't have land.'

As they looked towards the future few educated young men imagined that their factory wages alone would be sufficient to invest in the long-term upward mobility of their families. While factory labour offered some temporary guarantee against a fall into the day-to-day struggles of the labouring poor, it appeared to offer little prospect of upward mobility into an urban middle class. For Sai, and many others like him, the rising costs of goods and services on the edge of Visakhapatnam, the levels of remuneration in Worldwide Diamonds made it difficult, if not impossible, to imagine meeting the standards of living associated with being a successful householder, 'How can I get married like this?' Madhu once asked me:

> If you get married you need a minimum of 5000 rupees. Minimum. For one wife and one or two children. Day by day the cost of items is increasing. I need job security, that's the main thing. If you don't have it by the time you're at least 29 then you're finished.

Dreams in Motion

One evening in 2005, I visited Raju at his home in the Palle caste fishing village of Dippapalem. We walked out along the beach, avoiding the faeces, and stood scaring crabs while we watched contract workers from the steel plant take a short cut home, removing their trousers and lifting their bicycles over a tidal inlet that split the beach in two. In the near distance, smoke from the plant's cooling tower chimneys rose and merged with the sky. Out in the shallows, a line of fishermen cast their evening nets. 'This is the village of my grandfather's grandfather,' Raju said. 'Here there is sea, there is air. Even a man without money, without a job, can be here and have a good life, eating fish everyday, sleeping in the fresh air.'

Such wistful fantasies of a life of leisure and freedom from labour belied the lived experience of adolescence for young men like Raju in Visakhapatnam's hinterland. The prestige and security of permanent public sector employment in the local steel plant exerted a powerful influence over the dreams, desires and aspirations of young men and their families in villages like Dippapalem. His experiences of being educated, coupled with his parental expectations for social mobility through waged labour and his feelings of filial debt and obligation in return for their sacrifices made it impossible to live such a life of anti-labour even as it made it difficult to find appropriate forms of work.

As we walked along the beach that evening, the life of his fishing village was already coming to an end. Dippapalem had been earmarked for a major new infrastructure project, a shipping and container terminal that the government of Andhra Pradesh had declared necessary to release pressure on Visakhapatnam's port. When we first met in 2005, the land clearance and relocation process was well under way, with negotiations taking place on the terms of compensation and resettlement with members of the community. The villagers' principal demand was one permanent job in the port for at least one eligible boy from each household. Earlier on the day of this particular visit, revenue officers had arrived in the village accompanied by three vans of armed police to begin registering the names of family members. Around 1500 villagers had gathered at the road-head that leads into the village, refusing entry to all government officials until they had a written promise of employment from the port authorities. Months later, a member of Raju's peer group was killed in a tussle with police as they attempted to remove fishing boats from the shoreline so that construction work on the container terminal could begin. At the time Raju and his fellow villagers had been adamant: 'If there are no jobs we are not leaving. We can stay here, no problem.'

Five years later Dippapalem village had disappeared beneath the cranes and container terminals of Gangavaram Port. The people of Dippapalem had been resettled, higher-caste Kapu families securing the more valuable plots in a desirable highway township while lower-caste fishing families like Raju's were resettled just 2 km from their former homes, on the outskirts of the industrial township of Gajuwaka, where they constructed homes with financial support under a national government scheme for urban development. The promise of jobs for the displaced had led Raju to resign from the Worldwide Diamonds factory yet his expectation of employment in the new port had failed to materialise. Only 75 of 300 eligible young men from the village had found work in the port and, too proud to return to the Worldwide Diamond's factory, Raju had found contract work with one of the private sector contractors who won a tender to load and unload goods at the port. In the meantime, he had invested his portion of the compensation payment in a fixed deposit bank account, where it was accumulating interest for his son's future education.

Five years after I first met him on the floor of the Worldwide Diamonds Madhu, like Raju, had also left the factory's employment. A chance encounter on the streets of Visakhapatnam city put us back in contact. Driving past me on the back of a friend's motorbike in a dusty back street he shouted out my name. 'Worldwide Diamonds is gone,' he said. 'I walked away from that place and never looked back.' When I visited him later in his family home he elaborated. 'I just didn't want to work there any more. I lost all interest,' he told me:

A company should be like a mother to the worker. A company should think that the worker is their son and look after him and fulfil his needs. Why? Because the worker is working for the company. The company belongs to us. But this company doesn't think about people in this way. Instead it just makes people work, work, work, and gets profits from them. This company was never like a mother to workers, it was just interested in business.

One day, as Madhu explains, he simply decided not to go to work. Some of his work mates came looking for him at home, urging him to hand in a formal resignation letter that would allow him to collect his outstanding salary and his provident-fund contributions but Madhu refused. He left Visakhapatnam and travelled south, to the city of Vijayawada. He lived with a friend for three months and worked as a casual day labourer on a construction site, sending a portion of his earnings back home. 'My family didn't know how things were there,' he told me. 'They couldn't see. They thought it was good. I didn't tell them about the conditions I was living in, or what I was doing. I didn't tell them anything.'

Eventually his sister got him an interview for a post as a teaching assistant in a Visakhapatnam primary school and he came home. He successfully navigated the interview but his tenure at the school only lasted a few months. One day he was walking along the roadside in the highway township where he lived when he was involved in a road traffic accident. Distracted by thoughts of a young girl who had been the subject of his teenage affection but who was about to marry another man he had walked into a speeding auto-rickshaw. 'It was my mistake,' he says, 'completely mine. I was thinking about her and the future and things like that.' The accident had left Madhu bedridden for three months with a fractured leg and when he recovered he launched himself as a singer.

In 2008 he entered Eenadu TV's Saptaswaralu singing contest, winning a place in the final Top Ten. Later that year he was one of the finalists in the Voice of Vizag competition, performing a selection of Telugu, Hindi, Classical and Western pop songs to a huge crowd on the city's Ramakrishna Beach. Success was a catalyst for ambition:

> My dream is for everybody to recognise me as a singer! I want to be a performer and I want to hear my songs wherever I go. I want people to listen to my songs in the street. And when I'm walking down the road I want to be able to hear people say, 'Ah this is Madhu's song.' I want people to recognise my voice and say, 'Ah this is the voice of Madhu, this is his special voice, a voice that no other singer has.'

Over the next two years Madhu travelled to Hyderabad to record four songs for Telugu movies. His change in fortunes was immediately apparent in 2012 when he picked me up from a dusty Gajuwaka bus stand on a gigantic blue motorcycle that drew considerable attention from local commuters. Now 24 years old, he had been paid Rs. 40,000 for each recording and was being offered regular slots to sing at the gala functions organised by Visakhapatnam's up-market hotels. Madhu had used the money that he made from singing Telugu movie songs to restyle himself as a professional mentor or tutor for young children. He had started an after-school club for children, the 'Madhu Educational Society', in his parent's house and by 2012 he claimed to have 120 paying students, most of them from Gajuwaka's industrial middle-class households. The purpose of his 'school' as Madhu explained it to me, was to conjure up in his students the 'same love for knowledge' that he felt, and to share with them 'the lessons for following the correct path in life' that he had learned. 'More than anything I want to inspire them,' he said. 'Whatever dreams I have I want to inject them into my students,' he explained.

For other young men I first met in Worldwide Diamonds, however, the Visakhapatnam special economic zone remained a relatively constant island of low-waged and precarious factory labour in a sea of uncertainty, and they continued to arrive for work at the beginning of their shift, six days a week. With no other alternative Sai, for example, had stayed at Worldwide Diamonds. For him the factory had remained both 'source' and 'channel', and his continued commitment was reflected in his willingness to undertake unpaid retraining courses, to work long periods of overtime and his repetition of a managerial promise that productivity would reap future rewards. In 2008 this commitment appeared to have paid off. That year, 80 of the factory's blue-uniformed workers were employed at diamond manufacturing units in Southern Africa as part of a package of consultancy services offered by Worldwide Diamonds' corporate parent company (see chapter 4) and in December a new batch of five workers was chosen to join them. Sai was among them.

One day he was called off the factory floor in the middle of the A shift and offered a 24-month posting in Botswana. This dream of travelling outside India had captivated many of the young men employed in Worldwide Diamonds, who stood to benefit from a massive wage differential. As a shop floor supervisor in Southern Africa they would earn a salary equivalent to 25,000 rupees per month, an increase of 400 per cent on their current monthly wage in India, and Sai had jumped at the opportunity. 'Everyone works here for those chances only. To go and get more money. That was my sole aim, my goal, that is what I had been thinking about ever since I came to work here,' he told me.

Within a matter of weeks his visa and air tickets had been arranged. But Sai still had little idea what to expect in Botswana. As the date for his departure drew near his own enthusiasm and ambition were tempered.

> This is the biggest dream of all. I've been waiting six years for this but now ... But now my head is spinning. I thought I really wanted to go but now ... I don't feel it ... The company hasn't told me anything.

In an indication of how precarious this much sought after opportunity felt, Sai had not dared to ask any questions about where he was going, or what the specific terms and conditions of work in Botswana might actually be. 'I have so many questions but I am not asking anything,' he told me. 'When I am there, I will ask. But I don't want to ask all these questions now. You never know what people will think when you ask them, and you never know who will be in charge when you come back.'

As he reflected on why the opportunity had fallen to him and not to others, Sai presented this as a reward for his commitment to the company, his productivity and discipline.

> Why did they select me? Because I had the highest production in my section, and I had only taken leave once or twice in one or two years. That's why they selected me, my work and my behaviour. Some people here will be thinking, why did he get it, why did I miss this chance? See if one goes, nine will suffer. But only some people can win. Two people cannot win at the same time.

The dreaming and desiring voices of young men like Raju, Madhu and Sai capture something of the economy of anticipation that makes India's SEZs into particular places of work and labour. For these young men, like many others, the lived experience of employment is of a struggle to make sense of life and act strategically in a context of rapid social and economic transformation while attempting to fulfil kinship obligations, satisfy social expectations and realise material aspirations. Their ability to do so as they navigate into the future in search of security or stability magnifies differentials in the social and economic resources that have accrued to them and their families. Meanwhile their stories offer a reminder that the politics of work in India's new industrial economy is about consent as much as resistance.

6

The Struggles for Tomorrow

'Please don't be offended by what I'm about to show you,' said Siriyal, before turning to face the screen. We were sitting inside a large ground floor room in the compound of his parent's house in the market town of Atchutapuram, Visakhapatnam. At one end of the room was a small desk with a dusty computer and a huge pair of speakers. I had arranged this research interview, in November 2009, to talk about how rural industrialisation was affecting young men in north coastal Andhra Pradesh. As I described in chapter 3, during the 2000s Atchutapuram town had been transformed by the creation of a nearby special economic zone and I was interested in how young men were responding to the failure of the zone to realise promises of employment. Siriyal had recently opened a computer-training centre, offering certificated training courses in Microsoft Office, and had recently stood for election to local government as a youth candidate. Our conversation, however, was to take a disturbing and unanticipated turn that challenged my ideas about this small town as well as the direction of my fieldwork.

Siriyal pressed a button on his keyboard. On the screen in front of him a crisp colour video began to play, showing fluffy white clouds against a blue sky. The camera panned down to reveal lush hills and luminous grasses. The camera panned down still further to reveal a young woman kneeling on the ground, her head rising and falling over the videographer's pelvis. She stopped and pulled herself away, her face contorted with a combination of nausea and fear, and putting the palms of her hands together in supplication, looked towards the camera and said, 'Please Sir. Please Sir. Don't make me do it.' Siriyal turned to me and said, 'Everyone knows she must work in the SEZ. Village girls don't suck…'

I asked him to stop the film. I was deeply affronted by what I had just seen and heard. I was also unhappy and unsettled by the diverse ways in which, as a white man viewing this in South India, I had been suddenly implicated in the conditions of its production and circulation.

Rape and sexual violence against women in India has become a matter of heightened debate, critical commentary and public protest in recent years. In 2012, for example, the gang rape and death of a 23-year-old female medical student in Delhi saw thousands of people across India take to the streets demanding legal, political and social reforms (Yee 2013). The massive increase in the availability and use of mobile phones in India has also given rise to new forms of technologically mediated violence, as men record sexual assaults against women and circulate the images (e.g. Baishya et al. 2012; Majumder 2012). Yet sexual violence and their mediated forms continue to be noticeable by their absence from the ethnography of everyday life in small-town South Asia, and from the gendered politics of unemployment, work and labour in these places as they are represented by social scientists and progressive activists (see for example Chari 2004; Chopra 2006; de Neve 2005; Jeffrey 2010; John and Nair 2001; Srivastava and Kothari 2012).

As I have deliberated over how to describe the event above and reflected upon its analysis, I have come to ask how this video circulated among young men in the rural hinterland of Visakhapatnam, how it gained currency as an object of voyeuristic masculine fantasy and how it was eventually translated into an object of male outrage and indignation that catalysed men to action. Like critical theorists of gender and technology, I chose to focus less on the identity or life of the woman in the film than on her image as it was mobilised across this corner or Andhra Pradesh (cf. Wright 1999). The question as I saw it is how, in contexts of rural industrialisation, such 'techno-mediated forms' of sexual violence operate in ways that police the entry of women into new global workplaces and produce the masculine subject as capable of withstanding and contesting the terms and conditions of labour at these sites.

In 2009 this mobile phone video, depicting what appeared to be the oral rape of a young woman, was being shared through all-male social networks across the rural sub-districts of Rambilli and Atchutapuram. The video was accompanied by a story about its victim and perpetrator, alleged to be a young women employed inside the Brandix garment manufacturing zone that had been built across this hinterland and a factory supervisor respectively. Like factory women elsewhere in South Asia (Hewamanne 2008; Lynch 2007), the 2800 young Telugu women employed in 2009 to dye, cut and stitch brand-name ladies underwear in this Sri Lankan-owned facility aroused both desire and disgust in the imagination of local men. Rapid social and economic change, and the sudden entry of a large number of young women into the industrial workforce had been accompanied by new anxieties about their purity and virtue.

The morals of these women factory workers – the question of whether they were 'good girls' or 'bad girls' – was a matter of considerable male interest and fascination. At tiffin stalls, newspaper stands and roadside bars, in the town's police station, in the land revenue office, in the photographic studio, in one of many tea shops or tiffin parlours, or amid the lines of auto-rickshaws, the region's menfolk could be overheard telling stories about the vice and promiscuity of factory women to titillate and pass the time. These were stories about women who disembark from the fleet of factory buses that transport them in and out of the zone, only to be picked up by strange men who drive around the countryside in dark cars. They were stories of stalkers on the shift, of male colleagues and supervisors who single out a favourite woman and encourage her to feign a sickness so they can elope for the day. And they were stories of suicide, of the married young women who kill themselves after being accused of, or 'discovered' to be having an affair with their workmates.

These stories produced the SEZ as a space in which cultural values are contaminated or eroded by non-local forces, and in which women are the victims of its loss (cf. Wright 1999). Against this background the video fascinated and appalled, and it was watched by aspirant politicians and police officers, educated young men and school drop-outs, farm workers and auto-rickshaw drivers, teachers and journalists alike. 'How many people have seen it?' I asked Siriyal. 'Who knows?' he said. 'All my friends around here have seen it. The whole world has it now.' The technology did not just facilitate the video's circulation but also mediated its consumption, allowing it to be viewed with an unparalleled immediacy. At some point it was transferred to a computer and burned onto CDs for wider distribution.

For Siriyal, like other men with knowledge of this film in Atchutapuram town, responsibility for its production rested with the woman herself: with her clothes, her comportment and, most of all, her employment. 'Women around here used to be in the fields cutting grass with bare legs,' he said. 'Now they're wearing saris that cover them up, using face creams and going to beauty parlours. When they get into, so-called, up-lifted work, their attitudes change.'

Such commentaries were widely shared. 'At first a husband might be happy if his wife goes to work in the factory,' a middle-aged man told me in a small Atchutapuram tea shop one evening, as a convoy of buses swept past the doorway carrying workers back to the highway townships on the outskirts of Visakhapatnam at the end of the shift. 'But then things change. She will start to carry handbags and go on the bus.'

Across Atchutapuram questions about the film elicited similar commentaries. 'Women who work in the zone start being interested in other kinds of lifestyles,' I was once told by a young auto-rickshaw driver. 'They're not interested in farmers or labourers, or people who do manual work and wear dirty clothes. They're interested in other kinds of men: men who work as supervisors or managers, men who wear flashy clothes.'

In late January 2009 a journalist working for one of Andhra Pradesh's largest Telugu daily newspapers, *Andhra Jyoti*, picked up the story about the mobile phone film and filed a report with his editor. His reporting of the incident was vague on the details but strong on the rhetoric. 'Displaced people who were hoping for a peaceful life after the loss of their homes and lands now face an unprecedented and very serious challenge,' the article read, giving the false impression that women employed in the zone were primarily the daughters of families displaced by its construction (see chapter 3). 'Women workers in the SEZ are being harassed and blackmailed by male officials and employees.' The journalist tied the film directly to working conditions inside the zone, writing that women workers were being forced to work unpaid overtime and were being threatened with dismissal if they complained. This environment of fear and insecurity for women workers, he wrote, created the perfect conditions for sexual harassment and blackmail. 'Women who work inside the SEZ have to comply with whatever officials or managers tell them and unscrupulous people are cashing in on their vulnerability.'

In Visakhapatnam the editor decided to run the story on the front page of the newspaper's district edition and, in its translation to print, the oral rape of a young woman in a small town became a matter of salacious theatre. The newspaper's chief artist, a Hyderabad-based graphic designer, was commissioned to illustrate the piece. The artist produced a black and white line drawing that showed a woman cowering in the shadows with her hands folded under the chin and an eagle hovering above her, talons outstretched, a bald metaphor for predatory men. When the illustration was ready the story was published under a sensationalising headline:

BEWARE! MALE ANIMALS! Women workers are being bamboozled in the Andhra Pradesh SEZ. Managers are shooting blue films by luring women with the promise of work. Everything is possible on a mobile phone. Employees are prime actors. Suspicions of mafia involvement!

The story elicited an immediate response from Visakhapatnam's left-wing labour activists. The Centre for Indian Trade Unions (CITU) lodged a complaint at Atchutapuram police station demanding an independent probe into sexual harassment inside the Brandix garment factory and issued a press release condemning the exploitation of women workers there. Their response reframed the issue still further, nesting concern about violence against women workers in questions about the company's failure to generate employment. 'The Brandix company had been allowed to lease over 1,000 acres of land at very low cost by the government of Andhra Pradesh on the basis of its promise to create 60,000 jobs,' CITU leaders told journalists. 'But after three years they only employed 3,500 women who were not being paid minimum wages, were being refused a one-hour lunch break and were being asked to work beyond their eight-hour shift without payment of overtime' (*The Hindu*, 2009).

Several weeks after the video clip first surfaced the CITU mobilised several hundred for a rally at the entrance to the Brandix complex and a fast (*dharna*) to demand justice for the victim. They also handed over a formal written complaint addressed to company managers that demanded an immediate investigation. In June the members of a regional youth forum (Yuva Chetyna Vedika) tried to publicise their concerns about the negative impact of industrialisation on women and challenge local conceptions about the terms and conditions of employment in the SEZ by making a journey by foot (*padayatra*) from the rural market town of Anakappale to the Brandix SEZ, a distance of some 30 km. Meanwhile, persistent rumours about the woman's identity led journalists, trade union officials and youth activists to visit several nearby villages in search of the victim or her family. Yet no-one identifying herself as the woman in the film ever came forward or was identified, leading to stories that she had committed suicide.

These protests fitted into a pattern of labour activism focused on the SEZs built outside Visakhapatnam. During the 2000s trade union campaigns over low wages and working conditions inside the Worldwide Diamonds factory (see chapters 4 and 5), for example, had consistently focused on the specific vulnerability and unique risks to women workers here, repeatedly alleging that women were refused access to toilets and were subject to sexual harassment by managers.[1] Despite the rhetoric, however, the interests represented by India's trade unions are invariably those of their dominant constituencies, and while their mobilisations may appear to cut across gender, caste and religion union power remains contingent on existing social hierarchies and relationships (Fernandes

1997: 88). As feminist theorists have argued, when India's male political leaders mount campaigns to defend or protect women from sexual violence they do so by ascribing to women particular qualities and virtues that mark them as uniquely deserving of respect and protection and which also serve to constrain them within particular roles and identities (Mohan 2013). In north coastal Andhra Pradesh the representation of women workers as particularly at risk or vulnerable in new industries has done more to defend the continued participation of men in the workforce than to specifically protect women workers. Here trade union activism has, wittingly or not, worked to exclude or limit the participation of women in the labour force, by valorising, reaffirming and reproducing ideas about the sanctity of woman as mothers, sisters, wives and daughters and the capacity of men to provide for and protect them.

Fields of Protest

In this penultimate chapter I explore the fields of protest (Ray 1999) around India's special economic zones and show how social activism is embroiled in the making of these spaces, transforming the way that they appear in popular imaginaries. Across India economic zones have emerged as a locus for anxieties about the future, opening a window onto contemporary public life as well as relations of caste, class and gender. In and around these spaces concerns about the morality of working women and the reproduction of gendered norms and values overlap with concerns for economic security and stability, and with concerns about the transformation of citizenship and sovereignty as a consequence of liberalisation.

This book has set out to explore India's large-scale infrastructure projects as socially and culturally generative spaces. Doing so, I argue, means addressing a fuller range of actions, practices and politics than those represented by social activists. The dreamed-of futures that mobilise people in and around large-scale infrastructure projects take diverse forms, not all of them embraced by the politics of progressive social activists and campaigners concerned with the impacts of industrialisation. In the rural hinterland of Visakhapatnam, for example, the failure of SEZs to realise hopes of male employment has been mapped onto the bodies of women in ways that shape the rhetoric and form of protests over work, labour and employment. Against a background of high unemployment, protests by organised labour unions over the treatment of women workers are inextricably entwined with male anxieties over access to formal sector industrial work, and the discourses of labour activists hinge upon and reproduce a constellation of ideas about the female body and the proper place of women in society.

These protests diverge considerably from the demands for greater transparency and accountability in government that have animated a nationwide campaign against SEZs in India. As I explore in this chapter, anti-SEZ campaigners have worked to strategically foreclose the fields of protest around these sites in order to produce them as 'spaces of hope', in which to fashion radical geographies, possibilities and futures. Doing so means framing the struggles for tomorrow as left-liberal critiques of development rather than struggles over social reproduction, morality and virtue that reproduce patriarchal or hierarchical relations.

The terms under which land is acquired for industrialisation in India and the nature of employment being created has catalysed social and political activism, shaping novel forms of protest and bringing together diverse actors. In the late 1990s India's labour activists first began to voice concerns about the treatment of workers in the country's 'offshore' economy, drawing attention to alleged violations of labour rights and the ability of industrial capitalists to conduct business here with relative impunity (e.g. Chhachhi 1999; Ghosh 2002; ILO 2001). In the 2000s these concerns were eclipsed by questions over the terms and conditions under which land for SEZs was being acquired. The rapid proliferation of economic zones that followed the 2005 SEZ Act was accompanied by a multiplication of highly localised conflicts over the terms and conditions of land acquisition and displacement.

As India's SEZs have appeared to realise dystopian visions of contemporary capitalism they have also given rise to dreams of resistance and political mobilisations that contest dominant economic models, paradigms and trajectories. As India's SEZ projects emerged as a focus for protest and opposition to post-liberalisation era policies (Jenkins 2011) educated, middle-class social activists worked to link localised conflicts into a nationwide anti-SEZ campaign. Loosely allied under the banner of a 'progressive' or 'new' left, this campaign brought together diverse organisations and groups who identified themselves with struggles over the social impact of pro-market development policies. Just as the spectacular visions of growth that have been projected onto India's SEZs by politicians, planners and transnational investors have made them into particular spaces for global capital (see chapters 2–4) so too the counter-narratives of activists and campaigners have shaped these spaces as particular arenas of contestation. In their pursuit of different futures left-wing trade unionists, grassroots Dalit activists, new left social movement activists, environmental activists and caste-based associations of rural farmers have organised and strategised around these spaces in different ways. They advocate certain tactics or methods over others, magnifying their rhetoric over some issues while downplaying others, and they make different kinds of resources available to those most affected by large-scale industrial development projects (cf. Anand 2011: 544), drawing attention to activists and activism in the plural.

Anti-SEZ Activism

In 2009 a television documentary made JR into one of the most prominent social activists and filmmakers in north coastal Andhra Pradesh. Aired on all of the state's major Telugu news channels his film, 'Climate Crisis in AP' connected the investments of pharmaceutical companies and chemical industries in the region's economic zones to environmental degradation, rising disease, water and food shortages. Unchecked industrialisation heralds an apocalyptic future, the film concluded, that would see parts of the state abandoned as *nirgiva prantham* or dead zones.

The film was accompanied by graphic imagery. In one sequence a series of slides inverted a diagram of Darwinian evolution. Four drawings showed a black shape evolving from some unspecified primate ancestor, through the bipedal ancestors of modern humans, to the familiar shape of upright *Homo sapiens*. The sequence is interrupted by a nuclear mushroom cloud and the final drawing shows a creature with four legs and two heads. 'It's like a tidal wave, this so-called God: "Development"', JR told me, piling on the metaphors, as he talked me through the slides from his studio, a back-street office in central Visakhapatnam.

Born into a Kapu caste household and brought up in relatively austere circumstances in rural Srikakulum – his father employed as a driver in a city irrigation company – JR graduated in politics and public administration from Andhra University. His conversion to environmental journalism came when he was a feature reporter for *Vaata*, a Telugu newspaper. Posted to Visakhapatnam he began to cover the slew of new industrial projects in the city's hinterland and, with the rise of India's 24-hour television news channels, he branched out into documentary filmmaking. His friends tease him about his bombastic style and his habit of blowing stories up with rumour and speculation, but they also acknowledge his skills as an investigative journalist, with sympathetic contacts in the local government who leak him draft policy documents and presentations.

In 2008 he joined an online climate change campaign launched by Greenpeace (onehundredmonths.org), that asked people to collectively countdown to a global tipping point. His film took its cue from this campaign and linked a sequence of large-scale industrial projects in coastal Andhra Pradesh to an impending cataclysm. Footage for the documentary was shot by JR's associate, Sriram, a shy young man in his early twenties, also from Srikakulum. 'I was pro-SEZs and industrialisation when I came to Visakhapatnam,' he told me, 'I thought that if they can create jobs then it's good. But I changed my mind when I went to the field.' On his first visit to a SEZ dedicated to the production of pharmaceuticals just south of Visakhapatnam city, he was struck by the smell in the air, how the workers he interviewed complained of nausea and vomiting, and how his hair 'went all funny and stood up on end for a couple of days afterwards'.

'People around here don't want jobs,' JR said with conviction, from behind a desk strewn with CDs and DVDs, documents, files, press releases, cables, video tapes and laptops. 'They want food and water. The young men migrating here to the city don't have land at home to grow crops and agriculture is declining. People here need food not computers and chemicals.'

The 2005 SEZ Act focused and catalysed a small army of independent researchers, journalists, social science graduate students, and documentary filmmakers, like JR, who began to file reports and eye-witness accounts that documented the social and economic impact from the sites of proposed SEZs across the country, uploading them to websites and blogs, or publishing them in the print media. Meanwhile, international development agencies like ActionAid funded research into the social and economic impact of zones and the Ford Foundation (which once funded Indian policy makers on fact-finding missions to China's SEZs) began to support academic research aimed at better understanding the pattern of resistance to SEZs across India. In 2009 some of these activities coalesced into a nationwide anti-SEZ campaign, loosely coordinated by the National Alliance of People's Movements (NAPM), that sought to catalyse public opinion and fundamentally change the government of India's policy on economic zoning. Over the course of a year NAPM activists worked to organise public meetings at the sites of SEZs and to collect testimonies from some 400 people directly affected by zone projects in what they called a People's Audit of SEZs.

The anti-SEZ campaign drew strength from reports of grassroots opposition to SEZs in Nandigram (see chapter 1) and in Raigad, Maharashtra. In the 2000s Raigad had been identified as the site for a massive SEZ project, promoted by the Reliance corporation. In the face of popular opposition to plans in 2008 the state of Maharashtra held a referendum on the construction of the SEZ (the first of its kind in India) and over 85 per cent of voters rejected proposals. The apparent success of the struggle to oppose the SEZs in Raigad provided inspiration to organisations and activists across India, suggesting that the combination of grassroots political mobilisations, judicial activism and a media campaign, if sustained, could have a cumulative impact and successfully stop large-scale infrastructure projects (Srivastava 2009).

Modelled, in part, on the strategy and success of the Raigad movement, the People's Audit was an ambitious attempt to foster new kinds of social collectivity. On the one hand it set out to connect localised campaigns against SEZs into a national debate about SEZ policy, by amassing evidence about the social and economic impact of these projects that could critically interrogate official claims about their positive effect on employment, infrastructure development and investment and hold the state to account. On the other hand it set out to engineer or catalyse a national movement, producing and presenting a unified oppositional public face to state authorities and catalyse resistance to SEZs by lending solidarity and support to local groups. Anti-SEZ campaigners have approached localised conflicts over land and labour, for example, as opportunities to fashion broader opposition to 'development', and seen the challenge as that of connecting disparate struggles in ways that transcend their 'militant particularisms' and establish a common agenda for radical change (Harvey 2001; Maringanti 2008; Williams 1972).

For many activists, like JR, India's SEZ projects represented just one point of struggle that overlapped with struggles against nuclear power plants, steel plants, bauxite mines and international airports, and many drew the connections between the acquisition of land for SEZs and other struggles over natural resources (land, water and forest), as well as processes of financialisation. For these activists, conflicts and contestations around India's SEZs created a moment of opportunity in the creation of a broader, inclusive public movement in opposition to orthodox neoliberal economics, and capitalist globalisation.

For JR, like many other participants in these movements, contemporary struggles against rampant industrialisation in India are anchored in regional histories of rebellion and anti-imperialism. In his studio, next to the computer screen streaming a 24-hour Telugu television news channel, is a framed picture of Alluri Sita Ramu Raju. Between 1922 and 1923 this celebrated Telugu freedom fighter led a guerrilla war against the British empire in north-east coastal Andhra Pradesh. Moved by the repressive policies of the colonial administrators towards the region's tribal population and the actions of labour contractors, Ramu Raju led a series of successful armed raids against police stations. Following a massive campaign against him and after evading capture for several months, Rama Raju was caught and shot dead. His legend has inspired at least one Telugu film hit and his statues can found in prominent locations across the city. 'Rama Raju terrorised the Britishers with bows and arrows,' JR once told me me with pride and patriotism, but he left the allegory implicit: that activists like him are modern-day freedom fighters who fight corporate capital, political corruption, oppression and injustice with printed words and film.[2]

Announcing the People's Audit on SEZs, a concept note circulated by the NAPM invoked a similar legacy. 'At the turn of the 21st Century Special Economic Zones form the thorn bed of bitter resistance and struggle in India,' it read, 'much like British colonialism did at the turn of the previous century.' As I explore, however, while this anti-SEZ campaign took inspiration from repertoires of political action rooted in anti-colonial struggle it also took inspiration from the values and commitments of the postcolonial Indian state.

The People's Audit

'When we oppose a state policy based on rationality they say we are emotional. They say we are irrational, they say we are Naxalites (Maoists). So we have to use their kind of irrationality.' With these words one of India's most prominent social activists, Aruna Roy, introduced the 2009 People's Audit of SEZs to an audience of activists, academics and retired civil servants at a public meeting in the South Indian city of Chennai. In India today, she argued, social activists are compelled to draw on the very registers, practices and mechanisms that are the everyday foundations of the state and which their work is committed to critiquing. The audit, she explained, involved interrogating the promises, policies, legal and administrative structures of government against 'what is there on the ground'. 'We have to use facts, we have to use records, we have to use our access to information,' she went on to say. 'Whatever we do we have to do with documents and data. That's what this audit process is designed for. It offers the state a rational focus on its own contradictions.'

During the 2000s the social audit became an important fixture of civil society activism in India (Ackerman 2004; Goetz and Jenkins 2001). From its first use by Rajasthan-based Mazdoor Kisan Shakti Sangathan (Association for the Empowerment of Workers and Peasants) and the Mumbai-based Rationing Kruti Samiti (Action Committee for Rationing), the audit has emerged as a preferred mode of democratic action and engagement, with which social activist organisations work to hold government to account by auditing policies and expenditure, and by comparing them to the experiences and realities of purported beneficiaries through public hearings.

In their organisation these audits differ from the public hearings organised by government of India departments or industries on the side-lines of large-scale industrial development projects; the latter, which might be described as rituals of assent, invoke democratic procedures of public consultation (e.g. Kaur 2013). By contrast the social audit is organised independently of and autonomously from the state and are intended to reveal discrepancies between personal experiences and policies. Over the past decade the social audit has proved integral to India's pro-accountability movement. It was used to assess the implementation of India's National Rural Employment Guarantee Act and to hold bureaucrats and public officials to account for government expenditure, highlighting continued discrepancies in the use of public money or missing accounts with the intention of shaming people into returning 'misdirected' funds (Ackerman 2004).

'Only certain social practices take a form that will convince', the anthropologist Marylin Strathern wrote (2000: 1–2), exploring how the audit had broken free of its moorings in finance and accounting had come to be applied to a wide range of attempts to practice, achieve and perform accountability. The audit, she argued, has come to operate as a technology of political reason that carries the cultural stamp of accountability and which persuades people that 'accountability has been rendered' (2000: 1–2).

Like other technologies of reason the audit is globally mobile, operating in diverse contexts and environments as it is addressed to diverse problems (Ong and Collier 2005; Strathern 2005). In India it is the power of audit to appropriate the claims to rationality and objectivity at the heart of the modern bureaucratic state that have made it a key tool in campaigns for transparency and accountability in governance. To some anti-SEZ campaigners this power made the audit a more potent mechanism with which to challenge and reflect upon the problems posed by state-sanctioned industrial infrastructure projects than other forms of political activism.

In her speech Aruna Roy articulated the continued commitment of activists to planning as a utopian practice and to the ideal of an omnipotent, enlightened and procedurally perfect state peopled by a body of experts united by their commitment to the nation's progress (Fuller and Bénéï 2001: 8). What the state calls 'planning', they argue, is nothing of the sort and at the heart of their attempts to hold government accountable for its policies and politics is a demand for more planning not less. This is a vision in which decisions are made after bearing in mind the totality of possibilities for all parties, particularly the most vulnerable, and in which the stakes for different parties in the decision making process are judged according to how much they are going to be affected.

Similar concerns are vocalised across India by those scholars increasingly referred to as India's middle-class citizen-activists (Baviskar and Ray 2011; Mawsdley 2004); active, engaged citizens who see themselves explicitly as members of civil society, who voice demands for better governance and environmental management, but whose cultural politics and concerns for civility, cleanliness and order see them re-codifying urban landscapes in ways that disadvantage the poor or the working class.

One of Visakhapatnam's most energetic civil activists, for example, is E.A.S. Sharma, a retired officer in the Indian Administrative Service who has made prodigious use of the Right to Information Act, mounting successful cases against the municipal corporation and the state authorities in the Andhra Pradesh High Court, on one occasion winning a stay of execution under the Environmental Protection Act from planned development projects in the city. From his well-manicured residence in one of the city's leafy suburbs, he writes regular letters to Prime Minister Manmohan Singh. What drives him, he told me during an interview in late 2009, is a commitment to enlightenment values. 'I am dedicated to maintaining the sanctity of the law of the land, ensuring due process and procedure in local governance, and logical consistency in planning,' he said:

> If you look at master plans for the development of this country, for the development of cities like this one, if you are good at mathematics or any science, you will see that they are not internally consistent documents. My attention is focused on proper procedure and protocol, institutions and laws. If institutions are defective, I will attack them. If laws are defective, I will attack them. [He clapped his hands to emphasise the point.] Why, yesterday itself, I wrote another letter to the prime minister.

Yet just as fissures developed between India's postcolonial modernisers and its diverse publics – some of whom did not share the commitments to modern reason and their modernist discourse (Fuller and Bénéï 2001) – so too the language and practices of middle-class activists in India are also often at odds with those of vernacular activists. The grammar of protest and political claims making by left-wing labour unions in Visakhapatnam, for example, is often focused on eliciting the response of a powerful patron, either local politicians or government administrators, by appealing to them for patronage and by attempting to engender their passions and sentiments (*bhavodvegaalu*). In public demonstrations and rallies of SEZ workers could be heard the slogans: '*Manam Nyamu Kavali*' ('We Want Justice'); '*Mammalni Rakshimchindi*' ('Please Protect Us!') as well as, '*Mammalni Kaapaadandi*' ('Please Save Us').

Of course, as participants and supporters of the People's Audit of SEZs frequently recognised, the everyday efficacy of the audit as a political technology was no less about the mobilisation and management of sentiments. 'These audits are ritualised political events rather than information gathering exercises,' one South Indian participant told me:

> Research in our country doesn't go anywhere. These audits are political channels: their communication methods are more direct, they are quicker and faster in terms of the noise they generate. Senior civil servants and eminent members of civil society come to take the depositions. They are reported in the press and they create a groundswell of public interest. It's not about the information per se or about the quality of the information they generate but about the channel they create. That's what makes them politically important.

Frictions and Fault Lines

In 2009 I joined a group of independent researchers, academics, journalists, engineering students, social workers and the representatives of community-based organisations working to organise the audit of SEZs in Andhra Pradesh. In August I travelled from Visakhapatnam to Hyderabad, the state capital, for a preliminary meeting to discuss the logistics. As I will show, meetings like this one illustrate the work involved in institutionalising the audit as a political technology. These meetings opened a window onto the ideological battlegrounds upon which what counts as progressive social activism in India comes to be defined and defended. As such, they highlight the tensions between India's cosmopolitan left activists, who describe their politics in terms of wide-angled commitments to the non-local, national or even global, and vernacular activists who describe their politics in terms of commitments to particular places and constituencies of people; commitments that they and others sometimes glossed as the 'local'. Yet, as I explore, these frictions are also what allowed people to act together and they remind us, as Anna Tsing (2005) has argued, that the work of political mobilisation is that of negotiating difference.

The meeting in Hyderabad was hosted by an NGO that has received project grants from a range of international development agencies, including Oxfam and the European Union, to implement projects around rural livelihoods, sustainable agriculture and vocational education. The meeting took place around a large boardroom table with a facilitator making notes on a white board. At least half of the 12 participants were familiar with the idea of a social audit and had helped to organise a previous social audit of India's national rural employment guarantee scheme: 'If we can audit one government policy why can't we audit the others?' one of the organisers told me. For others, however, the concept was unfamiliar and there was nothing obvious, taken for granted or self-evident about its utility. 'What is an audit?' they asked. Or, 'What's the difference between a social audit, a public audit, and a people's audit?'

Invariably the degree of familiarity with this language marked people by class, identifying people as cosmopolitan activists, fluent in Telugu and English, who had been involved in earlier audits of government policies and programmes, and non-English-speaking provincial activists, who attended the meeting in response to localised conflicts over the acquisition of land for SEZs. For these participants the meeting was also a training programme, and the NAPM facilitators used the meeting to make the case to them for the audit as a legitimate and effective political tool.

The first items on the agenda were how an audit of SEZs should be organised. 'Should it take place in every district?' people asked. 'Should the visiting team visit every SEZ?' This, people quickly agreed, was impractical and undesirable. Contrary to the representation of the audit as an objective, positivist process by its national-level organisers, the choice of locations in Andhra Pradesh was determined entirely by the presence of active local organisers and by a concern to highlight, strengthen and showcase resistance. It was decided to hold the audit in three districts across the state, in locations where protest rallies had recently been held against SEZs or where farmers were working to block preliminary surveys of the lands for proposed zones. As a consequence, places like Visakhapatnam, home to the second highest concentration of SEZs in the state but with little history of outright opposition to these projects, were excluded altogether.

As the discussion continued the different political strategies of grassroots organisers and cosmopolitan activist groups revealed a line of tension. 'Could the social audit be translated into a mass political mobilisation?' vernacular activists asked. 'Will the audit just be a one-off event, a flash in the pan, or will it lead to something more sustained?' This meant ensuring that the audit left a legacy, strengthening anti-SEZ campaigns in the state and linking village-based groups to district-level and state-level groups. For the urban, educated new left activists, however, this focus on mobilisations risked embroiling the audit in mass politics and they argued that the process should be aimed at something more than political mobilisations, something, they suggested, with a specific legal outcome, like a judicial review of all SEZ projects in Andhra Pradesh or in India.

'People can't think about the wider issues,' the regional director for an Andhra Pradesh based human rights organisation, later complained, reflecting on the meeting. 'Faced with their circumstances. They can't see beyond their locality. They can't think about what is an SEZ or what is the SEZ Act.' For activists like him the work of political mobilisation in India is also one of cultural critique and, like others involved in the audit of SEZs, he saw an important element of pedagogy in the process. 'People in their little villages around here are more than willing to accept SEZs,' the director went on to tell me:

They say, give us a better deal and we'll hand over our land. They raise voices and slogans demanding more money, some promises of jobs, some more facilities, some better roads. But they never demand that the SEZ Act be repealed or protest because the land acquisition process is unjust. They never think about the national picture. All these things have to be critiqued.

For him, and other cosmopolitan activists, what counted as politics in the debates around India's SEZs was carefully delimited. 'Movements to increase the price of land or get jobs don't count. Movements to stop SEZs do,' he told me.

In Hyderabad, as discussion shifted to the question of how the audit would be funded or financed, the meeting highlighted the fault lines created by a history of financial flows from activists and organisations in India's urban centres to those in its provinces. The Hyderabad-based activists had, in advance of the meeting, tapped their overseas networks for contributions, asking friends and family who lived, worked or were studying in the US to help finance the audit process. But they also imagined that 'local' organisers would help to mobilise resources for the event. The suggestion was met with anger by activists from coastal Andhra Pradesh.

'How can you ask people who don't have jobs, people who haven't had jobs for years, people who don't have money to contribute so that outsiders can come and talk to them?' the representative of one community-based organisation from Kakinada asked:

There's always a gap in finances that our communities have to fill. After this movement has zoomed past us who will get us out of jail? Who'll stop us being harassed? Who'll pay for food? Unless I get some guarantees of financial support then I cannot participate in this audit programme.

Of course, such dramatic statements were also a negotiating gambit, and small-town Telugu activists played up their exclusion and marginalisation in order to make moral claims on urban activists and persuade them to raise funds on their behalf. But such questions also revealed a paradox: at the same time as the profile and capacities of individual activists hinged on their ability to secure financial resources for their organisations, they also hinged on their ability to assert their ideological purity and their distance from the mainstream 'development industry'.

Many cosmopolitan left activists in Andhra Pradesh are ambivalent towards NGOs that are involved in implementing development projects and programmes with the financial and technical support of larger, international organisations. Many have watched as small social welfare associations set up to educate, radicalise and mobilise Dalits or Adivasis are transformed by the inflow of funds from the global development industry. It is not uncommon to hear activists speak with dismay about 'the NGO-isation of political space' and the 'depoliticising' effects of development (see for example Ferguson 1990; Harriss 2002).

Such ambivalence became particularly apparent as Visakhapatnam-based activists hosted visitors from across India to discuss political strategies around the city's SEZ projects. In the wake of the 2005 SEZ Act the representatives of several Delhi-based NGOs had visited the city to explore the scope for projects or programmes on working conditions in the region's SEZs. Several meetings had been organised, to which left activists, journalists and social workers from across the region had been invited. These meetings had left a bad taste in the mouths of many activists. 'We all know how these meetings go,' one particular jaded activist, affiliated to an agricultural workers' union told me:

> They come here and organise an interaction. Then later there will be another meeting in another city, and we will be invited to go there and stay in a hotel. We never know what the motivation is. We don't know if people are driven because they wrote a project funding proposal in which they said they would organise meetings, or if people are coming to gather information for a new proposal. After the 2005 SEZ Act people came and offered us hundreds of thousands of rupees to conduct meetings. But we all know what happens afterwards, after the money and the meetings. Nothing. Nothing happens. The only duty of organisations like these is to eat money for the issue of the day and, today, SEZs are the issue.

Similar critiques are vocalised by anti-SEZ campaigners across India. These critiques frequently frame NGOs as vehicles for neoliberal ideology that reproduce relationships between state, capital and society under the auspices of radical change. A national convention on the acquisition of land for large-scale industrial infrastructure projects held in Bhubaneswar, Orissa, for example, concluded by resolving to carry forward an 'intensive and countrywide struggle against SEZs' and also called for 'the exposure and isolation' of the NGO 'forces of compromise' who 'play a divisive role in the movements'.

Around the planning meeting in Hyderabad the contours of this debate saw fissures and frictions between provincial activists, who whispered on the side-lines about the flow of funds from NGOs, and cosmopolitan activists who complained that the meeting was being hijacked by 'local politics'. As they worked to produce a final statement that would invite groups to contact them and join a state-wide Public Audit of SEZs they struggled to find a common ground, clashing on the specific choice of words or phrases. The wording of the final statement was conciliatory, referencing both the concerns of cosmopolitan activists with the 'audit process' and the interests of provincial activists who remained concerned about mobilising people in their particular areas. A People's Audit of SEZs in Andhra Pradesh, the final document read, sets out to 'institutionalise an official audit of SEZs with special reference to fundamental rights' and 'to evolve and strengthen local movements against SEZs'.

Depositions

The minibus stopped on the dusty roadside in the midday heat and the passengers got out to take photographs. With their camcorders, digital cameras, notebooks, sunglasses, and bottled water they created something of a spectacle and passing cyclists stopped to watch. 'It would once have been lovely and green around here,' someone said, 'Now look at it.' 'See those bodies of water,' another voice added, 'they must have once been so beautiful. Now look at them. They're all gone, destroyed by the zone.'

The bus passengers made for an eclectic group. There were two prominent public figures, both men, a Delhi-based Supreme Court advocate, well known for his opposition to big dam projects and the general secretary of a South Indian trade union. In addition the bus included a number of people who described themselves as activists; these included a group of women social workers who had helped block plans for a massive SEZ project in Raigad, Maharastra, three woman NGO workers from Chennai, a Tamil Catholic priest, two young men who were members of a Chennai activist collective, and a former IT professional who had recently returned to India from London where he had worked for a multinational energy company. There were several academics, a male professor of social work at a Chennai university, two women sociologists and myself.

All of us had been invited or had volunteered to join the 2009 People's Audit of SEZs and the bus was carrying us across the north-east corner of Tamil Nadu to hear public depositions from people most affected by SEZ projects. These depositions were the cornerstone of the People's Audit and they involved white-collar professionals (lawyers, retired civil servants, academics) listening to and recording the testimonies of people resettled by or employed inside SEZs, before making a series of recommendations. The presence of high-profile public celebrities on these panels guaranteed press coverage. 'You always need a star to bring attention the process,' as one South Indian activist told me. 'We need an activist poster-face for the outside world otherwise these spaces get taken by other people, like politicians.'

These depositions were a carefully stage-managed and formulaic moment of political theatre. In Tamil Nadu and Andhra Pradesh state-level organisers worked hard behind the scenes to ensure a continuity of process and content in depositions being held in diverse locations, sometimes hundreds of miles apart, and to communicate testimonies to a national committee. Yet, as I show, by working to make the depositions travel, the audit process also shaped their content and decontextualised them.

In advance of depositions in Andhra Pradesh and Tamil Nadu, local organisers were asked to pre-select participants in order to present to the panel a balanced representation of voices, including different communities of farmers, marginalised groups, women and Dalits. As one state-level organiser put it: 'We need to be aware of the gender balance and community representation to ensure someone from every social category is represented.' These social categories were often carefully documented, differentiating between labourers, farmers, share-croppers, fisher-folk, sand excavation workers, traditional artisans, construction workers, brick kiln workers, in ways that linked social identity and personhood with economic activity. In addition, some state-level committees issued more specific criteria, giving local organisers instructions or checklists, to manage who speaks and the content of their statements.

'We asked local organisers to bring five or six people from each affected village and we suggested some of the issues that they should speak about. After all, they can't speak about everything, otherwise the meetings will go on all day and we don't have enough time,' one state level organiser explained to me.

Speakers were asked to limit their statements to particular themes: the land acquisition process, the loss of lands previously assigned to the poor by the state, the loss of livelihoods, the loss of environmental resources including grazing land and water sources, and the general social impact of the zone on their lives. 'We have to keep them on the subject,' one organiser told me in Andhra Pradesh, 'otherwise people will use the opportunity to talk about all kinds of problems and issues.' 'We give people a format so they won't be all over the place when they speak and to make sure that the panellists will hear about the key themes,' another organiser told me. 'We explain to them, these are the issues you should talk about, you don't need to talk about everything.'

Sometimes the format of each meeting was meticulously planned, with state-wide organisers establishing in advance who would welcome the panellists with an overview of 'local-level issues' and providing them with information sheets that give background details on SEZ projects and figures on the amount of land acquired or number of people displaced. Inevitably this attention to organisation led to accusations of a top-down process and in Andhra Pradesh local activists repeatedly complained about a process that was being imposed upon them by people from Hyderabad or Delhi. 'They are the ones organising things, they are the ones talking to other people and planning what should happen,' I was told. These organisational hierarchies and differentials in information and organisational clout were keenly perceived and felt. 'People like them take decisions on our behalf,' I was told in coastal Andhra, by community-based activists. 'People like them live off people like us.'

The depositions that I attended all followed a similar format. The panellists were seated on a dais or on chairs. Those chosen to depose were asked to stand or sit in front of them. Each deposition began with people being asked for their name and age. While some of those asked to depose were shy or hesitant often the opposite was true and those who spoke displayed a keen understanding of the conventions around them. They often took the floor in self-conscious ways, positioning themselves directly in front of the panel's chair, and gesturing for their names and details to be recorded by a note taker.

Given the floor and the opportunity to speak, it was rare to hear people keep to the suggested format. In their depositions people frequently overran their time slot, taking the opportunity to see that their complaints about corrupt government officials, unpaid compensation payments, slow resettlement processes, mendacious factory managers, low wages or the costs of transport into and out of the zone were recorded. In these public depositions the panellists often took care to make people feel that their personal stories and the specificities of their situation were

Figure 11   Panel hearing a deposition, People's Audit of SEZs (2009)

important, noting the details of individual cases, the amount of land lost or monies never received. But sometimes even the most committed of panellists struggled to remain focused or keep their cool. After hours in the heat of the midday sun long depositions panellists were sometimes tired and grumpy. 'God! Let's forget about the numbers and get to the issues,' someone whispered to me at one public hearing as villagers went off message. 'Enough with the facts and figures. This is an audit, it's not a fact-finding mission.' Meanwhile, on the side-lines the organisers sometimes struggled to maintain control and, if speakers were perceived to have gone off-course, they tried to steer them back in particular directions. 'Somebody should talk more about land,' they could he heard saying. 'Get some old residents to talk about how it used to be here and how the village has changed,' or 'Get one of the women workers to talk about how they can't go to the bathroom.'

Underpinning the management of the process was a concern to produce similar or comparable knowledge about the impact of SEZs. By working to ensure that the same issues were raised again and again activists worked to build continuity across diverse places, contexts and communities. One implication was that the testimonials and public hearings began to follow a kind of template or script, making it possible to predict in advance what kinds of concerns and issues would be raised, and meaning that the issues that emerged from the social audit became virtually identical from place to place. The implications of managing the process in this way were that it established parameters for the discussion, circumscribing the kinds of information about place, relationships or impact that were collected. Loaded questions like, 'How many people here were dependent on agriculture before the SEZ?' left little scope to ask, for example, how people might have spent their compensation money or how the coming of a zone might have transformed caste relationships in an area.

As the depositions were brought to a close, panellists often bade goodbye to the gathering with statements of support and rabble-rousing speeches. 'Your opposition is mirrored across India!' Or 'These are the rights that have been given to you by the constitution so you have to fight for your rights.' At one meeting I listened as a panellist closed the deposition with a speech that evoked figures from Hindu mythology. 'Just like women prepare rice – tipping it forwards and backwards to pick out stones and grit – we need to remove the evils from government,' he said:

> It will take time but we should not give up in spite of the barriers. We cannot simply sit and wait for the government. We must raise our voices. We cannot wait for Rama, Krishna or even Lord Vishnu. We have to take care of things ourselves. We have to fight for our rights. If we start now we can make the future.

At the very end the organisers shouted slogans in Telugu or Hindi and led the audience in a chant, 'We will fight, We will win!' or 'Victory will be ours!'

In the aftermath of each deposition a process of interpretation took place as panellists worked to translate specific experiences into abstract recommendations or generalisable points that spoke to what they saw as the broader issues. In doing so they filtered, categorised and synthesised the public testimonies. Panellists shared information – 'What did he say?', 'What was his name?', 'How do you spell it?' – and read back over their notes, picking out key issues and observations, before passing a summary document up to the state-level committee.

On their visits to SEZs across South India participants in the social audit process frequently demonstrated a nuanced and sophisticated understanding of place. As they travelled by bus or by train across Tamil Nadu and Andhra Pradesh participants discussed the ways that India's rural and urban economies are tightly interwoven, or how the continued viability of agricultural livelihoods depends on a complex mixed economy and the household contributions of non-agricultural labour, or the man-made causes of declining agricultural fortunes as state governments fail to promote or invest in irrigation. Meanwhile people talked about the sociological nuances of caste, political affiliation and land ownership, and the complex desires and aspirations that people project onto SEZs as new sites of employment. They debated, for example, why people might choose to testify that they had never seen formal government notification of planned land acquisition when, in fact, they had been served notice of government plans but, in acts of everyday resistance, had refused to accept them.

Yet such nuanced conversation and reflection was frequently lost or erased in the ritual performance of audit. On location, panellists and activists often appeared hesitant or reluctant to probe these complex issues, wary of upsetting villagers or of appearing to interrogate them publicly, and anxious not to derail a collective politics of opposition or to undermine their own commitment to a wider public struggle. The questions that they asked in public and the information that they recorded often failed to address the complex social and material politics that activists discussed in private and meant that particular kinds of representations emerged. 'When I first came here with my urban activist thinking I looked at all these things differently,' one participant in the audit of SEZs told me, at the end of a long day hearing public depositions:

> I thought, people don't want to leave their land but after coming here again and again and interacting with people I came to see that it is much more complicated than that, I came to see that you can never generalise about land. It's not that they don't want to ever sell their land. It's just that they don't want to sell it now or they want to increase how much money they get for it and they don't have the bargaining power or machinery to negotiate with. But, of course, these things can't come out in a process like this.

Spaces of Hope

The People's Audit of SEZs culminated in 2010 with a national tribunal in Delhi that recommended India's SEZ Act be immediately repealed, all pending applications for SEZs be scrapped, a major review launched into all currently approved zones, the repatriation of all communities displaced by the construction of zones, and a full investigation into allegations of corruption and malpractice. Today, social activists claim this as a success, pointing to subsequent changes in the policy framework governing zones or to a slowdown in the proliferation of these enclave spaces. Yet we might also ask to what extent these recommendations had been determined in advance. To what extent they were prefigured by the form and content of the audit as a technology of political reason? And how might the outcomes have been different if Indian 'society' had been imagined as a site of illiberal and hierarchical relations rather than a site of resistance to state and capital?

Just as spaces, concepts and ideas associated with neoliberal capitalism have 'served as sources of hope' for planners and politicians (Miyazaki 2006), so too the spaces, concepts and ideas associated with critiques of neoliberal capitalism have been beacons of hope for activists. As I have sought to show throughout this book, India's SEZs have been produced as spaces of hope in this dual sense, becoming spaces in which hope in capitalism and hope in the critiques of capitalism overlap. In and around India's SEZs, we might say, hope is a capitalist and oppositional mode of anticipation that unites both the search for smoother spaces for capital and the search for alternatives to capitalism (Miyazaki 2006).

Left critics of India's contemporary political economy have been motivated not just by the anticipation of dystopian futures in which the violence of dispossession and the precariousness of labour is intensified, but also by the anticipation of utopian futures that are better than the present; futures in which other worlds are possible (Jameson 2005). The rejection of the SEZ as a model for development is also a question about alternatives, and campaigners have worked to bolster opposition by prompting policy debate about what a comprehensive land use policy might be or what a sustainable employment policy might look like, as well as by demanding the repeal of the SEZ Act. Yet it is important to remember that this anticipatory project remains committed to the capture or reform of the state, and to the idea of the state as an entity that can alter and transform outcomes. It is a politics that operates by presenting the state in India as a mask that conceals real power relations, interests and political practices behind the guise of public interest and, by so doing, makes the presence and possibility of a progressive state even more powerful (Hansen and Stepputat 2001).

Like other recent works of anthropology (e.g. Shah 2010) the ethnographic descriptions and analyses in this book sit uneasily with the premises and strategic representations from which many social activists on the Indian left draw energy. For some activists the only legitimate rationale for or value of 'social scientific research' is if it produces evidence, information or data that can be used, 'operationalised' or harnessed to campaign agendas (Kaur 2013). This is an argument over the utility of research and what it means to be politically engaged. In the debates over India's SEZs, for example, anti-SEZ campaigners have positioned themselves as marshals, carefully patrolling and monitoring the parameters of appropriate critical engagement.

Over the course of the research on which this book is based I have occasionally been on the receiving end of hostility, rigidity and dogmatism from India's anti-SEZ activists. 'If foreign researchers want to come here on fact-finding missions that's great,' I was once told by a young women activist involved in the campaign against SEZs. 'But we're here to build the resistance. We know what the facts are, we know what we believe in.' On another occasion, during a research interview with activists in an upper middle-class Delhi housing colony, a young Tamil-Brahmin man with a postgraduate degree in social science from a UK university challenged my integrity, 'Just explain, are you for zones or against them?', before adding, 'We don't trust anybody who doesn't belong to a mass-based movement.'

As I have explored in this chapter the oppositional narratives and practices of anti-SEZ campaigners frequently 'sanitise' (Ortner 1995) struggles over land and labour of their caste, class and gender politics, establishing a narrow definition of what constitutes political action and occluding the ordinary or everyday ways in which diverse communities of people living around these projects seek to make demands upon the state and upon each other as they navigate into insecure futures. In their strategic and tactical response to issues of forced displacement and resettlement around SEZs, for example, social activists excluded questions about the caste politics of land and the gender politics of employment. Instead the demands for transparency and accountability made by anti-SEZ campaigners emerged out of a particular set of ideas about what constitutes democratic action and mapped onto the occupation of India's public sphere by India's middle-class constituencies. As a result the audit process operationalised particular kinds of values – openness, transparency, and reason – that are tightly enmeshed in the country's elite politics. As contemporary observers of Indian politics in the post-liberalisation era have noted, the galvanisation of the middle classes around political problems – from corruption (Webb 2010, 2012) to the environment (Mawdsley 2004) – sees certain forms of protest celebrated as the 'voice of the people' while unpalatable voices are silenced.

7

Anticipation, Capitalism, Anthropology

On the coast of Andhra Pradesh, South India, a retired *Indian Express* journalist reflects on the local impact of the region's special economic zones. 'Visakhapatnam, a fishing village of yesterday and Steel-Industrial-Port city of today,' he writes, 'is all set to transform itself into the gigantic Industrial-Marine-Trade-Tourism-Mega-City of tomorrow.'

At a meeting in a rural market town a low-ranking state bureaucrat announces the compulsory acquisition of 10,000 acres of land for a special economic zone, promising financial compensation and jobs to all those who will be displaced. As plans for the zone inflate local land prices, a government secondary school teacher contemplates his next real estate purchase, calculating how to make the best deal by buying up plots of land when the price is low and selling them on when the price is high.

In one of South India's oldest manufacturing enclaves the general manager of an Anglo-Belgium diamond manufacturing company sits behind a computer screen and draws up plans for the creation of a world-class factory. His vision involves a complex reorganisation of factory space that will stamp a universal template for hyper-efficient manufacturing onto this outpost of the global economy. In the next-door office a human resources expert puts a team of Indian graduate students through a series of tests and exercises, telling them that they can become management revolutionaries.

In a dusty machine section two unmarried young men cut and polish rough fragments of carbon into round diamonds that will eventually be embedded in rings or watches or belts for Japanese or North American consumers. They discuss how to spend what remains of their monthly wage packet, after giving money to their parents, paying for rent, buying food, and putting some money aside for the future when they become grooms and fathers. How to spend it? A mobile phone? A jacket? A shirt? A watch? A belt? A knife?

On the stage of the World Social Forum in Mumbai an ageing Indian trade unionist imagines a pan-Indian surge of opposition to labour conditions in the country's industrial economy coalescing into a new kind of political organisation. Six years later on a bus travelling from zone to zone across South India a group of Indian political activists learn the refrain to a Bengali folk song, 'Don't sell your dreams'. At a rally in north coastal Andhra Pradesh a young social scientist and activist tells a group of farmers that their opposition is mirrored across India, and she leads their chant, 'SEZs? I say no!'

On an English-language blog dedicated to radical thought and politics a group of journalists, filmmakers, and scholars based in Delhi, Pune and New York upload a text about the political economy of India's special economic zones, referencing Marx and Baudrillard they construct a contemporary dystopia. 'The euphoria of chaos, the ecstasy of anarchy, living for a short while and for a fast buck,' it reads.

> This craveness [sic] for speed is what special economic zones offer ... Capital leads human and every relationship generating from humans into a simulacrum of no-tomorrow! Capital is the only tomorrow! Here speed is the Mantra – the faster you can fly befooling the producers the smarter you are!

*   *   *

In this book I have attempted to bring the diverse dreams that converge on India's large-scale infrastructure projects into the same analytic frame without attempting to derive from them a single logic, rationality or coherence. As I have set out to show, it is in the pursuit of conflicting and contradictory dreams that people produce the relationships and meanings that make these spaces of global capital. The politics of land and labour that shape India's SEZs are made in an economy of anticipation, as diverse ways of knowing about, imagining and living towards the future bring different kinds of people into conflict and into alignment. Rather than attempt to evaluate the successes and failures of India's SEZs by subjecting the claims that are made for them to empirical scrutiny this book has asked what it means to think of them as generative social and cultural spaces. Just as attempts to realise dreams and desires produce the relations of power that define our contemporary historical moment so too they bring new futures for capital and human subjects into being (Tsing 2005; Tsing and Pollman 2005).

Over the past 30 years critical engagements with the world's economic enclaves have remained remarkably stable, approaching them as unique sites of market-oriented calculations or rationality. Yet zones are also deeply affective spaces that depend upon the elicitation of speculative passions for their success. In order for land to be successfully acquired for a zone requires not just that people be forcibly dispossessed of it but also that they agree to exchange the futures invested in fields and homes for other, less known futures. In order for a zone to attract flows of capital it must inspire the sentiment of potential investors, inducing feelings of confidence and optimism in the prospects for short-term personal or corporate gain. Meanwhile, it is a fallacy to imagine that capitalist work regimes in these locations are founded only on brutal forms of domination. Today's factory managers, for example, must be able to incite the emotions of workers as much as their interests; work is both instrumental and affective. Employers seek to harness worker sentiments, appealing to collective feelings of patriotic, filial and religious duty, by referencing kinship, nation and God, and appealing to social and material desires. Large-scale infrastructure projects like India's SEZs are not just a product of dreams and schemes for the future – they also mediate them, and the zone is a place through which people come to know themselves afresh, a place that produces fear and anxiety, hope and desire.

India's economic enclaves may have acted as a pivot between specific regions and global flows, creating new arenas of non-state power and profit-making, but in this book I have asked that we challenge our accounts of these spaces as cohesive economic and political projects, as complete, finished and predictable, let alone as coherent and knowable. India's zones, I propose, are better understood as building sites, works-in-progress that are constantly under construction. Like all spaces they are constantly being made and remade through the speculative interventions and investments of planners, real estate speculators, capitalists, managers, employees and activists. Rather than see this array of speculative investments in the zone as ontologically or epistemologically distinct this book has set out to tie them together. Inside India's enclaves the schemes and dreams of transnational corporations are caught in what Anna Tsing (2005) has called the sticky grip or friction of worldly encounter, rubbing up against the expectations of regional politicians, local landowners, managers, labourers and activists. Instead of presuming to know the outcome of these encounters, this book has shown how zones can be unpredictable and generative spaces. At times the convergence of dreams in and around India's zones can make their operation more powerful and affective, at times these dreams collide in ways that disrupt their smooth operation.

Just as the history of these spaces is being written and rewritten, their futures are entirely unknowable. Zones can flourish, be expanded and renovated, and they can lie vacant and empty. The value of their real estate can rise and fall. They can succeed or struggle to attract the interests of investors. Just as their significance can be amplified so too can it diminish. Zones do not always work. There are gaps or contradictions between the hopes and desires that are invested in these spaces and their material outcomes. But these unmet dreams and expectations are the generative grounds from which anticipated and actual futures arise.

By the end of the 2000s the rampant proliferation of SEZ projects in India had slowed. Activists who campaigned for a review of government policies on industrialisation claim this as a success for a nationwide anti-SEZ movement, pointing to changes in the law governing land acquisition (which no longer allow states to compulsorily acquire land for private parties) and to changes in the tax regime for businesses located inside zones. It is worth noting, however, that these challenges to India's SEZ model from social and political activists reached a climax at the same moment as the effects of the 2008 global financial crisis began to be felt around the world, and as real estate and property developers struggled to finance new projects.

Indeed far from representing an obsolete or redundant model economic zones continue to proliferate. Whether they make economic sense or not they remain spaces onto which diverse dreams and schemes can be projected (Bach 2011). The planning and policy framework for India's SEZs, for example, now circulates as a model for other countries in the region. On India's north-eastern border, for example, in landlocked Nepal, a team from the International Financial Corporation (IFC) has been advising a fragile government on ways to institute a recovery from almost two decades of civil war. Economic zones are central to its recommendations. Since 2008 the World Bank's IFC team has been encouraging the development of special economic zones here as 'platforms' for piloting economic reform and encouraging private sector investment just as they once did in India.

In India too SEZs remain integral to social and economic planning, and SEZ projects have been incorporated into new programmes of industrialisation. In Andhra Pradesh the state government continues to present SEZs as engines of industrial growth and vehicles of social mobility, policy makers continue to present zones as 'trailblazers' that 'illustrate the employment benefits of less costly regulation' and development economists continue to conclude that SEZ employment can have a positive effect on human development indicators, make significant improvements in living conditions, and ensure better prospects for the education of their children.

Meanwhile, India's central government continues to encourage investment in existing SEZ projects, by offering tax exemptions to companies under new kinds of incentive schemes targeted at particular manufacturing sectors and by incorporating SEZs into new, long-term plans for industrialisation. Under a national programme to promote the use of renewable energy, for example, India's central government has incorporated SEZs into a wide range of tax incentives for the manufacturers of solar photovoltaic technology.

In 2013, as falling rates of growth and a devalued rupee saw triumphalist narratives of India's booming economy fade, large-scale infrastructure development projects remerged as dream projects capable of reviving the Indian growth story. Pro-business lobbyists pressed for the rapid implementation of a new manufacturing policy, and the creation of a new generation of national manufacturing and investment zones, once again arguing that India's 'infrastructural bottlenecks', 'cumbersome procedures' and 'inflexible labour legislation' continued to hold back growth, keeping the nation too slow to meet the needs of globally competitive business and preventing India's manufacturing sector from 'joining the race'. Some of these new visions for the future are being materialised by the government of India's policy for Petroleum, Chemical and Petrochemical Investment Regions (PCPIRs), a new generation of 'investment-friendly' spaces for exporters, that dramatically scale up the kinds of governance regimes once envisaged for SEZs. At the end of the 2000s, for example, a master plan for the development of north coastal Andhra Pradesh imagined the creation of an industrial 'coastal corridor'. These proposals incorporated the SEZs that had been built around Visakhapatnam city over the past decade into a massive new petro-chemical region, stretching over some 149,000 acres.

As I have sought to show in this book, the failure of large-scale infrastructure projects like India's economic zones to realise the expectations and promises invested in them does not only produce disenchantment and discontent. On the contrary, as James Ferguson (1999: 14) wrote, dreamed-of and desired futures continue to shape engagements with the present even when they remain unrealised.[1] Indeed, we might argue that the challenge for critical social science is not that people cease to believe in the ideas and promises of the market, development, or industrial modernity. Rather it is that people continue to believe in or have faith in these dreams, even when their fulfilment is perpetually deferred, and when their power, claims and effects are no longer entirely convincing.[2] Failure is to modernity, we might conclude, what crisis is to capitalism: the force through which dreams and desires for the future are renewed.

Notes

1   The Economy of Anticipation

1. In the early 1990s economic reforms granted India's state governments increased autonomy over economic development policies. Confident of its political control over the state West Bengal's communist leadership looked to emulate a Chinese model of state-controlled capitalism and rapid industrialisation (Bag 2011; Vanaik 2011).

2. The events in Nandigram prompted visits from numerous Indian journalists, some of whom explored the legacy of past industrial development projects. See, for example, Bhattacharya (2007) and Dutta (2011).

3. Anthropologists are increasingly alert to the material and social afterlife of institutions, structures and sensibilities – and to the way that ruination weighs on the future and shapes the present. See for example, Stoler (2008: 194, 2013), Street (2012), Navaro-Yashin (2009).

4. The precise relationship between these parties and their involvement in the events at Nandigram is a matter of considerable debate, see for example, in the commentaries by Palit and Bhattacharjee (2008), Sarkar and Chowdhury (2009), McConnochie (2012).

5. West Bengal's main opposition parties include the Trinamool Congress, the Socialist Unity Centre of India (SUCI), Jamiat Ulema-e-Hind and Indian National Congress.

6. For committed Marxist analyses of India's special economic zone projects, which locate them within an overarching logic of accumulation, see for example Levien (2011, 2012), Sarkar and Chowdhury (2009), Banerjee-Guha (2008), Sampat (2010).

7. For a more detailed exposition of the term 'accumulation by dispossession' and its intellectual genealogy see, for example, Ramachandraiah and Srinivasan (2011), Harvey (2003), Bidwai (2006), Zoomers (2010), Levien (2012), Corbridge et al. (2012: 206), Gardner (2012: 14).

8. This is to take seriously a non-representational theory of space, to approach capitalist zones and enclaves as spaces that are constantly in the process of being constructed rather than 'inert containers of action' (Hetherington 1997; Massey 2005; Thrift 1996).

9. The 'dream' occupies a pivotal place in a twentieth-century tradition of Marxist cultural theory, particular the work of Walter Benjamin and the Frankfurt School (Benjamin 1969; Buck-Morss 1995; Gilloch 2013; Williams 1982). For Benjamin the legacy of industrial capitalism was a 'dreamworld' in which our collective human consciousness had become increasingly

subject to the domination and delusions of the material world, and in which commodities, machines, inanimate things and the built environment disguise real human aspirations and desires. In this book I borrow the language of dream and nightmare from Susan Buck-Morss (2002), who used it to describe the construction and collapse of mass utopias in the twentieth century. For Buck-Morss the 'dreamworlds' of capitalist modernity were those large-scale projects of social and economic transformation that express a desire for arrangements that transcend existing forms.

10. As Bruno Latour puts it, outlining the contours of an actor-network theory that is rooted in the sociology of Gabriel Tarde: 'a dream … [can have] the same qualities as a political idea, or a mathematical formula, a piece of poetry or an industrial good: they are all social productions and "quanta of change" that have lives of their own' (Latour 2005: 15).

11. For Latour (1993: 125–6) these totalities help to foster a sense of exceptionality; of an era that remains separate, distinct and unique, definitively cut off from the past.

12. In institutions of incarceration (Taussig 2004) and education (Bénéï 2001), science (Redfield 2000) and biomedicine (Street 2012), and in sites of urban planning (Holston 1989) and sites of rural development (Li 2007), the pursuit of a future that is better than the past has been inscribed on spaces, bodies and persons.

13. For Graeber debt is a temporal relationship in which the future is an obligation to pay. Global financial markets make this future obligation into something that can be bought and sold. Yet just as people can bet on the future rise or fall in the price of stocks, shares, currencies and commodities so too they can trade in the probability of future payments. It was the complex trade in obligations to make future debt repayments that spread the risk of credit defaults in the US sub-prime mortgage market and precipitated the 2008 global financial crisis (see also Zaloom 2007, 2008).

14. For recent writing on modes of prediction, calculation and prophecy in anthropology see da Col (2012), da Col and Humphrey (2012), and Anderson and Fenton (2009). Riles and Reed (2006) and Mosse (2005) both explore the anticipatory power of documents, while Zaloom (2007) is focused on charts and models. The work of economic sociologists MacKenzie (2007) and Callon et al. (2007) draws on actor network theory to explore how ways of knowing the future construct economic markets, while geographers like Castree (2009: 47) remain firmly committed to the implications for political economy.

15. This anthropology of imagination has become most clearly formulated in the work of Moore (2013) and Appadurai (1996).

16. For many anthropologists the contours of this affective economy are inspired by Massumi's (1995) conceptual writings, and elaborated ethnographically

in work by Yanagisako (2002: 11) and Mole (2008, 2012) on Italy and Rofel (2007: 7) on China.

17. This interplay of reason and affect has also proven important for anthropologists writing about the virtual frontiers of capitalism, at sites of financial trading in London or New York (e.g. Ahmed 2004; Richard and Rudnyckyj 2009).

18. For ethnographic writing that engages with the centrality of de-industrialisation to contemporary economic processes see, for example, Ferguson (1999), Burawoy et al. (2000) and Mollona (2009).

19. While old industrial towns like Kanpur in Uttar Pradesh (Joshi 2003) and Ahmedabad in Gujarat (Breman 2004) saw rapid deindustrialisation during the 1990s, emerging centres of informal manufacturing like the knitware capital Tirrupur in Tamil Nadu (Chari 2004; de Neve 2005) or the slums of Dharavi in Mumbai (Norris 2010) were incorporated into the global economy as new sites of production and accumulation.

20. The same is true of struggles over urban resettlement and gentrification (Baviskar 2003; Ghertner 2010).

21. In this grand view regional investments in transportation and communication networks, as well as national trade agreements and legal treaties are part of a wider trend aimed at reducing or reconfiguring all spatial, temporal and cultural barriers to the movement, circulation and exchange of money (Bach 2011; Harvey 2005; Hilgers 2012).

22. From state spaces that were planned, built and operated by states and governments, economic zones have also become sites of non-state activity. Where in the 1980s only some 25 per cent of the world's economic zones were privately owned and operated, by the mid 2000s this had risen to 62 per cent (see Arnold 2012; Farole and Akinci 2011).

23. The proliferation of economic zones has given rise to a wide body of literature on the changing role of women in a global labour force (Mills 2003; Nash and Fernandez-Kelly 1983; Ong 1987, 2004, 2006; Salzinger 2003; Wright 2003) and on the regimes under which they work (Cross 2010; Palan 2003, Roy 2009; Tsing 2009) which will be addressed more fully in chapters 4–6.

24. Harvey traced the ramifications of this speed-up through diverse fields of culture and politics. The drive for efficiency and flexibility in industrial production and a shortening of time horizons for decision making in international financial markets, he argued, were mirrored in an increasingly rapid change in lifestyle fashions, as well as in aesthetic shifts taking place in literature and the arts.

25. For Ong (2006), when governments establish economic zones they make a departure from generalised political norms and the rule of law in order to create market-oriented spaces of political exception. Under conditions of neoliberalism, she argues, states make positive exceptions from the rule of law – creating new territories with extraordinary political benefits or economic

gains and setting aside some citizens for special privileges, new opportunities and forms of pastoral care that foster market-oriented values (Ong 2006: 5). But, Ong argues, states also make negative exceptions in ways intended to exclude spaces and subjects from market-driven calculations, neoliberal governance regimes, and juridical-legal protections. The application of the negative exception can see the suspension of legal, civil or constitutional rights for specific regions or groups of people, effectively 'fragmenting citizenship' and attaching 'different values to different categories of person' (2006: 101).

26. The history of India's economic liberalisation has been extensively documented (e.g. Gupta 2012). The 1991 budget was preceded by a balance of payments and foreign exchange crisis. Dominant analyses of the crisis place the blame on public spending in the 1980s, as well as the disintegration of the Soviet Union leading to a collapse in overseas markets for Indian-made goods, and the fallout from the first US-led invasion of Iraq, which led to an increase in oil prices and a fall in remittances from Indians working in the Gulf.

27. The 1990s were also marked by shifts in political power in India. The Indian Congress Party, which had ruled India since independence, lost control over central government as the right-wing Hindu Nationalist Bharatya Janata Party and regional lower-caste political parties emerged as important players in a new era of national coalition politics. These changes were accompanied by sectarian violence that marked a symbolic end to an era of secular nationalism.

28. In our time, Guyer has argued, the 'distant future' has gained social, cultural and political traction – that corresponds to the importance of the 'long-run' in the macro-economic and monetary theories that we have come to refer to in shorthand as neoliberal. The ideological parameters or norms within which people have come to imagine, envisage or anticipate the future today, she argues, place a renewed value on long-term, or distant time horizons.

2   The Vision of Growth

1. What is now Visakhapatnam has been a significant maritime base for global trade since the seventeenth century, when the Coromandel coast provided important harbours and trading stations for the Dutch and British East India companies. The natural harbour around which the city is built gained prominence in the eighteenth and nineteenth century under the British colonial administration and maritime industry has been central to the city's twentieth-century growth.

2. This will remain only a fractional 3 per cent of the 75 million people expected to populate Andhra Pradesh by 2021.

3. Indeed India's steel towns provided a model for the construction of new economic enclaves that those involving in drawing up new legislation for the organisation of zones drew on directly.

4. In 1957, under its second five-year plan, the government of India embarked on the construction of several industrial townships to house workers in the nation's new steel plants.

5. As required by the Minimum Wages Act (1948), Section 13, 'Fixing hours for a normal day'.

6. As required by the Minimum Wages Act (1948), Section 18, 'Maintenance of registers and records'.

7. As required by the Industrial Employment (Standing Orders) Act, 1946.

8. This funding was provided via the Indian Council for Research on International Economic Relations (ICRIER).

9. For examples of life cycle modelling with respect to economic zones in India and elsewhere, see Schrank (2001) and Omar and Stoever (2008).

10. In 1993–4 this stood as approximately Rs 9955.83 crore. Five years later in 1997–8 this debt had more than doubled to Rs 20,430.28 crore and just under a fifth of all public expenditure (16.78 per cent) went towards servicing its debt.

11. Writing against the social realism and positivism of political anthropology, Begoña Aretxaga stressed 'the centrality of fantasy to the political'. Her challenge to social realist portraits was to illuminate the phantasmatic aspect or fictional reality of politics, to see fantasy 'as an essential drive in the shaping of politics' (Aretxaga 2005: 202 in Navaro-Yashin 2007b: 80–94; see also Navaro-Yashin 2007a).

12. To many political commentators Rajshekhara Reddy proved more efficient and aggressive at marshalling the institutional mechanisms and cultures of politics that the Chandrababu Naidu had introduced. Midway into its first term in office the Reddy government issued a new policy document, 'Doing business with Andhra Pradesh', advertising to investors the government's continued commitment to facilitating investments and to building the infrastructure for business through public–private partnerships.

13. The process has been variously described as a 'national real estate scam in the making' (Chakraverti 2006) and 'the biggest land grab movement in the history of modern India' (Sumit Sarkar quoted in Sridhar 2006a).

3   The Land of Speculation

1. In 2008, for example, a group of landowners in Anantapur district, further south along the Andhra Pradesh coastline, won a High Court order rejecting the planned acquisition of land for a high-tech IT-SEZ. The success of their case hinged on claims about the area's biodiversity and the annual migration

of a bird, the Siberian Painted Stork, to the area. The farmers had enlisted local conservation societies and, eventually, the World Wildlife Federation to support their opposition. Yet a closer examination of the case by a Hyderabad-based researcher and social activist (Seethalakshmi 2009) found that these claims about the environmental impact of the zone in fact concealed the famers' illegal occupation of land that they had no legal right to. The farmers in question were Reddys, the dominant landowning caste. Their land holdings far exceeded a legal ceiling on land ownership in the state. Indeed, much of the land under their control had been formerly 'assigned' to Dalit communities in the land reforms. Over time, however, these more powerful farmers had either evicted, forcibly purchased or encroached upon their land and repossessed it, a fact that plans for the SEZ risked bringing to light.

2. Under India's Land Acquisition Act, the acquisition of land for public purpose requires that owners be compensated at a market rate. The value is usually set at the district level by administrators and politicians but, as Michael Levien (2011) has written, these groups often seek to keep compensation below the market rate in order to minimize taxes on land transactions.

3. Just over 80 per cent of this area is used for agriculture. Only 7 per cent of land in Atchutapuram and Rambilli was recorded as 'uncultivable' and only 12.7 per cent as used for non-agricultural purposes.

4. In 2012, for example, the Velama landowner and Congress MLA Kannababu became the subject of a probe by the Anti-Corruption Bureau, the Central Bureau of Investigations and the Income Tax Department following allegations that he illegally acquired property around the APSEZ.

5. He joined a new political party, the Prajya Rrajam Party, launched by the Telugu cinema star Chiranjevi, and in 2009 was elected as one of the party's representatives to the Mandal Parishad Territorial Committee for a five-year term.

6. Of course, even two years after the first families were resettled, many plots remained vacant. Stories abounded of wealthy farming families who – though entitled to a plot in the new colony – had used their compensation money to move out of the area altogether, or of families who remained in limbo, their compensation payments delayed by disputes with siblings or government officials and who had not yet begun to construct new homes for themselves.

4   The Factory of the Future

1. A year later LID had closed all operations in Israel and opened its new headquarters in Visakhapatnam. The move primarily enabled the company to cut out the financial costs of transporting goods through Israel *en route* to their markets in the United States.

2. An image of this scene taken by a local photographer for a booklet designed to advertise the company, unwittingly captured this sign. In a move that was characteristic of the concerns for corporate appearances that extended across all aspects of the factory's production, when the photograph was eventually noticed by managers it was altered for inclusion in the brochure and the notice-board was digitally erased.

3. As in, for example, A.H. Maslow's (1943) hierarchy of needs.

4. This is what Holmes and Marcus (2005) have called 'para-ethnographic' knowledge.

5. As John Law (1994) has written, modernity consists in ordering rather than order.

6. Factory comes from the Venetian word *feitoria*, and was first used by the Venetians and then by the Portuguese in Goa to mean the places where agents reside and do business (see Ghosh 2011: 172).

7. This is what Michael Burawoy (1985) called hegemonic despotism.

8. On the mechanics of control in the post-Fordist industrial workplace see: Jenkins (1994), Miller and Rose (1995), Rose (1989), du Gay, (2010: 660), Bahnisch (2000: 61).

9. For a discussion of the industrial panopticon and the nature of visibility and control in the modern workplace see Sewell and Wilkinson (1992), Jenkins (1994), Thompson and Ackroyd (1995), Webster and Robins (1993).

10. On the production and management of affect see: Thrift (2007) and Navaro-Yashin (2009).

5   *The Labour of Aspiration*

1. These suspect politics surface in accounts of the generational politics between communities of farmers who seek to defend their land against India's SEZs and their young sons who can be bought off with petty sums of money, liquor and promises of 'urban excitement' (Srivastava and Kothari 2012: 5–6). They can also be discerned in the distinction between the consumption practices of India's new middle classes and its new industrial workers: the haves enjoy a carnival of consumption that rests on the bloodied shoulders of the have-nots, maltreated, over-exploited workers (Srivastava and Kothari 2012: 115). In these accounts the hopes and dreams of radical social and political transformation rest on the possibility of political subjectivities that lie outside of capitalism; perspectives or vantage points that are used to bring authenticity and legitimacy to critique.

2. As Jeffrey (2008, 2010) has written, in some contexts they appear in common cause with the poor or the disenfranchised, as they struggle against the state or entrenched social interests in pursuit of equality and social justice, but in other contexts, such as anti-Muslim pogroms in India's cities, their

actions appear aimed at securing narrowly defined communal advantage and interests.

3. In their essay on 'anticipation' Adams et al. (2009) present liberalism as a political project that registers in the normative values and ideas that constitute society's designs for persons, relationships and ways of living in the future, as well as the forms of conduct that people come to expect of themselves in the present (see also Rose (1999).

4. Ethnographic writing on the role of education in projects of upward social mobility in India includes Bear (2005), Fuller and Narasimhan (2006), Jeffrey et al. (2004, 2008), Chopra and Jeffery (2004), Gardner and Osella (2003), Klenk (2003), Osella and Osella (2000b).

5. Embedded in these institutions were postcolonial associations between gender, technology, nationalism and progress. Outside Visakhapatnam's largest state-run ITI, for example, a large signboard is emblazoned with images of a spanner, a hammer, a cog and a bolt of electricity alongside the slogan, 'Building the youth, building the nation'.

6. At the bottom end of the factory's wage scale in 2005 was the trainee who earned around 60 rupees (US$1.48) a day, a wage comparable to that of day labourers in Visakhapatnam's construction industry. At the top end was a senior diamond polisher whose earnings might average around 150 rupees (US$3.70) per day, comparable to day wages as a restaurant waiter. Since the factory opened in 1997, the wages of labourers had risen with inflation, but managers had introduced piece-rate systems, incentive schemes and production targets that were designed to extract ever-greater value from workers' labour.

7. See, for example, the work of Mains (2007), Argenti (2007), Osella and Osella (2006).

8. Christian Strümpell (2008) makes similar observations in the small power plant in nearby southern Orissa where he conducted fieldwork.

9. Across South Asia consumption has emerged as a key cultural practice through or against which the region's 'new middle classes' have come to be defined (e.g. Liechty 2003) and many accounts of India's post-liberalisation transformation valorise consumption as a social or economic force.

6 The Struggles for Tomorrow

1. As ethnographies of gender, work and labour attest (e.g. Salzinger 2000; Wright 2003) this language often jars with the ways that women may choose to represent their own experiences of work and labour at these sites in the zones. In Sri Lanka, for example – as at other sites where young women are incorporated into a global labour force – the workplace can also be experienced

as a transgressive space, a space of relative freedoms and liberations from the outside world.

2. Like many other parts of India north coastal Andhra Pradesh has a diverse and vibrant culture of social and political activism. Around Visakhapatnam city, for example, statues of Alluri Sita Rama Raju sit alongside Potti Sreeramulu, commemorating the region's anti-colonial struggle against the British as well as its post-independence struggle for Telugu state-hood (see chapter 2). In 1968 north coastal Andhra Pradesh gained notoriety as a hub for left-wing radicalism when Maoist activists – inspired by a peasant uprising in Naxalbari, West Bengal – declared some 500 square km of Srikakulum district to be under 'red rule', securing the area for several months before being put down by the police and armed forces.

7   *Anticipation, Capitalism, Anthropology*

1. In India, for example, we might think of the ways that unemployed young men (Jeffrey 2010), marginalised and criminalised castes (Pandian 2009) or labour migrants (Osella and Osella 2000a) respond to the failures of modernisation and development not by calling into question the premises or desirability of progress but by holding more closely to its idea and future prospects.

2. In Slavoj Žižek's (2010) critical or materialist psychoanalysis it is precisely this impossibility of satiating subconscious desire that defines the lived experience under contemporary capitalism.

Bibliography

Abram, Simone and Gisa Weszkalnys. 2011. 'Introduction: Anthropologies of Planning – Temporality, Imagination, and Ethnography.' *Focaal* 61: 3–18.

—— 2013. *Elusive Promises: Planning in the Contemporary World*. Oxford: Berghahn.

Ackerman, John. 2004. 'Co-governance for Accountability: Beyond "Exit" and "Voice".' *World Development* 32(3): 447–63.

Adams, Vincanne, Michelle Murphy and Adele E. Clarke. 2009. 'Anticipation: Technoscience, Life, Affect, Temporality.' *Subjectivity* 28(1): 246–65.

Aggarwal, Aradhna. 2012. *Social and Economic Impact of SEZs in India*. New Delhi: Oxford University Press.

Agrawal, Arun and Kalyanakrishnan Sivaramakrishnan. 2000. *Agrarian Environments: Resources, Representations, and Rule in India*. Durham, NC: Duke University Press.

Ahmed, S. 2004. 'Affective Economies.' *Social Text* 22: 117–39.

Alexander, P.C. 1963. *Industrial Estates in India*. New Delhi: Asia Publishing House.

Almor, Ya'akov. 2004. 'Israel Diary', *Solitaire: The International Gem and Jewelry Magazine* December.

Amin, Ash (ed.) 1994. *Post Fordism: A Reader*. London: Blackwell.

Amis, Philip and Sashi Kumar. 2000. 'Urban Economic Growth, Infrastructure and Poverty in India: Lessons from Visakhapatnam.' *Environment and Urbanization* 12(1): 185–96.

Anand, Nikhil. 2011. 'PRESSURE: The PoliTechnics of Water Supply in Mumbai.' *Cultural Anthropology* 26(4): 542–64.

Anderson, Ben and Jill Fenton. 2009. 'Spaces of Hope.' *Space and Culture* 11(2): 76–80.

Appadurai, Arjun. 1996. *Modernity at Large: Cultural Dimensions of Globalisation*. Cambridge: Cambridge University Press.

—— 2008. 'The Capacity to Aspire: Culture and the Terms of Recognition.' In *Cultural Politics in a Global Age*, edited by David Held and Henrietta L. Moore, pp. 29–35. London: Oneworld.

—— 2013. *The Future as Cultural Fact: Essays on the Global Condition*. London: Verso.

Aretxega, Begoña. 2003. 'Maddening States.' *Annual Review of Anthropology* 32(1): 393–410.

Argenti, Nicolas. 2007. *The Intestines of the State: Youth, Violence, and Belated Histories in the Cameroon Grassfields*. London: University of Chicago Press.

Arnold, Dennis. 2012. 'Spatial Practices and Border SEZs in Mekong Southeast Asia.' *Geography Compass* 6(12): 740–51.

Bach, Jonathan. 2011. 'Modernity and the Urban Imagination in Economic Zones.' *Theory, Culture & Society* 28(5): 98–122.

Bag, Kheya. 2011. 'Red Bengal's Rise and Fall.' *New Left Review* 70.

Bahnisch, Mark. 2000. 'Embodied Work, Divided Labour: Subjectivity and the Scientific Management of the Body in Frederick W. Taylor's 1907 "Lecture on Management".' *Body & Society* 6(1): 51–68.

Baishya, Anirban K., Shaheen S. Ahmed and Amit R. Baishya. 2012. 'News Pornography and Mediated Cultures of Violence.' *Kafila*, 20 August.

Balagopal, K. 1995. 'Politics as Property.' *Economic & Political Weekly*, 7 October: 2482–4.

—— 2007. 'Illegal Acquisition in Tribal Areas.' *Economic & Political Weekly*, 6 October.

Balch, Oliver. 2012. *India Rising: Tales from a Changing Nation: Travels in Modern India*. London: Faber & Faber.

Bandyopadhyay, D. 2001. 'Andhra Pradesh : Looking beyond Vision 2020.' *Economic & Political Weekly* 36(11): 900–903.

Banerjee-Guha, Swapna. 2008. 'Space Relations of Capital and Significance of New Economic Enclaves: SEZs in India.' *Economic & Political Weekly* 43(47): 51–9.

Baviskar, Amita. 2003. 'Between Violence and Desire: Space, Power, and Identity in the Making of Metropolitan Delhi.' *International Social Science Journal* 55(175): 89–98.

—— 2004. *In the Belly of the River: Tribal Conflicts over Development in the Narmada Valley*. Oxford: Oxford University Press.

—— 2008. 'Pedagogy, Public Sociology and Politics in India: What Is to Be Done?' *Current Anthropology* 56(3): 425–33.

—— 2009. 'Breaking Homes, Making Cities: Class and Gender in the Politics of Urban Displacement.' In *Displaced by Development: Confronting Marginalisation and Gender Injustice*, edited by Lyla Mehta. London: Sage.

Baviskar, Amita and Raka Ray. 2011. *Elite and Everyman: The Cultural Politics of the Indian Middle Classes*. New Delhi: Routledge.

Bear, Laura. 2001. 'Making a River of Gold: Speculative State Planning, Informality, and Neoliberal Governance on the Hooghly.' *Focaal* 61: 46–60.

—— 2005. 'School Stories and Internal Frontiers: Tracing the Domestic Life of Anglo-Indian Citizens.' In *Manufacturing Citizenship: Education and Nationalism in Europe, South Asia and China*, edited by Veronique Bénéï, pp. 236–61. London: Routledge.

Bénéï, Veronique. 2001. 'Teaching Nationalism in Maharashtra Schools.' In *The Everyday State and Society in Modern India*, edited by Veronique Bénéï and Christopher J. Fuller, pp. 194–217. London: Hurst & Co.

Benjamin, Walter. 1995. 'Paris: Capital of the Nineteenth Century.' Edited by Philip Kasinitz. *Perspecta* 12: 163–72.

Berlant, Lauren. 2007. 'Nearly Utopian, Nearly Normal: Post-Fordist Affect in La Promesse and Rosetta.' *Public Culture* 19(2): 273–301.

—— 2011. *Cruel Optimism*. Durham, NC: Duke University Press.

Bhattacharya, Ravik. 2007. 'Here's Why the Chemistry in Nandigram Failed.' *The Indian Express*, 7 April.

Bidwai, Praful. 2006. 'The Great Land Grab.' *Frontline* 23(18): 9–22.

Boltanski, Luc and Eve Chiapello. 2007. *The New Spirit of Capitalism*. London: Verso.

Bourdieu, Pierre. 1979. 'Symbolic Power.' *Critique of Anthropology* 4(13–14): 77–85.

Braverman, Harry. 1974. *Labour and Monopoly Capitalism: The Degradation of Work in the Twentieth Century*. New York: Monthly Review Press.

Breman, Jan. 2004. *The Making and Unmaking of and Industrial Working Class: Sliding Down the Labour Hierarchy in Ahmedabad, India*. New Delhi: Oxford University Press.

Buck-Morss, Susan. 1995. 'The City as Dreamworld and Catastrophe.' *October* 73: 3–26.

—— 2002. *Dreamworld and Catastrophe: The Passing of Mass Utopia in East and West*. Cambridge, MA: MIT Press.

Burawoy, Michael. 1985. *The Politics of Production: Factory Regimes under Capitalism and Socialism*. London: Verso.

Burawoy, M., J.A. Blum, S. George, Z. Gille and M. Thayer. 2000. *Global Ethnography: Forces, Connections, and Imaginations in a Postmodern World*. Berkeley: University of California Press.

Business Weekly. 2002. 'A Tale of Two Indias.' April.

Callon, Michel, Yuval Millo and Fabian Muniesa. 2007. *Market Devices*. London: Wiley-Blackwell.

Carrier, James G. 1992. 'Emerging Alienation in Production: A Maussian History.' *Man* 27(3): 539–58.

Carsten, J. and S. Hugh-Jones. 1995. *About the House: Lévi-Strauss and Beyond*. Cambridge: Cambridge University Press.

Castree, Noel. 2009. 'The Spatio-temporality of Capitalism.' *Time & Society* 18(1): 26–61.

Chakraverti, S. 2006. 'Company Towns.' *The Times of India*, 21 August.

Chalfin, Brenda. 2008. 'Sovereigns and Citizens in Close Encounter: Airport Anthropology and Customs Regimes in Neoliberal Ghana.' *American Ethnologist* 35(4): 519–38.

Chari, Sharad. 2004. *Fraternal Capital: Peasant Workers, Self Made Man, and Globalisation in Provincial India*. New Delhi: Permanent Black.

Chhachhi, Amrita. 1999. 'Gender, Flexibility, Skill, and Industrial Restructuring: The Electronics Industry in India.' *Gender, Technology and Development* 3(3): 329–60.

Chopra, Radhika. 2006. 'Muted Masculinities: Introduction to the Special Issue on Contemporary Indian Ethnographies.' *Men and Masculinities* 9: 127–30.

Chopra, Radhika and Patricia Jeffery. 2004. *Educational Regimes in Contemporary India*. New Delhi: Sage.

Comaroff, Jean and John Comaroff. 2000. 'Millennial Capitalism: First Thoughts on a Second Coming.' *Public Culture* 12(2): 291–343.

Corbridge, Stuart and John Harriss. 2000. *Reinventing India: Liberalization, Hindu Nationalism and Popular Democracy*. London: Polity Press.

Corbridge, Stuart, John Harriss and Craig Jeffrey. 2012. *India Today: Economy, Politics and Society*. Cambridge: Polity Press.

Cross, Jamie. 2009. 'From Dreams to Discontent: Educated Young Men and the Politics of Work at a Special Economic Zone in Andhra Pradesh.' *Contributions to Indian Sociology* 43(3): 351–79.

—— 2010. 'Neoliberalism as Unexceptional: Economic Zones and the Everyday Precariousness of Working Life in South India.' *Critique of Anthropology* 30(4): 355–73.

—— 2012a. 'Technological Intimacy: Re-engaging with Gender and Technology in the Global Factory.' *Ethnography* 13(2): 119–43.

—— 2012b. 'Sweatshop Exchanges: Gifts and Giving in the Global Factory.' *Economic Anthropology* 32(2): 3–26.

da Col, Giovanni. 2012. 'Introduction: Natural Philosophies of Fortune – Luck, Vitality, and Uncontrolled Relatedness.' *Social Analysis* 56: 1–23.

da Col, Giovanni and C. Humphrey. 2012. 'Introduction: Subjects of Luck – Contingency, Morality, and the Anticipation of Everyday Life.' *Social Analysis* 56(2): 1–18.

Damodaran, Harish. 2008. *India's New Capitalists: Caste, Business, and Industry in a Modern Nation*. New York: Palgrave Macmillan.

de Neve, Geert. 2005. *The Everyday Politics of Labour: Working Lives in India's Informal Economy*. New Delhi: Social Science Press.

Deb, S. 2012. *The Beautiful and the Damned: Life in the New India*. London: Faber & Faber.

Deleuze, Gilles and Félix Guattari. 2004. *Anti-Oedipus: Capitalism and Schizophrenia*. London: Continuum.

Dhara, Tushar. 2008. 'Nandigram Revisited: The Scars of Battle.' *Infochange*, April.

du Gay, P. 2010. 'Making Up Managers : Bureaucracy , Enterprise and the Liberal Art of Separation.' *British Journal of Sociology* 45(4): 655–74.

Dutta, Sujan. 2011. 'From Nandi Womb: Resolve.' *The Telegraph*, 3 May.

Elyachar, Julia. 2005. *Markets of Dispossession: NGOs, Economic Development and the State in India*. Durham, NC: Duke University Press.

Errington, F. and D. Gewertz. 2004. *Yali's Question: Sugar, Culture and History*. Chicago: University of Chicago Press.

Falzon, M.A. 2004. 'Paragons of Lifestyle: Gated Communities and the Politics of Space in Bombay.' *City & Society* 16(2): 145–67.

Farole, Thomas and Gokhan Akinci. 2011. *Special Economic Zones: Progress, Emerging Challenges and Future Directions*. Washington, DC: World Bank.

Ferguson, James. 1990. *The Anti-Politics Machine: Development, Depoliticisation, and Bureaucratic Power in Lesotho*. Minneapolis: University of Minnesota Press.

—— 1999. *Expectations of Modernity: Myths and Meanings of Urban Life on the Zambian Copperbelt*. Berkeley: University of California Press.

—— 2006. *Global Shadows: Africa in the Neoliberal Economy*. Durham, NC: Duke University Press.

Fernandes, Leela. 1997. *Producing Workers: The Politics of Gender, Class and Caste in the Calcutta Jute Mills*. Philadelphia: University of Pennsylvania Press.

Freeman, Carla. 1998. 'Femininity and Flexible Labor: Fashioning Class through Gender on the Global Assembly Line.' *Critique of Anthropology* 18(3): 245–62.

—— 2000. *High Tech and High Heels in the Global Economy: Women, Work and Pink-collar Identities in the Caribbean*. Durham, NC: Duke University Press.

Fuller, Christopher J. and Véronique Bénéï. 2001. *The Everyday State and Society in Modern India*. London: C. Hurst & Co.

Fuller, Christopher J. and Haripriya Narasimhan. 2006. 'Engineering Colleges, "Exposure" and Information Technology Professionals in Tamil Nadu.' *Economic & Political Weekly* 41(3): 258–62.

Gardner, Katy. 2012. *Discordant Development: Global Capitalism and the Struggle for Connection in Bangladesh*. London: Pluto Press.

Gardner, Katy and Filippo Osella. 2003. 'Migration, Modernity and Social Transformation in South Asia: An Overview.' *Contributions to Indian Sociology* 37(1–2): v–xxviii.

Ghertner, D. Asher. 2010. 'Calculating without Numbers: Aesthetic Governmentality in Delhi's Slums.' *Economy and Society* 39(2): 185–217.

Ghosh, Amitav. 2011. *River of Smoke: A Novel*. New York: Farrar, Straus & Giroux.

Ghosh, Aparism. 1999. South Asian of the Year: Chandrababu Naidu. *Time Magazine* (Asia Edition), 31 December.

Ghosh, Jayati. 2002. 'Globalisation, Export Oriented Employment for Women and Social Policy: A Case Study of India.' *Social Scientist* 30(11–12): 17–60.

Giddens, Anthony. 1991. *The Consequences of Modernity*. London: Polity Press.

Gilloch, Graeme. 2002. *Walter Benjamin: Critical Constellations*. Cambridge: Polity Press.

Goetz, Anne Marie and Rob Jenkins. 2001. 'Hybrid Forms of Accountability: Citizen Engagement in Institutions of Public-sector Oversight in India.' *Public Management Review* 3(3): 363–83.

Government of Andhra Pradesh (1999) *Swarna Andhra Pradesh Vision 2020*. Hyderabad: State Secretariat, Government of Andhra Pradesh.

Government of India Parliamentary Standing Committee on Commerce. 2007. *83rd Report on the Funcitoning of Special Economic Zones*. New Delhi: Rajya Sabha Secretariat.

Government of India Planning Commission. 1999. Record of Discussions: 48th Meeting of the National Development Council. In *Summary Record of Discussions of the National Development Council Meetings*. New Delhi: Government of India.

Graeber, David. 2011. *Debt: The First 5,000 Years*. New York: Melville House.

Gramsci, Antonio. 1971. *Selections from the Prison Notebooks of Antonio Gramsci*, edited by Quintin Hoare and Geoffrey Nowell Smith. London: Lawrence & Wishart.

Gregory, Steven. 2007. *The Devil Behind the Mirror: Globalisation and Politics in the Dominican Republic*. Berkeley: University of California Press.

Greider, William. 1997. *One World, Ready or Not*. London: Simon & Schuster.

Guha, Ramachandra. 2007. *India after Gandhi: The History of the World's Largest Democracy*. New Delhi: Picador India.

Gupta, Akhil. 1998. *Postcolonial Developments: Agriculture in the Making of Modern India*. Durham, NC: Duke University Press.

—— 2012. *Red Tape: Bureaucracy, Structural Violence, and Poverty in India*. Durham, NC: Duke University Press.

Gupta, S.P. 1996. *China's Economic Reforms: Role of Special Economic Zones and Economic and Technological Development Zones*. New Delhi: Indian Council for Research on International Economic Relations.

—— *Report of the Committee on India Vision 2020*. New Delhi: Planning Commission of India.

Guyer, Jane I. 2007. 'Prophecy and the Near Future: Thoughts on Macroeconomic, Evangelical, and Punctuated Time.' *American Ethnologist* 34(3): 409–21.

Hansen, Thomas Blom. 1999. *The Saffron Wave*. Princeton, NJ: Princeton University Press.

—— 2001. 'Governance and State Mythologies in Mumbai.' In *States of Imagination: Ethnographic Explorations of the Postcolonial State*, edited by Thomas Blom Hansen and Finn Stepputat, pp. 221–254. Durham, NC: Duke University Press.

—— 2012. *Melancholia of Freedom: Social Life in an Indian Township in South Africa*. Princeton, NJ: Princeton University Press.

Hansen, Thomas Blom and Stepputat, Finn. 2001. 'Introduction: States of Imagination.' In *States of Imagination: Ethnographic Explorations of the Postcolonial State*, pp. 1–40. Durham, NC: Duke University Press.

Harriss, John. 2002. *Depoliticizing Development: The World Bank and Social Capital*. London: Anthem Press.

Harvey, David. 1990a. 'Between Space and Time: Reflections on the Geographical Imagination.' *Annals of the Association of American Geographers* 80(3): 418–34.

—— 1990b. *The Condition of Postmodernity*. London: Blackwell.

—— 2001. 'Militant Particularism and Global Ambition: The Conceptual Politics of Place, Space and Environment in the Work of Raymond Williams.' In *Spaces of Capital: Towards a Critical Geography*, edited by David Harvey, pp. 158–88. London: Routledge.

—— 2005. *A Brief History of Neoliberalism*. Oxford: Oxford University Press.

Hetherington, Kevin. 1997. *The Badlands of Modernity: Heterotopia and Social Ordering*. London: Routledge.

Hewamanne, Sandya. 2008. *Stitching Identities in a Free Trade Zone: Gender and Politics in Sri Lanka*. Philadelphia: University of Pennsylvania.

Hilgers, Mathieu. 2012. 'The Historicity of the Neoliberal State.' *Social Anthropology* 20(1): 80–94.

The Hindu. 2008. 'We Will Replicate China's SEZ Model, Says APIIC CMD.' 17 June.

——— 2009. 'CITU Alleges Violation of Labour Laws by Brandix.' 5 February.

Hobsbawm, E. and T. Ranger (eds). 1983. *The Invention of Tradition*. Cambridge: Cambridge University Press.

Holmes, Douglas R. and George E. Marcus. 2005. 'Cultures of Expertise and the Management of Globalisation: Toward the Re-functioning of Ethnography.' In *Global Assemblages: Technology, Politics, and Ethics as Anthropological Problems*, edited by Aihwa Ong and Stephen Collier, pp. 235–52. London: Blackwell.

Holston, J. 1989. *The Modernist City: An Anthropological Critique of Brasília*. Chicago: University of Chicago Press.

ILO. 2001. *Labour Issues in Export Processing Zones in South Asia: Role of Social Dialogue*. New Delhi: ILO.

Inda, Jonathan Xavier. 2000. 'A Flexible World: Capitalism, Citizenship, and Postnational Zones.' *PoLAR: Political and Legal Anthropology Review* 23(1): 86–102.

Jameson, Fredric. 2005. *Archaeologies of the Future: The Desire Called Utopia and Other Science Fictions*. London: Verso.

Jeffrey, Craig. 2008. '"Generation Nowhere": Rethinking Youth through the Lens of Unemployed Young Men.' *Progress in Human Geography* 32(6): 739–58.

——— 2010. 'Timepass: Youth, Class, and Time Among Unemployed Young Men in India.' *American Ethnologist* 37(3): 465–81.

Jeffrey, Craig, Patricia Jeffery and Roger Jeffery. 2004. 'Degrees without Freedom: The Impact of Formal Education on Dalit Young Men in North India.' *Development and Change* 35(5): 963–86.

——— 2008. *Degrees without Freedom? Education, Masculinities and Unemployment in North India*. Stanford, CA: Stanford University Press.

Jenkins, A. 1994. 'Just-in-Time, Regimes and Reductionism.' *Sociology* 28(1): 21–30.

Jenkins, Rob. 2011. 'The Politics of India's Special Economic Zones.' In *Understanding India's New Political Economy: A Great Transformation?* edited by Sanjay Ruparelia, Sanjay Reddy, John Harriss and Stuart Corbridge , pp. 49–65. Abingdon: Routledge.

John, Mary and Janaki Nair. 2001. *A Question of Silence? The Sexual Economics of Modern India*. London: Zed Books.

Joshi, Chitra. 2003. *Lost Worlds: Indian Labour and Its Forgotten Histories*. London: Permanent Black.

Kabeer, Naila. 2000. *The Power to Choose: Bangladeshi Women and Labour Market Decisions in London and Dhaka*. London: Verso.

Kapferer, Bruce. 2005. 'New Formations of Power, the Oligarchic-corporate State, and Anthropological Ideological Discourse.' *Anthropological Theory* 5(3): 285–99.

Kaur, R. 2013. 'Sovereignty without Hegemony, the Nuclear State, and a "Secret Public Hearing"' in India.' *Theory, Culture & Society* 30(3): 3–28.

Klenk, Rebecca. 2003. '"Difficult Work": Becoming Developed.' In *Regional Modernities: The Cultural Politics of Development in India*, edited by Kalyana-krishnan Sivaramakrishnan and Arun Agrawal, pp. 99–121. Oxford: Oxford University Press.

Latour, Bruno. 1993. *We Have Never Been Modern*. Cambridge, MA: Harvard University Press.

—— 2005. *Reassembling the Social: An Introduction to Actor-Network Theory*. Oxford: Oxford University Press.

Law, John. 1994. *Organizing Modernity*. Oxford: Blackwell.

Levien, Michael. 2011. 'Special Economic Zones and Accumulation by Dispossession in India.' *Journal of Agrarian Change* 11(4): 454–83.

—— 2012. 'The Land Question: Special Economic Zones and the Political Economy of Dispossession in India.' *Journal of Peasant Studies* 39(3–4): 933–69.

—— 2013. 'Regimes of Dispossession: From Steel Towns to Special Economic Zones.' *Development and Change* 44(2): 381–407.

Li, Tania. 2010. 'Indigeneity, Capitalism, and the Management of Dispossession.' *Current Anthropology* 51(3): 385–414.

—— 2011. 'Centering Labor in the Land Grab Debate.' *Journal of Peasant Studies* 38(2): 281–98.

Li, Tania Murray. 2007. *The Will to Improve: Governmentality, Development, and the Practice of Politics*. Durham, NC: Duke University Press.

Liechty, Mark. 2003. *Suitably Modern: Making Middle Class Culture in a New Consumer Society*. Princeton, NJ: Princeton University Press.

Low, Setha M. 2001. 'The Edge and the Center: Gated Communities and the Discourse of Urban Fear.' *American Anthropologist* 103(1): 45–58.

Lukose, Ritty. 2005. 'Consuming Globalisation: Youth and Gender in Kerala, India.' *Journal of Social History* 38(4): 915–35.

Lynch, Caitrin. 2007. *Juki Girls, Good Girls: Gender and Cultural Politics in Sri Lanka's Global Garment Industry*. London: ILR Press.

MacKenzie, Donald A., F. Muniesa and L. Siu. 2007. *Do Economists Make Markets? On the Performativity of Economics*. Princeton, NJ: Princeton University Press.

Mains, D. 2007. 'Neoliberal Times: Progress, Boredom, and Shame among Young Men in Urban Ethiopia.' *American Ethnologist* 34(4): 659–73.

Majumder, Sanjoy. 2012. 'Why Rural Sexual Violence Remains Rife in India.' *BBC News India*, 21 October.

Maran, Murasoli. 2000. 'If Removal of Quantitative Restrictions Has Adverse Impact, We'll Counter It through the Weapon of Tariff.' *Rediff.com*, 31 March, available at: http://www.rediff.com/money/2000/mar/31maran.htm.

—— 2002. 'Exim Policy 2002–2007.' *Outlook India*, available at http://www.outlookindia.com/articlefullwidth.aspx?215045.

Maringanti, Anant. 2008. 'The Million Mutinee Question.' *Kafila*, 1 September. http://kafila.org/2008/09/01/the-million-mutinee-question-anant-maringanti/

—— 2010. 'Telangana: Righting Historical Wrongs or Getting the Future Right?', *Economic & Political Weekly* 45(4): 33–8.

Maslow, A.H. 1943. 'A Theory of Human Motivation.' *Psychological Review* 50(4): 370–96.

Masquelier, Adeline. 2002. 'Road Mythographies: Space, Mobility, and the Historical Imagination in Postcolonial Niger.' *American Ethnologist* 29(4): 829–56.

Massey, Doreen B. 2005. *For Space*. London: Sage.

Massumi, Brian. 1995. 'The Autonomy of Affect.' *Cultural Critique* 31: 83–109.

Mawdsley, Emma. 2004. 'India's Middle Classes and the Environment.' *Development and Change* 35(March): 79–103.

Mazzarella, William. 2003. *Shovelling Smoke: Advertising and Globalisation in Contemporary India*. Durham, NC: Duke University Press.

—— 2006. 'Internet X-ray: E-governance, Transparency, and the Politics of Immediation in India.' *Public Culture* 18(3): 473–505.

—— 2010. 'Beautiful Balloon: The Digital Divide and the Charisma of New Media in India.' *American Ethnologist* 37(4): 783–804.

McConnochie, Adam. 2012. '"The Blessed Land": Narratives of Peasant Resistance at Nandigram, West Bengal, in 2007.' Unpublished MA thesis, Victoria University of Wellington, New Zealand.

McGoey, Linsey. 2007. 'On the Will to Ignorance in Bureaucracy.' *Economy and Society* 36(2): 212–35.

—— 2012. 'The Logic of Strategic Ignorance.' *British Journal of Sociology* 63(3): 533–76.

Menon, Nivedita and Aditya Nigam. 2007. *Power and Contestation: India Since 1959*. London: Zed Books.

Mertes, Tom. 2002. 'Grass-roots Globalism.' *New Left Review* 17(September–October): 101–10.

Miller, Peter and T. O'Leary. 2008. 'The Factory as Laboratory.' *Science in Context* 7(3): 469–96.

Miller, Peter and Nikolas Rose. 1995. 'Production, Identity, and Democracy.' *Theory and Society* 24(3): 427–67.

Mills, Mary Beth. 1999. *Thai Women in the Global Labour Force: Consuming Desires, Contested Selves*. New Brunswick, NJ: Rutgers University Press.

—— 2003. 'Gender and Inequality in the Global Labour Force.' *Annual Review of Anthropology* 32(1): 41–62.

Mitchell, Lisa. 2009. *Language, Emotion, and Politics in South India: The Making of a Mother Tongue*. Bloomington: Indiana University Press.

Mitchell, Timothy. 1999. 'Dreamland: The Neoliberalism of Your Desires.' *Middle Eastern Report* spring.

—— 2002. *Rule of Experts: Egypt, Techno-politics, Modernity*. Berkeley: University of California Press.

Miyazaki, Hirokazu. 2006. *The Method of Hope: Anthropology, Philosophy, and Fijian Knowledge*. Stanford, CA: Stanford University Press.

Mody, Anjali. 2010. 'The Politics of India's Special Economic Zones: A Briefing Note'. New Delhi. http://www.indiasezpolitics.org/article.php?id=184

Mohan, Anupama. 2013. 'The Languages of Sexual Violence.' *Kafila*, 11 February. http://kafila.org/2013/02/11/the-languages-of-sexual-violence-anupama-mohan/

Mol, Annemarie and John Law. 1994. 'Regions, Networks and Fluids: Anaemia and Social Topology.' *Social Studies of Science* 24(4): 641–71.

Mole, N.J. 2008. 'Living It on the Skin: Italian States, Working Illness.' *American Ethnologist* 35(2): 189–210.

—— 2012. *Labor Disorders in Neoliberal Italy: Mobbing, Well-being, and the Workplace*. Bloomington: Indiana University Press.

Mollona, M. 2009. *Made in Sheffield: An Ethnography of Industrial Work and Politics*. Oxford: Berghahn Books.

Mooiji, Jos. 2003. 'Smart Governance?: Politics in the Policy Process in Andhra Pradesh, India.' Working Paper 228, Overseas Development Institute, London.

Moore, Henrietta L. 2013. *Still Life: Hopes, Desires and Satisfactions*. Cambridge: Polity Press.

Mosse, David. 2005. *Cultivating Development: An Ethnography of Aid Policy and Practice*. London: Pluto Press.

Naidu, Chandrababu. 2000. *Plain Speaking*. New Delhi: Penguin Books.

Nash, June and Maria Fernandez-Kelly. 1983. *Women, Men and the International Division of Labour*. New York: State University of New York Press.

Navaro-Yashin, Yael. 2007a. 'Make-believe Papers, Legal Forms and the Counterfeit: Affective Interactions between Documents and People in Britain and Cyprus.' *Anthropological Theory* 7(1): 79–98.

—— 2007b. 'Introduction: Fantasy and the Real in the Work of Begoña Aretxaga.' *Anthropological Theory* 7(1): 5–8.

—— 2009. 'Affective Spaces, Melancholic Objects: Ruination and the Production of Anthropological Knowledge.' *Journal of the Royal Anthropological Institute* 15(1): 1–18.

Ngai, Pun. 2003. 'Subsumption or Consumption? The Phantom of Consumer Revolution in "Globalizing" China.' *Cultural Anthropology* 18(4): 469–92.

—— 2005. *Made in China: Women Factory Workers in a Global Workplace*. Durham, NC: Duke University Press.

Norris, Lucy. 2010. *Recycling Indian Clothing: Global Contexts of Reuse and Value*. Bloomington: Indiana University Press.

OECD. 2008. *Labour Regulation and Employment Dynamics at the State Level in India*. Paris: OECD.

Omar, K. and W. Stoever. 2008. 'The Role of Technology and Human Capital in the EPZ Life-cycle.' *Transnational Corporations* 17(1): 135–59.

Omvedt, Gail. 1995. *Dalit Visions: The Anti-caste Movement and the Construction of an Indian Identity*. Hyderabad: Orient Longman.

Ong, Aihwa. 1987. *Spirits of Resistance and Capitalist Discipline: Factory Women in Malaysia*. Albany: State University of New York Press.

—— 2004. 'The Chinese Axis: Zoning Technologies and Variegated Sovereignty.' *Journal of East Asian Studies* 4(1): 69–96.

—— 2006. *Neoliberalism as Exception*. Durham, NC: Duke University Press.

Ong, Aihwa and Stephen Collier. 2005. *Global Assemblages: Technology, Politics, and Ethics as Anthropological Problems*. London: Blackwell.

Ortner, Sherry B. 1995. 'Resistance and the Problem of Ethnographic Refusal.' *Comparative Studies in Society and History* 37(1): 173–93.

Osella, Caroline and Filippo Osella. 2006. *Men and Masculinities in South India*. New Delhi: Anthem Press.

Osella, Filippo, and Caroline Osella. 2000a. 'Migration, Money and Masculinity in Kerala.' *Journal of the Royal Anthropological Institute* 6(1): 117–33.

—— 2000b. *Social Mobility in Kerala: Modernity and Identity in Conflict*. London: Pluto Press.

Palan, Ronen. 2003. *The Offshore World*. Ithaca, NY: Cornell University Press.

Palit, A. and S. Bhattacharjee. 2008. *Special Economic Zones in India: Myths and Realities*. New Delhi: Anthem Press.

Pandian, Anand. 2009. *Crooked Stalks: Cultivating Virtue in South India*. Durham, NC: Duke University Press.

Panjwani, N. 1984. 'Living with Capitalism: Class, Caste and Paternalism among Industrial Workers in Bombay.' *Contributions to Indian Sociology* 18(2): 267–92.

Parry, Jonathan P. 1999a. 'Lords of Labour: Working and Shirking in Bhilai.' *Contributions to Indian Sociology* 33(1–2): 107–40.

—— 1999b. 'Two Cheers for Reservation: The Satnamis and the Steel Plant.' In *Institutions and Inequalities, Essays in Honour of André Betteille*, edited by Jonathan P. Parry and Ranajit Guha. New Delhi: Oxford University Press, pp. 128–69.

—— 2000. 'The "Crisis of Corruption" and "The Idea of India": A Worm's Eye View.' In *Morals of Legitimacy. Between Agency and the System*, edited by Italo Pardo. London: Berghahn Books, pp. 27–55.

Peck, Jamie and Nik Theodore. 2012. 'Reanimating Neoliberalism: Process Geographies of Neoliberalisation.' *Social Anthropology* 20(2): 177–85.

Peck, Jamie and Adam Tickell. 2002. 'Neoliberalizing Space.' *Antipode* 34(3): 380–404.

Petryna, Adriana. 2003. *Life Exposed: Biological Citizens after Chernobyl*. Princeton, NJ: Princeton University Press.

Poster, Winifred R. 2002. 'Racialism, Sexuality, and Masculinity: Gendering "Global Ethnography" of the Workplace.' *Social Politics* 9: 126–58.

Prakash, Gyan. 1999. *Another Reason: Science and the Imagination of Modern India*. Princeton, NJ: Princeton University Press.

Rajan, Kaushik Sunder. 2006. *Biocapital: The Constitution of Postgenomic Life*. Durham, NC: Duke University Press.

Ramachandraiah, Chigurupati and Ramasamy Srinivasan. 2011. 'Special Economic Zones as New Forms of Corporate Land Grab: Experiences from India.' *Development* 54(1): 59–63.

Rancière, Jacques. 2002. '"Preface" to Proletarian Nights.' In *The Everyday Life Reader*, edited by Ben Highmore, pp. 246–50. London: Routledge.

Rao, P. Narasimha and K.C. Suri. 2006. 'Dimensions of Agrarian Distress in Andhra Pradesh.' *Economic & Political Weekly* 41(16): 1546–52.

Ray, Gautama. 2008. *Nandigram and Beyond*. Kolkata: Gangchil Publications.

Ray, Raka. 1999. *Fields Of Protest: Women's Movement in India*. Minneapolis: University of Minnesota Press.

Reddy C., A. Prasad and Kumar G. Pavan. 2010. 'Employment Generated by Special Economic Zones in Southern India.' *Journal of Economics* 1(1): 1–11.

Redfield, Peter. 2000. *Space in the Tropics: From Convicts to Rockets in French Guiana*. Berkeley: University of California Press.

—— 2002. 'The Half-life of Empire in Outer Space.' *Social Studies of Science* 32(5–6): 791–825.

Richard, A. and D. Rudnyckyj. 2009. 'Economies of Affect.' *Journal of the Royal Anthropological Institute* 15: 57–77.

Riles, A. and Adam Reed. 2006. 'Documents Unfolding.' In *Documents: Artefacts of Modern Knowledge*, , pp. 158–81. Ann Arbor: University of Michigan Press.

Robins, Nick. 2006. *The Corporation that Changed the World: How the East India Company Shaped the Modern Multinational*. London: Pluto Press.

Rofel, Lisa. 2007. *Desiring China: Experiments in Neoliberalism, Sexuality and Public Culture*. Durham, NC: Duke University Press.

Rose, Nikolas. 1989. *Governing the Soul: The Shaping of the Private Self*. New York: Free Association Press.

—— 1999. *Governing the Soul*. London: Free Association Books.

Rosenberg, D. and S. Harding. 2005. *Histories of the Future*. Durham, NC: Duke University Press.

Roy, A. 2009. 'Why India Cannot Plan Its Cities: Informality, Insurgence and the Idiom of Urbanization.' *Planning Theory* 8(1): 76–87.

Roy, Srirupa. 2007. *Beyond Belief: India and the Politics of Postcolonial Nationalism*. Durham, NC: Duke University Press.

Rudnyckyj, D. 2009. 'Market Islam in Indonesia.' *Journal of the Royal Anthropological Institute* 15: S183–S201.

Salzinger, Leslie. 2000. 'Manufacturing Sexual Subjects: "Harassment", Desire, and Discipline on a Maquiladora Shopfloor.' *Ethnography* 1(1): 67–92.

—— 2003. *Genders in Production: Making Workers in Mexico's Global Factories*. Berkeley: University of California Press.

—— 2004. 'Revealing the Unmarked: Finding Masculinity in a Global Factory.' *Ethnography* 5(1): 5–27.

Sampat, Preeti. 2010. 'Special Economic Zones in India: Reconfiguring Displacement in a Neoliberal Order?' *City* 22(2): 166–82.

Sarkar, Tanika and Sumit Chowdhury. 2009. 'The Meaning of Nandigram: Corporate Land Invasion, People's Power, and the Left in India.' *Focaal* 54: 73–88.

Schrank, A. 2001. 'Export Processing Zones: Free Market Islands or Bridges to Structural Transformation?' *Development Policy Review* 19(2): 223–42.

Searle, Llerena G. 2010. *Making Space for Capital: The Production of Global Landscapes in Contemporary India.* Publicly Accessible Penn Dissertations, University of Pennsylvannia.

Seethalakshmi, S. 2009. *Special Economic Zones in Andhra Pradesh: Policy Claims and People's Experiences.* Hyderabad: Society for Rural Development and ActionAid.

Seminarist. 2008. 'Betting on Growth.' *Seminar* 582: 51–6.

Sennett, R. 2008. *The Craftsman.* New Haven, CT: Yale University Press.

Sewell, Graham and Barry Wilkinson. 1992. '"Someone to Watch Over Me": Surveillance, Discipline and the Just-in-time Labour Process.' *Sociology* 26(2): 271–89.

Shah, Alpa. 2006. 'The Labour of Love: Seasonal Migration from Jharkhand to the Brick Kilns of Other States in India.' *Contributions to Indian Sociology* 40(1): 91–118.

—— 2010. *In the Shadows of the State: Indigenous Politics, Environmentalism, and Insurgency in Jharkhand, India.* Durham, NC: Duke University Press.

Shrivastava, A. and A. Kothari. 2012. *Churning the Earth: The Making of Global India.* New Delhi: Penguin Viking.

Sidaway, James D. 2003. 'Sovereign Excesses? Portraying Postcolonial Sovereigni-tyscapes.' *Political Geography* 22(2): 157–178.

—— 2007. 'Enclave Space: A New Metageography of Development?' *Area* 39(3): 331–9.

Sivaraman, Satya, Amit Sengupta and Jharna Jhaveri (eds). 2007. *What Really Happened: Report of the People's Tribunal on Nandigram.* New Delhi: Daanish Books.

Sivaramakrishnan, Kalyanakrishnan and Arun Agrawal (eds). 2003. *Regional Modernities in Stories and Practices of Development.* Oxford: Oxford University Press.

Sridhar, V. 2006a. 'Subversive Enclaves.' *Frontline* 23(10). http://www.frontline.in/static/html/fl2320/stories/20061020003601900.htm

—— 2006b. 'Why Do Farmers Commit Suicide? The Case of Andhra Pradesh.' *Economic & Political Weekly* 41(16): 1559–65.

Srinivas, S.V. 2008. 'Cardboard Monuments : City , Language and "Nation" in Contemporary Telugu Cinema.' *Singapore Journal of Tropical Geography* 29(1): 87–100.

—— 2009. 'Megastar: Chiranjeevi and Telugu Cinema After NT Rama Rao.' *Contributions to Indian Sociology* 45(1): 113–56.

Srinivasulu, K. 2002. *Caste, Class and Social Articulation in Andhra Pradesh: Mapping Differential Regional Trajectories*. London: Overseas Development Agency.

Srivastava, Aseem. 2009. 'The Peasant Mutiny Of 2009.' *Tehelka*, 18 July.

Srivastava, Aseem and Ashish Kothari. 2012. *Churning the Earth: The Making of Global India*. New Delhi: Penguin.

Srivastava, Rajeev and Anand Rai. (2007) 'SEZs in India – New Avatar of Globalisation: An Analytical Perspective.' Paper presented at the Conference on Global Competition and Competitiveness of Indian Corporates, Indian Institute of Management, Khozikode, Kerala, India.

Stoler, Ann Laura. 2008. 'Imperial Debris: Reflections on Ruins and Ruination.' *Cultural Anthropology* 23(2): 191–219.

—— 2013. *Imperial Debris: On Ruins and Ruination*. Durham, NC: Duke University Press.

Strathern, Marilyn. 2000. 'Introduction: New Accountabilities.' In *Audit Cultures: Anthropological Studies in Accountability, Ethics and the Academy*, edited by Marilyn Strathern. London: Routledge.

—— 2005. 'Robust Knowledge and Fragile Futures.' In *Global Assemblages: Technology, Politics, and Ethics as Anthropological Problems*, edited by Aihwa Ong and Stephen J. Collier, pp. 464–81. Malden, MA: Blackwell.

Street, Alice. 2012. 'Affective Infrastructure: Hospital Landscapes of Hope and Failure.' *Space and Culture* 15(1): 44–56.

Strümpell, Christian. 2008. '"We Work Together, We Eat Together": Conviviality and Modernity in a Company Settlement in South Orissa.' *Contributions to Indian Sociology* 42(3): 351–81.

Tarlo, Emma. 1996. *Clothing Matters: Dress and Identity in India*. Chicago: University of Chicago Press.

Taussig, Michael. 2004. *My Cocaine Museum*. Chicago: University of Chicago Press.

The Economist. 2000. 'The State that Would Reform India', 2 September.

Thompson, Paul and Stephen Ackroyd. 1995. 'All Quiet on the Workplace Front: A Critique of Recent Trends in British Industrial Sociology.' *Sociology* 29(4): 615–33.

Thrift, Nigel. 1996. *Spatial Formations*. London: Sage.

—— 2006. 'Space.' *Theory, Culture & Society* 23(2–3): 139–46.

—— 2007. *Non-representational Theory: Space, Politics, Affect*. London: Routledge.

Tsing, Anna. 2000a. 'Inside the Economy of Appearances.' *Public Culture* 12(1): 115–44.

—— 2000b. 'The Global Situation.' *Cultural Anthropology* 15(3): 327–60.

—— 2005. *Friction*. Princeton, NJ: Princeton University Press.

—— 2009. 'Supply Chains and the Human Condition.' *Rethinking Marxism* 21(2): 148–76.

Tsing, Anna and Pollman, E. 2005. 'Global Futures: The Game.' In *Histories of the Future* edited by Daniel Rosenberg and Susan Harding. Durham, NC: Duke University Press.

Upadhya, Carol. 1988. 'The Farmer Capitalists of Coastal Andhra Pradesh.' *Economic & Political Weekly* 23(28): 1376–82.

—— 1997. 'Social and Cultural Strategies of Class Formation in Coastal Andhra Pradesh.' *Contributions to Indian Sociology* 31(2): 169–93.

Vanaik, Achin. 2011. 'Subcontinental Strategies.' *New Left Review* 70.

Vijayabaskar, M. 2010. 'Saving Agricultural Labour from Agriculture: SEZs and Politics of Silence in Tamil Nadu.' *Economic & Political Weekly* 45(6): 37–43.

Wacquant, Loïc J.D. 2000. 'Inside "The Zone": The Social Art of the Hustler in the American Ghetto.' In *The Weight of the World*, edited by Pierre Bourdieu. Stanford, CA: Stanford University Press.

Webb, M. 2010. 'Success Stories: Rhetoric, Authenticity, and the Right to Information Movement in North India.' *Contemporary South Asia* 18(2): 293–304.

—— 2012. 'Activating Citizens, Remaking Brokerage: Transparency Activism, Ethical Scenes, and the Urban Poor in Delhi.' *PoLAR: Political and Legal Anthropology Review* 35(2): 206–22.

Webster, Frank and Kevin Robins. 1993. '"I'll Be Watching You": Comment on Sewell and Wilkinson.' *Sociology* 27(2): 243–52.

Weeks, Kathi. 2011. *The Problem with Work: Feminism, Marxism, Antiwork Politics, and Postwork Imaginaries*. Durham, NC: Duke University Press.

Williams, Raymond. 1972. *Marxism and Literature*. London: Verso.

Williams, Rosalind H. 1982. *Dream Worlds: Mass Consumption in Late Nineteenth-century France*. Berkeley: University of California Press.

Wright, M.W. 1999. 'The Dialectics of Still Life: Murder, Women, and Maquiladoras.' *Public Culture* 11(3): 453–73.

Wright, Melissa. 2003. 'Factory Daughters and Chinese Modernity: A Case from Dongguan.' *Geoforum* 34(3): 291–301.

Yanagisako, Sylvia. 2002. *Producing Culture and Capital: Family Firms in Italy*. Princeton, NJ: Princeton University Press.

Yee, Amy. 2013. 'Reforms Urged to Tackle Violence against Women in India.' *The Lancet* 381(9876): 1445–6.

Zaloom, Caitlin. 2007. 'Future Knowledge.' *American Ethnologist* 34(3): 444–6.

—— 2008. 'How to Read the Future: The Yield Curve, Affect, and Financial Prediction.' *Public Culture* 21(2): 245–68.

Žižek, Slavoj. 2010. *Living in the End Times*. London: Verso.

Zoomers, Annelies. 2010. 'Globalisation and the Foreignisation of Space: Seven Processes Driving the Current Global Land Grab.' *Journal of Peasant Studies* 37(2): 429–47.

Index

CPSIA information can be obtained
at www.ICGtesting.com
Printed in the USA
FSHW01n2316161018
53052FS